THE HANDLOOM WEAVERS

A STUDY IN THE ENGLISH COTTON INDUSTRY
DURING THE INDUSTRIAL REVOLUTION

THE HANDLOOM WEAVERS

A STUDY IN THE
ENGLISH COTTON INDUSTRY DURING
THE INDUSTRIAL REVOLUTION

DUNCAN BYTHELL

Lecturer in Economic History
University of Durham

WITH AN INTRODUCTION BY

R. M. HARTWELL

CAMBRIDGE
AT THE UNIVERSITY PRESS
1969

Published by the Syndics of the Cambridge University Press
Bentley House, 200 Euston Road, London N.W.1
American Branch: 32 East 57th Street, New York, N.Y. 10022

Library of Congress Catalogue Card Number: 69-10487
Standard Book Number: 521 07580 7

Printed in Great Britain
at the University Printing House, Cambridge
(Brooke Crutchley, University Printer)

TO MY PARENTS

CONTENTS

PREFACE

THIS book is the outcome of research begun in Oxford in the years 1962–5, and its completion owes a good deal to the kindly advice of my supervisors, Dr Max Hartwell, of Nuffield College, and Mr Michael Brock, of Wolfson College. My debt to Dr Hartwell has been further increased by his generous offer to provide an introduction to this, my first book. Among other scholars who have helped me, I must particularly thank Dr W. H. Chaloner, of Manchester University, for allowing me at the outset of my research to draw on his vast knowledge of the source materials for English industrial history, and Mr John Prest, of Balliol College, who at a later stage offered detailed criticisms of my original draft. Last but by no means least, it is a pleasure to record my gratitude to Mr A. F. Thompson, of Wadham College, who first aroused my undergraduate interest in the history of England in the nineteenth century, and who has been an unfailing source of encouragement and reassurance during the past six years.

I was courteously received at many Libraries and Record Offices in Lancashire, Oxford, and London in the course of working on the scattered materials which have gone into this book, but I am especially obliged to Misses Lofthouse and Leach, of Chetham's Library, Manchester, whose helpfulness much exceeds anything that one can reasonably expect. It was also my privilege and pleasure to be able to consult Messrs W. Bennett of Burnley and W. Spencer of Colne, both of whom gave me very freely of their detailed knowledge of the local history of north-east Lancashire.

The object of this book is to fill one of the many gaps in our knowledge of the English cotton industry, and to contribute towards restoring this now comparatively neglected industry to something like the primacy it once enjoyed in studies of 'the first industrial revolution'. Since my typescript was delivered to the Press, there have been several welcome developments with the same tendency. A number of the classic nineteenth-century texts, including the works of Edward Baines and Samuel Bamford, have

recently been reprinted with introductions by Dr Chaloner, and it is gratifying that these important writings are widely available once again. As for original work, *The Growth of the British Cotton Trade 1780–1815* by M. M. Edwards (1967) appeared too late for me to refer to, but has filled many serious gaps in our information about the development of the general organization of the whole industry and particularly about its marketing side. Although there is little direct overlap with my work, Dr Edwards's study does amplify and clarify points which I have sketched rather lightly, especially in chapters 2 and 5, and I would commend any student anxious to pursue these aspects of the subject more deeply to see what Dr Edwards has to say.

For their assistance in preparing this book for publication, I must first of all thank Mrs Kathleen Wilkinson and Mrs Lilian Bragger, who typed it in different versions. My friends Mr P. J. Rhodes, of the Department of Classics at Durham, and Mr A. P. Burton, of the Victoria and Albert Museum, have put me under a great obligation by their willingness to help check the proofs. And I am grateful to Messrs Michael Fenn and Allan Hill, of University College, Durham, who respectively compiled the index and drew the sketch-map.

Finally, I wish to record my debt to the many undergraduates at Oxford and Durham Universities whose companionship, as friends and as pupils, sustained and encouraged me during the six years that this book was in the making.

DUNCAN BYTHELL

Department of Economic History
University of Durham

INTRODUCTION

by R. M. Hartwell

No other group of workers in the history of the English working classes has received more sympathy and less scholarly attention than the handloom weavers of the Lancashire cotton industry during the industrial revolution. Always in the cast, but rarely on the stage, they are mentioned, without close scrutiny, in every book on the industrial revolution. Although the leading example of technological unemployment during English industrialization, their heads have never been accurately counted. Although the most quoted example of deteriorating living standards, their wages have never been exactly computed. Although an alleged prime source of radical discontent and action, their role in politics has never been fully analysed. Indeed, Mr Bythell's study is the first book-length and detailed examination of the handloom weavers—their numbers, their varying history of employment, their standard-of-life, their industrial and political actions, their displacement and disappearance. This is surely strange? And even stranger when one remembers that so much of the best English economic history has come out of Manchester, from the pens of a long line of distinguished historians from Unwin to Ashton, and that much of this writing has been concerned with the industrial revolution. Yet no Manchester historian took up the history of the handloom weavers.

It is fitting, even at this late date, that the first full-length study should come from Lancashire. Mr Bythell was born and schooled in Lancashire, before going to Wadham College, Oxford, to read history and subsequently to write the thesis which is this book. His interest in the general theme of the social problems of the industrial revolution was roused by a special subject in the Oxford history syllabus on the administration of Sir Robert Peel. His interest in Lancashire and the cotton industry sprang directly from his home environment. He was born and reared in the village of Haggate, near Burnley, a place which he himself notes was a

centre for Chartist enthusiasm during the years when the hand-loom weavers were in full decline. His great-great grandfather was born in the same village in 1824 and as a boy was a handloom weaver, although much later, in the 1870s, he actually started a small power-weaving factory; he certainly played an active part in the history of decline and transition of the weavers which his great-great grandson here describes. All four of Mr Bythell's grandparents were also employed for the whole of their working lives as factory weavers, and both of his parents began their working lives in the mill. It is not surprising, therefore, that when Mr Bythell was looking for a research project he turned to Lanca-shire and to the cotton industry for inspiration.

Nevertheless, when the specific subject of the handloom weavers came up as a possible topic for research, Mr Bythell was sceptical that the subject had not already been covered, and, when satisfied that it had not been, was worried lest neglect had been rationally based on the inadequacy of the sources. The 'feeling' that the weavers had been adequately studied reflected a general view, a view built up by frequent references but few facts. Everyone had heard of the handloom weavers; everyone had some but not very definite ideas about their fate, and on closer examination every fact softened, every distinction blurred. Suspicion about the adequacy of the sources, however, was well founded. Beyond the parliamentary papers, fortunately massive, evidence thinned rapidly, although diligence and luck turned up many sources, which, fragmentary as they were, nevertheless allowed Mr Bythell to add flesh to the substantial bones of the great parliamentary inquiries of the period. The final result is impressively detailed and Mr Bythell was able to answer the many questions which we want answered about the history of the handloom weavers. In so doing he not only throws light on the progress of technology in the cotton industry (in itself an important subject), but also on radical politics. Indeed, no other working-class group of this period has been subjected to such close scrutiny. And only when similar studies of many other labour groups are made, will many of the tantalizing questions raised by the standard-of-living debate be settled

It is neither necessary nor appropriate that I should here summarize Mr Bythell's book, or underline his main conclusions. It is appropriate, however, to discuss Mr Bythell's work in the context of modern research in economic history, both as regards subject-matter and methodology. In subject-matter, the book reflects a greatly revived interest in the industrial revolution, an interest which is partly a response to the contemporary interest in economic growth, but, from the historian's point of view, more definitely a response to an increasing interest in 'the great discontinuity' of modern history which began with the industrial revolution. The industrial revolution, according to Carlo Cipolla, created a deep breach in the continuity of the historical process. And along with the French Revolution, it achieved, according to Eric Hobsbawm, 'the transformation of the world between 1789 and 1848'. Among economic historians, it is now fashionable to look at this change as economic growth; but such abstraction, even in deference to hard figures and exact analysis, disguises the complexity and diversity of history. However, historians should welcome the interest and techniques of the economists, for as Mr Bythell demonstrates, these can be useful if combined with the virtues of historical research, understanding, and sympathy.

Mr Bythell's method cannot be neatly labelled as quantitative, or sociological, or economic, or 'new'; it is solidly empirical in the traditions of English historical scholarship. Mr Bythell's history is firmly based on facts and chronology, and, where it is appropriate, he counts and is analytical. Mr Bythell asks 'what?', 'when?', 'why?', and 'how much?'. He is concerned not only with numbers and living standards, but also with political and social response. However, although his book contains much economic and political history, it is essentially social history in depth; he has documented and analysed a great social problem, its creation and its final solution.

R. M. H.

The weaving towns and villages of north-east Lancashire in 1821.

CHAPTER I

PROBLEMS AND SOURCES

AT one time, the story of the English cotton industry held pride of place in accounts of those many social and economic changes which are conventionally labelled 'the industrial revolution', and it is not difficult to understand why. Cotton was, after all, the first major industry to use power-driven machinery in factories; contemporary observers tended to be particularly impressed because its growth in the late eighteenth and early nineteenth centuries was on a far bigger scale than that of the traditional woollen, silk, and linen textiles;[1] and most important of all, cotton's interests became very closely involved in national politics in the 1830s and 1840s. To a very large degree, the controversies over factory regulation and free trade concerned cotton more than any other industry, since, in the popular imagination at least, 'factories' meant cotton mills, and 'free traders' meant Lancashire mill-owners. From the crucial importance of these controversies to the development of the new urban-industrial society, it necessarily followed that the cotton trade should come to be widely regarded as the centre-piece of the new order.

More recently, however, the emphasis in industrial revolution studies has changed, and the cotton industry has been dethroned from the position it formerly occupied.[2] This has come about largely through the study of the more basic general developments in transport, in power supplies, in the making of capital goods, and in capital formation—all of which can be termed the *sine qua non* of industrial growth. Thus it is now recognized that exaggerated notions formerly prevailed as to the size and importance of cotton

---

[1] This interest was demonstrated in the 1830s and 1840s not only in the serious social commentaries of P. Gaskell, A. Ure, and J. P. Kay, but also in contemporary fiction, especially the works of Mrs Gaskell. No other industry attracted public attention on this scale.

[2] The decline in interest is, of course, in part symptomatic of the diminishing importance —gradual in the nineteenth century but very marked since 1914—of cotton in the economy as a whole.

in relation to the rest of the economy; even at the end of the Napoleonic war, when it was still the only industry to have adopted the factory system on a large scale, it probably represented no more than $7\frac{1}{2}$ per cent of the national income.[1] It is also admitted that it is misleading to concentrate on the cotton trade, because its very newness in the late eighteenth century makes its history during a period of general economic growth untypical of developments in older-established industries.

But untypical as it was, and exaggerated as it has been, the development of the English cotton industry in the period from 1780 to 1850 was still, as Professor Court says, 'a revolutionary and transforming event',[2] in at least three major directions. First, the growth of a large industry saw the emergence of a powerful and cohesive class of entrepreneurs, the millowners. Secondly, cotton was overwhelmingly dependent on foreign trade; the raw material came from abroad, and in the first half of the nineteenth century between 50 and 60 per cent of the manufactured article was exported as cloth or yarn.[3] For this reason, no other industry was more influential in changing the basis of the British economy from the old-fashioned ideas of imperial self-sufficiency to the Manchester School's doctrines of free trade and world markets. And thirdly, as the first industry to employ power-driven machines in large factories, cotton was important in changing the status and the working conditions of the numerous labour force which it employed. All three factors were of fundamental significance in the industrial development of Britain.

It might be supposed, from the early tendency to regard 'industrial revolution' and 'cotton' as synonymous, that there already existed a substantial body of information readily accessible on the cotton industry during the period of the classic 'industrial revolution'. A recent writer has said, for instance, that 'no industry has been so frequently investigated and written about as the cotton industry'.[4] However, anyone who attempts to compile a biblio-

[1] P. Deane and W. A. Cole, *British economic growth, 1689–1959* (Cambridge, 1962), p. 163.
[2] W. H. B. Court, *A concise economic history of Britain since 1750* (Cambridge, 1954), p. 57.
[3] Deane and Cole, *op. cit.* p. 187.
[4] M. Blaug, 'The productivity of capital in the Lancashire cotton industry during the nineteenth century', *Economic History Review*, XIII (1961), 359.

graphy of the industry's history will soon realize that the volume of available work is quite small, and its value is even smaller. There have been some useful studies of limited aspects of the subject,[1] but no attempts at comprehensive treatment which do not derive from a very small number of sources: the same statements from a handful of contemporary writers, such as Baines, Gaskell, and William Radcliffe;[2] the same quotations from a narrow range of parliamentary papers; and the same statistics from late nineteenth-century authorities such as Ellison and Wood, appear time and time again.[3] Our knowledge of what happened in the English cotton industry during this important period could profitably be extended.[4]

II

Particularly obscure is the transition from the so-called domestic system to the factory system in cotton weaving, although it is probably true that the most popularly held image of the 'industrial revolution' depicts the cruel displacement of the hardy domestic textile worker by the dark satanic mill. And rightly so; for this was in many ways the crucial development in the cotton trade during the first half of the nineteenth century. It affected a substantial proportion of England's industrial labour force and changed the organization and structure of what was now her chief manufacturing industry; it had profound effects on the normal patterns of life and work for the weaver and his family; and in the critical social problem which resulted from the co-existence for many years of hand and power weaving, it provided the biggest blot on the whole history of the industrial revolution

---

[1] Such as G. Unwin, *Samuel Oldknow and the Arkwrights* (Manchester, 1924); R. S. Fitton and A. P. Wadsworth, *The Strutts and the Arkwrights* (Manchester, 1958); N. J. Smelser, *Social change in the industrial revolution* (London, 1959); and A. Redford, *Manchester merchants and foreign trade, 1794–1858* (Manchester, 1934).

[2] E. Baines, *History of the cotton manufacture* (London, 1835); P. Gaskell, *The manufacturing population of England* (London, 1833), and *Artisans and machinery* (London, 1836); W. Radcliffe, *The origin of the new system of manufacture, commonly called powerloom weaving* (Stockport, 1828).

[3] T. Ellison, *The cotton trade of Great Britain* (London, 1886) and G. H. Wood, *History of wages in the cotton industry during the past hundred years* (London, 1910).

[4] Cotton is not unique in this respect; few major British industries have been comprehensively studied over the period 1780–1850.

3

—a blot so big, indeed, that even the 'optimistic' school of economic historians have to excuse it by attributing it to an unusual combination of adverse factors which normally ought not to have been found occurring together.[1] The purpose of the present study is to examine this important development in an effort to discover what really happened when England's first major modern manufacturing industry experienced its principal technological development. The line of approach to be adopted will probably not commend itself to all students of the industrial revolution, since the end product will be a piece of 'macro-history' which will examine this development in general and 'total' terms, rather than a piece of 'micro-history' which would consider the same subject from the point of view of the personal experience and problems of actual individual handloom weavers who were involved in it. Like all economic history written in these terms, it will say a good deal about various apparently impersonal 'factors' and 'forces', rather less about real people, and as such it can be rightly criticized as a one-sided approach to a many-sided question. The best defence of the present procedure is simply that, in the past, much discussion of this and related topics has been carried on in terms of myth, half-truth, and, often, sheer ignorance. Not until the general background has been clarified can we begin properly to understand and profitably to discuss the predicaments and the responses of a few known individuals.

Much of what has been said about the handloom weavers has been confused, and much can be seen, after a little reflection, to be highly implausible. In the present chapter, the object is to indicate how little we really know about this phase of economic development, and to suggest at what points our need for enlightenment is greatest.

First, the current state of opinion on these various problems will be presented; secondly, the plausibility of that opinion will be considered; and thirdly, the lines of approach and the kinds of material which will have to be employed to amplify or revise the current orthodoxy will be indicated.

[1] See the explanation of T. S. Ashton, *The industrial revolution* (London, 1947), p. 117.

At the outset, it is imperative to have a clear picture of the organization and structure of the cotton industry as a whole, and to consider the relationships which existed between its several branches. In particular, the links between the master spinners and the master manufacturers (whether hand or power) need to be established, in order to explain why, for example, the first weaving sheds were set up by spinners who already owned factories and machines. Professor A. J. Taylor has suggested that the spinner, unlike the simple handloom manufacturer, had the resources with which to purchase costly machinery.[1] But is it in fact correct to apply the late nineteenth century's organizational pattern, in which there was a sharp division between these two major processes, to the situation in the industrial revolution proper? Is it not true rather that the 'trend' towards the combination of these processes, which was certainly a marked feature of the early days of the powerloom, was not a new 'trend' at all, but merely the logical continuation of a combination which had hitherto been normal? Certainly, the evidence, for example, of trade directories at the end of the Napoleonic war suggests that a considerable number of entrepreneurs in cotton were both spinners and manufacturers. Only if the structural pattern is clarified will the peculiar way in which the powerloom came to be adopted be explicable.

On the introduction of the powerloom in cotton, historians are in general agreement, at least as to the chronology. It is usually maintained that it came into general use only gradually, and that the social readjustments became painful because it existed alongside the handloom for some years. Thus Professor Ashton writes: 'Whereas the water-twist and mule-spinning factories had sprung up almost overnight, the power-operated weaving mills came very slowly.'[2]

As to timing, Professor Redford's view would be generally accepted: 'Even so late as 1830, it was estimated that there were in England and Scotland not more than 60,000 powerlooms, while there were about 240,000 handlooms. Power weaving was

---

[1] A. J. Taylor, 'Concentration and specialization in the Lancashire cotton industry', *Economic History Review*, I (1949), 118.

[2] Ashton, *op. cit.* p. 117.

by that time entering upon a period of rapid development after a generation of struggle; and by the middle of the century the victory of the power-driven machine was virtually complete.'[1]

Economic historians have found it less easy to agree on an explanation for the long delay in the powerloom's adoption—after all, Edmund Cartwright patented his first powerloom in 1785. Professor Ashton, again, has furnished the most comprehensive statement; the slowness of the transition from hand to power 'was due partly to imperfections in the powerloom itself, partly to the long war with France (which by raising the rate of interest discouraged investment in plant), and partly to the reluctance of the weavers, many of them women, to leave their homes.'[2]

However, Halévy (and his compatriot Mantoux) found the chief cause of delay in the unwillingness of the manufacturer to risk outbreaks of machine-breaking by the enraged hand workers: 'It would be nearer the truth to say that the fear inspired by their threats and numbers was the real cause why machinery was not introduced earlier into this department.'[3]

On balance, the first part of Ashton's thesis—that the power-loom was for long an imperfect machine—is both the most plausible and the most widely-held explanation. The mechanization of weaving was not a simple matter, and, so long as the new looms had technical imperfections and were liable to become obsolete fairly quickly, entrepreneurs would be unwilling to invest heavily in them, especially when handloom weaving involved cheap labour and little fixed capital. Despite the power-loom's obvious advantages of 'saving labour, improving the quality of the goods, and bringing all the operations of the manu-facture under the immediate eye of the master',[4] its adoption would necessarily be limited until it could be applied to quality as well as coarse goods, and until such difficulties as the need for an automatic device to stop the loom whenever any of a number of things went wrong had been overcome. And, as Messrs Briggs

---

[1] A. Redford, *An economic history of England, 1760–1860* (2nd edn, London, 1960), p. 124.
[2] Ashton, *op. cit. loc. cit.*
[3] E. Halévy, *England in 1815* (English paperback edn, London, 1961), p. 289.
[4] Speech of the prosecuting counsel during the trial of the 1826 loombreakers at Lancaster Assizes as reported in *Wheelers Manchester Chronicle*, 19 August 1826.

and Jordan remind us, 'the powerloom...did not approximate to its modern form until 1840.'[1]

The second part of Ashton's thesis, which attributes the slow adoption of the powerloom to the French war which diverted capital from industry, seems much less plausible. For heavy investment in spinning mills up to at least the time of the Orders in Council and the war with America has been noted by Professor Briggs;[2] whilst 1810, in the very midst of the period of economic warfare, saw the cotton industry at a record level of activity and prosperity.[3] To the third and final part of Professor Ashton's thesis, that the handloom weavers were 'reluctant' to enter the factory, fundamental objections will be brought later.[4]

Besides studying the spread of the powerloom in cotton by asking when and why, it is also important to ask where and why. Who were the people who first found it worthwhile to invest in the powerloom? Professor Taylor has shown that in 1835 the great majority of powerlooms were in south Lancashire and Cheshire, and that only 12,000 out of a total of 90,000 were to be found in the north Lancashire towns[5]—Preston, Blackburn, Burnley, and Colne—which in the later nineteenth century were the centres of the weaving branch of the industry; even in Bolton there were fewer than 1,500 powerlooms in 1834.[6] Since north Lancashire had previously been the centre for weaving plain, coarse goods by hand, as Bolton traditionally was for fancy goods, it is necessary to explain why these districts were slower in adopting powerlooms than were the south Lancashire towns, where the handweaving tradition was apparently less strong. Was it only the result of the existing accumulation of capital in the hands of the master spinners in Manchester, Stockport, and Ashton, or were there other special inhibiting factors at work in the northern districts?

The examination of the adoption of the powerloom leads naturally to the consideration of the converse problem—the decrease in the number of handlooms—and so raises the question of

[1] M. Briggs and P. Jordan, *An economic history of England* (8th edn, London, 1958), p. 245.
[2] A. Briggs, *The age of improvement* (London, 1959), p. 162.
[3] F. Crouzet, *L'économie britannique et le blocus continental* (2 vols, Paris, 1958), p. 510.
[4] See below, p. 11.   [5] Taylor, *op. cit.* p. 117.
[6] *PP. 1834 (556)* x, Q. 5627.

the nature, size, composition and distribution of the labour force engaged at cotton hand weaving during the industrial revolution. The first problem is that of recruitment in the years before the powerloom became practicable. Before the spinning inventions of the 1770s which made possible the production of cotton yarn for both warp and weft, there were virtually no English weavers producing all-cotton cloth. The fustian weavers of Lancashire, who used a mixture of linen and cotton, came nearest to it, but they were too few to have provided more than a bare nucleus for the new labour force. For in view of the popular favour which cotton soon acquired as a substitute for woollen and linen cloth, the recruitment of weavers for the new industry must have occurred on a massive scale. Yet no-one seems to have considered seriously where they all came from.

Nor is there any real agreement as to when the period of recruitment ended and the numbers began to decline. How long did it take for the powerloom to become so widespread as to affect the number of hand weavers? Some writers imply that although the number of handlooms was still considerable in 1830, it had in the past been even bigger; others infer from the parliamentary papers that the number was at its peak in the 1830s, and only declined thereafter. Could it be perhaps that both are right, in the sense that the progress of technical change differed greatly from one district to another?

The problem is particularly difficult, because the evidence for numbers is extremely slender, and most of the estimates go back to the same two or three sources. Several witnesses before the 1833 committee on manufactures, commerce and shipping made round-figure estimates of 200,000 or 250,000 weavers,[1] and since they were men conversant with the cotton trade their estimates have been accepted by all who have dealt with the subject from Edward Baines onwards. In particular, they form the basis for the detailed calculations of G. H. Wood, who drew up a table tracing the growth and decline of the hand-weaving force; but the mathematical regularity with which Wood's total falls by 25,000 every two years between 1831 and 1835, and then by 10,000

[1] PP. *1833* (*690*) VI, QQ. 9449 and 10171.

every three years until it vanishes, leads to the suspicion that the table was based on a desire for symmetry, rather than on a wish to set down hard facts diligently acquired.[1]

Despite the slim basis of evidence on which they rest, Wood's estimates have been extensively quoted as proven facts. And even those writers who have gone back to the various original estimates in the parliamentary papers of the 1830s have sometimes been misled, because it is not always clear whether the figures relate to both England and Scotland, whether they refer to all textiles or to cotton only, or whether by the phrase 'dependent on the hand-loom' they mean actual weavers or weavers and their families. Because of this imprecision, some extremely misleading statements have been made about the number of handloom weavers. Thus Dr P. Gregg writes of 'the handloom weavers...declining from half a million in 1838 to 50,000 in 1848',[2] which appears to be derived from Clapham's estimate of half a million weavers in all textiles in the 1820s[3] and Wood's guess at the number of cotton weavers in 1848.

If there are few hard facts about the numbers of weavers, there are equally few about the composition of the labour force. It is generally acknowledged that not all the weavers were adult men although, in the 'golden age' of domestic manufacture, weaving was, in contrast with spinning, allegedly a man's job. Sir John Clapham, speaking of the workers, whether domestic or factory, in the cotton industry in the 1830s, concluded that 'the majority were probably women and girls';[4] and contemporary evidence in the parliamentary papers makes it abundantly clear that children of both sexes formed a considerable proportion of the labour force.[5] How considerable, no-one has attempted to say. Yet the question is an important one, since it is clear that, for many women, children and old people, who might be called the 'sub-ordinate' members of a family, handloom weaving was not

[1] Wood, *op. cit.* pp. 127–8. Wood, of course, admitted that his figures could not be exact.
[2] P. Gregg, *A social and economic history of Britain* (3rd edn, London, 1962), p. 223.
[3] J. H. Clapham, *The early railway age, 1820–1850* (2nd edn, Cambridge, 1930), p. 179.
[4] *Ibid.* p. 72.
[5] The 1,200 calico weavers employed by James Massey and Sons in North Lancashire were said to be 'principally women and children' by the firm's manager, G. Smith (*PP. 1833 (690)* VI, Q. 9343).

a full-time trade, but rather the same kind of domestic by-occupation that spinning had formerly been—a factor of considerable significance when, for example, one is attempting to assess the meaning of wage statistics in the industry. At the same time, the labour force did contain a substantial proportion of adult men to whom the loom was the only source of income; three-fifths of the 3,500 weavers employed by P. Dixon and Co. in a wide stretch of country around Carlisle were men.[1] These were likely to be the real sufferers when wages fell.

It is usually asserted that Irish immigrants bulked large among the cotton handloom weavers, particularly in the industry's last years, and the competition which resulted from the Irishmen's lower standard of living has been alleged to have increased the distresses of the English weavers. A number of historians quote the statement of W. E. Hickson, one of the royal commission on the weavers in 1837–41, that the Irish formed at least one half of the cotton weavers,[2] apparently forgetting that Hickson's statements were solely the result of personal observations on a short fact-finding tour of a district with which he had no previous acquaintance. According to the 1841 census, however, the place of the Irish has been much exaggerated. This showed that virtually half the 100,000 Irish-born persons in Lancashire were in Liverpool (not noted for any large-scale weaving), and it is highly unlikely that the 50,000 living elsewhere were all weavers.[3] Some writers have developed this theme by claiming that, as the English moved out of handloom weaving when it became unprofitable, the Irish, willing to accept lower wages, moved in.[4] But although this argument may apply in Manchester and Glasgow, it can have little relevance in north-east Lancashire, where hand weaving lingered a long time on a large scale, but where there were few Irishmen.

The final problem about the labour force concerns, of course, its ultimate displacement and disappearance. Were the handloom weavers, having been rendered technologically redundant by the powerloom, willing or able to find alternative employment else-

[1] PP. 1840 (220) XXIV, p. 606.   [2] Ibid. p. 693.
[3] A. Redford, Labour migration in England, 1800–50 (Manchester, 2nd ed. 1964), p. 155.
[4] For example, D. Read, 'Chartism in Manchester', in Chartist Studies, ed. A. Briggs (London, 1960), p. 31.

where? In particular, did they, as Professor Ashton claimed, add to their miseries by their 'reluctance' to enter factories? When one reflects that the earliest power weavers were women and children working for quite low wages, it is clear that something more than 'reluctance' kept adult men, at least, out of the factory. Some may indeed have been unwilling to adapt themselves to the new working conditions, but it is surely far more likely that many were simply unable to find alternative work, either because there were at that stage relatively few factory jobs for men, or because there were no factories in a particular locality, or because the weavers in question were too old to be trained for a new trade.

III

On matters connected with the labour force, little is known, and that little is confused. When the subject of the weaver's wages and standard of living is examined, the sum total of facts is much greater, but the confusion is in no way diminished. Historians have made extensive use of the wealth of material on this topic in the various parliamentary papers from 1803 onwards, and have been unanimous in concluding that the domestic weavers in the first half of the nineteenth century became a class who suffered, in the contemporary phrase, 'distress'. To the 'optimistic' school of economic historians the decline in the real wages of the handloom weavers is the major exception to the rule that the working population of England was materially better-off in the year of Sir Robert Peel's death than in the year of his birth. Sir John Clapham, for example, summarized their plight as 'a crying national tragedy'.[1]

Within this general framework, however, there are elements of ignorance and confusion. In the first place, the information in the blue books does not give a consistent coverage for the whole period 1780–1850.

Our knowledge of wages in the so-called 'golden age' at the beginning of the period, when the new industry was just developing, is very slender. Witnesses at parliamentary committees

[1] Clapham, *op. cit.* p. 551.

who claimed to trace back the piece-rates for particular cloths to the 1790s, and embittered old men like William Radcliffe, gave the impression that wages had formerly been very high. This impression is not borne out, however, by Professor Unwin's account of Samuel Oldknow's weavers in the 1780s and 1790s.[1] Just how 'golden' things were, and how far the prosperity of the early years was the result of freak conditions which attended the widespread demand for a new and initially scarce fabric, is a subject which requires serious consideration. Somewhat surprisingly, even less is known about wages in the last years of handloom weaving, chiefly because there was no further public inquiry into the weavers' condition after the royal commission of 1837–41. Even G. H. Wood, who produced a table of average weekly earnings, was obliged to admit that for the 1840s and 1850s (by which time the number of cotton handloom weavers was small) his figures were pure conjecture.[2]

Secondly, even assuming that the information in the parliamentary papers is on the whole factually correct for the period 1800–40, it can still be very misleading. There is not much advantage in simply taking an average of all the available figures, as Wood did,[3] since variety rather than similarity was the essential feature of earnings in this industry. Even in the same town and for the same type of cloth, the piece-rates offered by different manufacturers were alleged to vary by as much as 10–15 per cent, particularly in fancy goods.[4] Yet it is this kind of average which is generally quoted in books on the subject; the most recent full-scale work on the cotton trade in this period, by N. J. Smelser, simply copies Wood's table in its entirety without any critical comment.[5]

Apart from differences in piece-rates for the same cloth, we should expect to find a number of criteria according to which weavers' wages might vary. First, wages would differ according to locality, town weavers being generally better paid than those in the country, where labour was more plentiful, and those near

[1] Unwin, *op. cit.* pp. 112–13.
[2] Wood, *op. cit.* pp. 127–8.
[3] *Ibid.* p. 112.
[4] PP. *1833 (690)* VI, Q. 1828.
[5] Smelser, *op. cit.* p. 140.

Manchester than those further away. Secondly, wages would vary according to the quality of the work being done; fine, fancy, and patterned cloths, involving greater skill, being generally more highly paid than coarse and plain cloths. Thirdly, when considering the standard of living, we should remember that actual weekly earnings are more important than piece-rates, and these would depend on the weaver's strength, skill, and application, and on the efficiency of his tools. Thus an adult male weaver might normally expect to earn more than his wife, his young children, or his aged parents. Any set of wage figures which fails to specify to what class of weavers, as determined by the above criteria, they were paid, is not a great deal of use, when we are studying the progress of wages or the household economy of a weaving family.

Other points must also be borne in mind before the significance of any particular group of figures can be assessed. In the first place, many of the wage statistics given in the parliamentary papers are estimated, not actual, earnings, and they tend to assume, first, that the weaver was in permanent employment and earned the same sum every week, and, second, that his output changed little over time. But the whole question of unemployment and under-employment has received scant attention, and it is by no means clear for how much of his time a weaver was idle—whether voluntarily or of necessity. Secondly, contemporary estimates varied considerably as to the amount which had to be deducted from the gross wage to cover 'working expenses' such as the cost of shuttles, paste and brushes for dressing the warp, and of heating and lighting the workshop. Thirdly, the important point in determining the standard of living is the total income of the family, not the earnings of individual members; and the family income might well include such incidentals as the value of garden produce if the weaver lived in the country, the rent of looms and living accommodation provided for a journeyman, the expense saved by having children to wind the bobbins, extra income from seasonal farmwork in rural areas, and parish relief for a large family.

It is also necessary to distinguish between the distress which the weavers suffered before and after the powerloom came into use,

for the nature of their problems changed substantially in the 1820s. In the latter part of the Napoleonic war, when powerlooms were quite insignificant, the plight of the cotton weavers was at times very serious, its chief symptoms being low money wages at a time of inflation, and spells of unemployment because of the dislocation of trade with both Europe and America. Later, as the powerloom spread and became more efficient in producing an ever-widening range of cloths, there opened a period of permanent distress, with wages driven lower by the unequal competition. But it would be wrong to assume that the cotton weavers suffered a long and unrelieved decline from the time of the Orders in Council until their last survivors vanished some time after the cotton famine. There were times when the slump which affected the weavers was merely part of a general commercial depression, and, equally, there were always some branches of the trade which suffered less than others. There were even periods of prosperity for the hand weavers after the French war: one such spell followed the reopening of the continental market after the battle of Leipzig and lasted into 1815; another came in 1821–2, after the post-war slump, but before the first wave of heavy investment in powerlooms and mills in 1823–5 had taken place.[1]

It is not difficult to explain the catastrophic fall in wages. Before the coming of the powerloom, the labour supply was insufficiently responsive to the fluctuating demands of the industry, and under slump conditions competition to obtain employment inevitably forced down piece-rates. In addition to reducing the costs of weaving, the introduction of the powerloom had the effect of further increasing the weaving capacity of the whole industry and thereby widening the gap between labour supply and demand which occurred in periodic trade depressions. In these circumstances, Clapham's argument, that from the 1830s the handloom weavers formed a true 'reserve army of labour', which was able to find work only when the factories were fully occupied, seems the fairest description of their economic

[1] One of the best illustrations of the prosperity of 1821–2 will be found in the diary and account book of William Varley, a country calico weaver near Burnley. See W. Bennett, *History of Burnley* (Burnley, 1948), vol. III, appendix 1.

role.[1] Another contributory factor, much criticized by contemporaries, especially during wartime when markets fluctuated wildly, was the defective organization of the weaving side of the industry, with its preponderance of small manufacturers, who, lacking large reserves of capital, were obliged to indulge in cutthroat competition with one another and to accept whatever price a merchant would give them for their cloth. At the same time, however, contemporaries often had alternative explanations of the weavers' troubles: many blamed the iniquitous tax structure, which lay heavily on such luxuries as tea and sugar which were in general consumption; and many argued that the contraction of the currency at the end of the war, which caused money wages to fall but fixed incomes to rise in real terms, had made the burden of taxation even heavier;[2] others attacked the whole basis of the existing tariff, which by protecting British farming hindered the export of British manufactured goods to agrarian countries and also kept the cost of living at home unnecessarily high, to the great advantage of our foreign competitors.[3]

IV

So far, this chapter has dealt with economic aspects of the cotton handloom weavers' problems. These have needed most explanation, because it is here that our existing knowledge seems to be most defective. But the social and political consequences of the economic developments are in themselves of major interest; and although certain topics have been covered by historians, there still remain substantial unmapped areas.

Fortunately, many of the sociological problems have been illuminated by Dr Smelser's recent book, which examines in detail the problems involved in the change from the joint family effort which characterized domestic manufacture to work in the

---

[1] Clapham, op. cit. p. 557.
[2] These points were frequently raised in Commons debates in the 1830s. See e.g. Debate on the reduction of public salaries and wages of the working classes, 7 March 1833, in 3rd Series Hansard, vol. 16, cols. 353–69.
[3] The view, for instance, of Lord King in a Lords debate on the depression of 1826. New Series Hansard, vol. 15, col. 742.

factory where the members of the family were separated according to the particular functions they fulfilled. Other developments, such as the changed status of the worker who, with the passing of the 'domestic system', lost the freedom to regulate his working day, the ownership of his tools, and the privileges inseparable from the idea of a working-class hierarchy of apprentice, journeyman, and master, have long been recognized. But some interesting social questions are yet unexplored. For example, many writers have made the distinction between the class of weavers who lived in the country and carried on some small-farming and the wholly urban class of full-time cellar weavers.[1] What is uncertain is the relative importance of each group within the labour force as a whole; was Clapham right to describe the former as 'half-mythical' and to regard them as virtually non-existent by the 1830s?[2] Then again, no-one has ever tried to establish whether the formal master–apprentice relationship and the other features of a classical 'domestic craft' such as existed in the older textile industries ever held the same place in cotton. But detailed investigation may well reveal that in its social and organizational basis the cotton-weaving trade, because of both its newness and its rapid growth, was untypical of older industries and their traditional patterns.

The social implications of the changes in weaving in the first half of the nineteenth century attracted the attention of such contemporary observers as Gaskell, Kay, and Engels. But probably more concern was shown for the weavers' plight as a result of the political and semi-political activities in which they indulged in a vain effort to improve, or at least to bolster up, their position. These activities took different forms at different times. In descending order of respectability, they included: efforts to enlist the support of the central government to remedy their grievances by legislation; direct industrial action to put pressure on their employers to pay higher wages; opposition to any enactments of the government which, like the 1834 Poor Law Amendment Act,

---

[1] Both Clapham (*op. cit.* p. 180) and Smelser (*op. cit.* p. 141) make the distinction, which derives largely from the evidence of the Bishop of Chester to the 1826–7 s.c. on emigration (*PP. 1826/7 (237)* v, Q. 2262).

[2] Clapham, *op. cit.* p. 552.

appeared to put an end to what the weavers regarded as their natural rights; outright opposition to the existing political regime when it seemed unlikely to remedy their grievances, and a consequent demand for reformed political institutions over which they would have greater influence; and finally, in the last extremes of despair, the wanton destruction of the machines which the handloom weavers regarded as chiefly responsible for their troubles.

If we exclude the history of the weavers' unionism and the attacks on the steamlooms,[1] none of the main activities in which the handloom weavers are generally thought to have indulged has received detailed treatment. The most 'respectable' of these, the story of the frequent petitions to parliament for the relief of distress, provides a fascinating sidelight on the workings of upper-class politics in the first half of the nineteenth century. In the first place, the speeches in the House and the questions in the various select committees are indicative of the divergent schools of thought which prevailed on such crucial questions as the weavers' plans for a minimum wage enforced by the legislature. But perhaps even more significant are the ways in which interested parties manipulated the committee system, and the consequent doubts which must arise as to the value of the information which the different committees unearthed and caused to be printed in the parliamentary papers.

The possibilities of bias in the parliamentary papers can be appreciated if one remembers that the select committees of 1834–5 pronounced in favour of a scheme of wage regulation by statute, whilst the royal commission of 1837–41, composed of professional political economists, declared its implacable hostility to the plan.[2] There are in fact many indications that the report of the 1835 committee was the work of a pressure group inspired by John Maxwell and John Fielden. It is clear that the problems of the

---

[1] See J. L. and B. Hammond, *The skilled labourer, 1760–1832* (London, 1919), chapters 4 and 5 *passim*, and also H. A. Turner, *Trade union growth, structure, and policy* (London, 1962), pp. 51–105.

[2] A study of the 'professionalism' of the royal commission will be found in G. J. Stigler, 'The classical economists—an alternative view', in *Five lectures on economic problems* (London, 1949).

handloom weavers were regarded with apathy by most M.P.s,[1] and consequently a determined minority might go a long way in its efforts to undermine the current ideas of political economy by proposing such outlandish plans as wage-fixing by statute. According to Dr Bowring, an M.P. who opposed the minimum wage idea, of the sixty-seven members of the 1835 committee, only twenty-five attended the session at which the final report was drawn up, and only fifteen of those voted in favour of its adoption.[2]

Further doubts as to the reliability of the parliamentary papers arise when the witnesses who appeared before the committees are considered. In 1834–5, few of those called expressed hostility to the idea of wage regulation, although it is not unlikely that many manufacturers would be opposed to such a limitation on their individual freedom in business matters; one can only suspect that there was some judicious selection on the part of the committee's managers. Moreover, there seem to have been a few 'professional' witnesses who kept on appearing year after year at the various committees: one Bolton weaver, Richard Needham, appeared no less than four times between 1803 and 1834—at the select committees of 1803 on the Cotton Arbitration Act, of 1824 on artisans and machinery, of 1833 on manufactures, commerce and shipping, and of 1834 on handloom weavers—and from the copious evidence he gave it would almost be possible to write a brief sketch of his life. Taken altogether, one cannot help feeling that, useful as they are, the parliamentary papers may not always tell the full story of the changes in the industrial revolution.

The second type of political activity means in effect the reaction of the weavers to a major piece of social legislation like the 1834 Poor Law. It has long been known from the parliamentary papers that in some of the cotton-weaving areas in the 1820s low wages were being subsidized out of the poor rates; indeed, the system is condemned by Professor Ashton for helping to persuade the weavers to stay in their homes.[3] It has also been assumed that,

---

[1] There were less than fifty M.P.s present on 15 May 1834 when the motion for a select committee was first debated (*3rd Series Hansard*, vol. 23, col. 1097).
[2] *3rd Series Hansard*, vol. 29, col. 1164.
[3] Ashton, *op. cit.* p. 117.

since wages were no longer to be made up under the Act of 1834, the weavers must have suffered severely, and that consequently they formed the backbone of the anti-Poor Law agitation in the north of England which eventually merged into Chartism.[1] But neither the working of the relief system under the old law, nor the rigidity with which the new law was enforced, particularly in its early years, has been fully studied. A certain amount of regional work has, however, been done, and the general impression is that the severe hardship which was at first expected under the new system did not occur because of the lenience of the guardians, who were subject to strong local pressures. A recent study of the Poor Law in north-east Lancashire concludes that although the new machinery of administration by unions and guardians was set up in the late 1830s, the principles on which relief was given were for many years unchanged.[2] Clearly the view that the domestic weavers were the chief sufferers, and therefore the chief complainers, under the new Poor Law calls for a reappraisal.

The same can be said, too, of the third aspect of the weavers' political activities—their advocacy of parliamentary reform. This was a cry which they seem to have taken up at various times. They were involved in the reform movement in Manchester during the post-war slump, which culminated in the 1817 march of the Blanketeers and the Peterloo meeting of 1819.[3] But it is with Chartism around 1840 that the handloom weavers, by now in full decline, have been particularly associated. This association seems to have resulted partly from the assumption that the weavers were strongly behind the anti-Poor Law agitation, and partly from the belief that, as Chartism was most flourishing at times of general economic depression, then the class which usually suffered most in such catastrophes must have furnished its staunchest supporters.[4]

It would certainly have been strange if many handloom weavers had failed to support a movement like Chartism, which offered a

[1] See M. Hovell, *The Chartist movement* (Manchester, 1925), p. 16.
[2] R. Boyson, 'The new Poor Law in north-east Lancashire', in *Transactions Lancashire and Cheshire Antiquarian Society*, LXX (1960), 35.
[3] D. Read, *Peterloo: the massacre and its background* (London, 1958) *passim*.
[4] See D. Read's essay in *Chartist Studies*, ed. A. Briggs (London, 1960), p. 31.

vague but immediate panacea for men who, in general, had been suffering poverty for years. What is dubious, however, is whether the weavers as a body were more strongly pro-Chartist than were the factory workers, the Irish labourers, or any other particular group in the cotton areas. If it is true that the cotton handloom weavers more than any other class in Lancashire supported the Charter, one might expect first that Chartist demonstrations and meetings would be particularly frequent and violent in areas where hand weaving still predominated, and second that the local Chartist programme would refer specifically to remedies for the weavers' peculiar problems. None of the historians of Chartism, however, has really tried to prove the assumption that the handloom weavers were the most loyal Lancashire Chartists by producing evidence to illustrate either of the above points. Until they do, the idea must be regarded as a rather crude hypothesis.

V

It will be obvious, therefore, that there are many directions in which our knowledge of the fate of the cotton handloom weavers in the period 1780–1850 might be extended. The more one considers the narrow range of facts, the many unproven assumptions, the misleading statements, and the dependence on a small and not necessarily wholly reliable group of sources which has been revealed, the more one is tempted to echo Gaskell's view, expressed in a slightly different context as early as 1833: 'The little amount of information on all these subjects is very extraordinary, especially when it is borne in mind how large a proportion of the national wealth and of the entire population are involved in them.'[1]

The information with which we may hope to answer these various questions must be gathered piecemeal from a wide range of sources. There is no one type of material, no one collection of manuscripts or papers, which can tell us all we want to know. Like any group which fights a losing battle, the cotton handloom weavers and their problems became an almost forgotten bad

---

[1] P. Gaskell, *The manufacturing population of England* (London, 1833), p. 5.

dream as soon as they lost their place in the social and economic structure. Many of the traces of their way of life—their tools and their houses, as well as their habits and their institutions—were quickly obliterated. And in common with other long-vanished groups of poor, ill-organized and badly-educated working men, the weavers left very few literary remains in the form of letters, diaries, notebooks, or memoirs which might give in their own words an indication of their complaints and aspirations. As a result, they must largely be seen through the eyes of outsiders—journalists, employers, magistrates or politicians —who interested themselves in the weavers' problems, and whose views have proved more able to survive.

Even with this drawback, however, enough material remains to suggest answers to the questions which have been posed. And although some of their limitations have been suggested above, it is in the parliamentary papers that the best start can be made. With all their faults, these reports must carry a great deal of authority, having been officially published by the rulers of society who had to examine the weavers' complaints; the fact that they are sometimes one-sided does not make them untrue. Furthermore, they do provide the first-hand opinions of a good number of intelligent individual weavers, which would otherwise not have survived. Nor is it merely from the select committees and the royal commission of the 1830s which dealt specifically with the weavers that this useful information can be obtained. A whole range of reports in the first half of the nineteenth century, covering such diverse topics as foreign trade, emigration, the employment of children, trade unionism, poor relief, and even drunkenness can yield incidental material which has a bearing—often trivial, but sometimes crucial—on the fate of the handloom weavers.

This great but uneven body of fact needs to be supplemented or confirmed from outside, and contemporary books and pamphlets touching wholly or in part on the subject form the first source of help. Hansard, for instance, furnishes the background of parliamentary manoeuvre and discussion which must be read alongside the blue books. The works of serious journalists and economists—such as Peter Gaskell, Andrew Ure, or Charles Babbage—illustrate

the wide range of viewpoints held by thoughtful and well-informed individuals on a topic of considerable public concern.

At the local level, there are, among others: the factual, on-the-spot reports of living conditions from bodies like the Manchester Statistical Society, or such individuals as J. P. Kay and Joseph Adshead; early local histories of parts of Lancashire—for example, those written in the 1820s by James Butterworth of Oldham; topographies, or accounts of individual visits to the weaving districts, whether by foreigners—such as Simond (1810–11), D'Eichthal (1828) or Engels (1845)—or by Englishmen like Aikin in the 1790s, or Cooke Taylor in the 1840s; the first histories of the cotton industry, by John Kennedy (1815), Richard Guest (1823), William Radcliffe (1828) and Edward Baines (1833); and the published reminiscences of the few handloom weavers—of whom Samuel Bamford was the most prominent—who acquired fame in other spheres.

After the books and pamphlets, other local sources help greatly to expand the basic material from the parliamentary papers. In some directions, the surviving local records are very thin. There are few manuscripts left by weavers themselves—the diary and account book of William Varley being one of the most useful[1]— or, for that matter, by their employers. The destruction of business records for all periods of the cotton industry's history has been on a massive scale, and as early as 1852, a local historian was complaining of 'a sad neglect in the paucity of records respecting the rise and progress of the cotton manufacture in Blackburn, which we are afraid can never be amply given to the public'[2] and apart from a few minor local exceptions, those which survive have long since been worked over by historians.[3]

Local government records, fortunately, are more abundant. First, there are the reports of magistrates to the central government at times of stress or disturbance. Historians have long been aware of the value of these documents in the Home Office papers: the

[1] See above, p. 14, n. 1.
[2] P. A. Whittle, *Blackburn as it is* (Preston, 1852), p. 230.
[3] See, for example, F. Collier, *The family economy of the workers in the cotton industry, 1784–1833* (Manchester, 1964) and G. Unwin, *Samuel Oldknow and the Arkwrights* (Manchester, 1924).

Hammonds drew heavily on them in their account of the hand-loom weavers' activities in *The skilled labourer*, and Professor Aspinall published many in his book *The early English trade unions*. Then again, the actual records of those local authorities concerned with the relief of poverty both before and after 1834 illustrate the degree of success with which the weaving districts tackled the problem of the weavers' declining economic well-being.

Another valuable, if cumbersome, source of local information in this period is the Lancashire press. Tucked away among the excerpts from the London papers, the advertisements for stage-coaches, patent medicines and lottery tickets, and the stories of 'horrid murders'—which bulk large in the provincial newspapers of the period—are countless details of both the normal and the unusual events in the economic life of the handloom weaving area. The business advertisements, whether relating to property or to jobs, demonstrate the growth and day-to-day working of the industry in all its variety; whilst correspondence, editorials, and reports of public meetings all illustrate local reactions to the weavers' different problems and the various attempts at their solution. The yield from such newspapers tends, however, to be patchy—after all, the papers of the period were written neither by the poor nor for the poor—and although there are the pleasant surprises from the occasional unexpected discovery, the extraction of information is in general a slow and time-consuming business. Since, however, the Manchester newspapers circulated most widely in the cotton districts and also reported news at second hand from the papers of the other towns, these may be taken to be the most useful and informative, as well as the most accessible and long-lived; accordingly, a detailed study of the leading Manchester newspapers has been made over the whole period from the late 1770s to the early 1840s, supplemented by the selective reading of other newspapers (in so far as these exist for the late eighteenth and early nineteenth centuries), in order to obtain fuller reporting of specific local events, where appropriate.[1]

[1] The full reporting of specific local events proved most valuable in tracing the work of the royal commission on the handloom weavers, 1837–41 (see below, pp. 165–6). The published report which Mr Muggeridge, the assistant commissioner, made on Lancashire (*PP. 1840 (220)* XXIV) was a highly condensed summary of the mass of evidence which he

Even when facts have been gathered from all these sources, there must, by the very nature of the subject, remain some uncertainties, and some surmises. Yet the combination of the little-used local material with the traditional printed works does make it possible to offer plausible solutions to many of the interesting problems connected with this significant aspect of the industrialization of England in the early nineteenth century.

had collected, and omitted much of the detail; by tracing Muggeridge's route through the weaving districts and studying the local press reports of the meetings which he held, many of these details have fortunately been recovered.

THE ORGANIZATION OF THE INDUSTRY

THE complete history of the cotton industry during the industrial revolution, like that of many other industries, has never been written. To study its many ramifications during the crucial period of change from the last decades of the eighteenth century to the middle of the nineteenth—the development of sources of raw materials and of markets, the expansion of output, the social consequences of technical change in the various branches, the internal organization of the industry, and the place of cotton within the whole economy—would be a vast undertaking. In a study of only the weaving section of the industry during this period, many of these aspects must be ignored completely. Yet weaving must be seen within its proper context of the industry as a whole, and before the particular problems which came to face the hand workers in this one section of the industry can be examined, a few general points about the structure of the English cotton trade during the industrial revolution need to be established.

The size of cotton as compared with other contemporary industries during the first half of the nineteenth century must never be forgotten. Measured by the imports of cotton wool, the industry's raw material, which came entirely from abroad, the cotton industry grew in the last three decades of the eighteenth century from almost nothing to a position where it provided more employment and more exports than any other in the kingdom.[1] For the first half of the nineteenth century, its output increased at an estimated rate of more than 5 per cent per annum.[2] In 1830, cotton goods accounted for half the value of British exports, and

---

[1] F. Crouzet, *L'économie britannique et le blocus continental* (Paris, 1958), I, pp. 55 and 64.
[2] P. Deane and W. A. Cole, *British economic growth, 1689–1959* (Cambridge, 1962), p. 186.

even twenty years later, when other industries had begun to catch up, the figure was still two-fifths.[1]

It is important to remember that until the 1830s, when the handloom was rapidly disappearing from the industry, the home trade was of almost equal importance to the export trade. In money value, the proportion of the cotton industry's final product which was exported fluctuated fairly closely around 50 per cent between the end of the French wars and the early 1840s, although by the end of that decade it had risen to over 60 per cent.[2] Thus the cotton trade owed as much to the disposal of its goods by waggoners, riders-out, and drapers in the towns and villages of the United Kingdom as it did to the more spectacular efforts of merchants and their factors in Hamburg, Philadelphia, and Rio de Janeiro. For this reason, the demand for cotton goods was as liable to be affected by high food prices at home as by hostile tariffs or other barriers to trade abroad.

The foreign markets for cotton until the 1830s were largely confined to Europe and the Americas. In 1805, Europe and America took nearly three-quarters of all cotton exports, and north and west Europe alone took nearly one-third.[3] In 1820, half the piece-goods Britain exported went to Europe, over a fifth to south America and nearly a tenth to the U.S.A.[4] By 1840, the proportion of goods going to Europe had fallen by a half, but that to south America had increased to 35 per cent. It was only after the late 1830s that the direction of cotton exports shifted substantially, with the beginnings of the great trade to the Ottoman empire and the Far East.

Cloth was not the only product exported by the cotton industry in this period. Some of the yarn spun in England was also exported directly. In 1820 19·5 per cent of the cotton spun in England was exported as yarn, 47 per cent as cloth, and the rest was retained for home consumption. By 1830, the first figure had risen to 30 per cent, and the second had fallen to only 38 per cent; a strong indication of the inability of the weaving industry, still heavily

---

[1] Deane and Cole, *op. cit.* p. 31.   [2] *Ibid.* p. 187.
[3] Crouzet, *op. cit.* p. 70.
[4] T. Ellison, *The cotton trade of Great Britain* (London, 1886), p. 64.

dependent on the handloom, to make use of all the yarn the spinning industry could produce.[1] Yarn exports still continued thereafter, but it was in the 1830s and 1840s, thanks to the power-loom and the new eastern markets, that the real increase in cloth exports took place. Plain calico exports rose from 366 million yards in 1842 to 613 million in 1845.[2] The transitional period in the history of cotton weaving—from the 1820s to the 1840s—also witnessed an important change in the types of cloth exported. There was an absolute decline in the export of fancy goods— cambrics, dimities, ginghams and cords—after the 1830s, yet between 1820 and 1846 the export of printed calicoes doubled and that of plain calicoes shot up from 113 million yards to 618 million.[3] This again reflected the increasing use of the powerloom for plain cloth to satisfy the less sophisticated new markets, and the gradual reduction of both the demand for fancy cloth and the supply of hand weavers to produce it.

These figures illustrate an important general point—the sharp contrast between the unmechanized weaving section of the cotton industry and the spinning section, which used the water-frame and the mule. Before the coming of the powerloom, cotton spinning not only supplied the home weaving industry, but also acted as a major exporting industry in its own right; thus in one particular item, Britain in the early nineteenth century was an exporter of an important semi-manufactured article on an appreciable scale. Weaving, on the other hand, was as much concerned with pro-ducing for the home market as with supplying a relatively re-stricted group of foreigners. The situation was markedly different in the late nineteenth century, when yarn exports were pro-portionally less important, and when the vast bulk of the cloth woven was intended for export. As an integral part of the whole cotton industry, therefore, the weaving section in the handloom days was in a position very different from that which it was to occupy in the decades immediately before 1914.

[1] Ellison, *op. cit.* p. 59.
[2] R. Burn, *Statistics of the cotton trade* (London, 1847), table 6.
[3] *Ibid. loc. cit.*

II

Yet cotton weaving remained Britain's biggest manufacturing industry in the early nineteenth century, and the organization of the human and material resources to produce so much cloth was complex and widespread. Cotton handloom weavers might have been found in almost any part of Great Britain north of the Thames, and in much of Ireland. But they were particularly concentrated in north-western England, western Scotland, and Ulster. In the first district, the majority of the weavers lived in Lancashire south of the Ribble and in the adjoining parts of Cheshire and the West Riding, but they were also scattered in smaller groups throughout the villages of north Lancashire, the Yorkshire dales, and the border country around Carlisle. Probably three-quarters of them were producing plain calico cloth, but in some districts there were important local specializations on fancy goods:[1] cambrics and fine muslins were woven in Bolton, Stockport and Paisley, the first-named being also noted for its bed-quilts and its counterpanes; stripes, checks, and ginghams were the specialities of Manchester, Preston and Carlisle; old-fashioned fustians and remnants of the eighteenth-century woollen industry lingered on for many years in Bury, Rochdale, Oldham and Rossendale. North-east Lancashire provided the bulk of the plain cloth; at the height of the trade in the early 1820s, Blackburn produced nearly 50,000 pieces of calico a week, Burnley and district 25,000–30,000 pieces and Todmorden 7,000.[2] On the whole, it appears that the fancy and skilled weavers were more usually concentrated in the big towns, whereas many of the plain weavers were dispersed in the villages over the countryside.

Unfortunately, there is little detailed information on the development of industrial organization in our period; as a writer on the Scottish cotton industry put it, 'it is so much the sort of thing that in "normal times" everyone takes for granted'.[3] Clearly,

---

[1] For the details of local specialities in the 1830s, see E. Baines, *History of the cotton manufacture* (London, 1835), p. 418.

[2] E. Baines, *History, directory and gazeteer of the county palatine of Lancaster* (Liverpool, 1824–5), I, 505 and 567; II, 565.

[3] W. H. Marwick, 'The cotton industry and the industrial revolution in Scotland', *Scottish Historical Review*, XXI (192–34), 210.

Manchester was always not merely an important seat of manufacture, but also the main commercial centre for the whole industry.[1] Yet a glance at the commercial directories for the post-war years when the handloom weaving trade was at its height will show that each sizable town in the manufacturing area had its own resident manufacturers. Wardle's directory for 1814–15, for instance, lists 400 'country manufacturers attending the Manchester market'.[2]

This large body of entrepreneurs in cotton weaving can be divided into two groups—those who undertook weaving only, and those who owned spinning mills and also put out work to domestic weavers. The latter appeared most frequently in the country districts, whereas the former, often concentrating on specialities, were more likely to be found in the larger towns. In 1816–17, the Colne–Burnley district, where there were many small towns and villages, had a predominance of 'spinners-and-manufacturers', twenty-eight being listed in Wardle's directory as against seventeen 'manufacturers only'. Bolton, however, had only eleven who combined the two processes, but had fourteen counterpane and nearly one hundred muslin manufacturers, whilst Blackburn, with only nine 'spinners-and-manufacturers', had over sixty calico manufacturers.

In terms of numbers, some of the great handloom manufacturers employed even more workmen than did their better-known contemporaries among the leading factory lords. Of the latter, George and Adam Murray of Manchester employed 1,215 factory hands in 1816, McConnel and Kennedy employed 1,020, Philips and Lee 937, and Thomas Houldsworth 622; whilst outside Manchester, Horrockses of Preston had 700, and Birley and Hornby of Blackburn had nearly 550.[3] By contrast, even in the 1830s, Dixons of Carlisle employed 3,571 handloom weavers scattered over the Border country and Northern Ireland, James Masseys of

---

[1] See R. Smith, 'Manchester as a centre for the manufacture and marketing of cotton goods, 1820–1830', *University of Birmingham Historical Journal*, IV (1953–4).
[2] The references in the ensuing paragraph are to the trade directories published annually by Wardle and Bentham, of Manchester.
[3] R. S. Fitton and A. P. Wadsworth, *The Strutts and the Arkwrights* (Manchester, 1958), p. 195.

Manchester put out work to over 1,200 weavers in north-east Lancashire, Hardy and Andrew still employed 1,000 in the country around Stockport, and Fieldens provided work on the same scale in the Todmorden area.[1] Large weaving businesses were not unknown in the early days of the industry, either: William Radcliffe claimed to employ over 1,000 in 1801, Patrick Milne employed between 3,000 and 4,000 around Aberdeen in 1803, whilst 'a whole countryside of handloom weavers' accounted for the great bulk of the 7,000 workers in Horrockses', Preston, business in 1816.[2] In neither factory nor out-working systems, however, were figures of this order the norm. The average manufacturer, regardless of whether he combined spinning with weaving, probably numbered his workers in a few hundreds, or in the case of some of the small Bolton manufacturers in tens and scores.

Very little is known about the origins of the handloom manufacturers as a class of entrepreneurs, but contemporaries often asserted that they began in very humble circumstances.[3] Bishop Blomfield spoke disparagingly of those who 'rise from the loom, and as soon as they can make a small sum of money, build a factory... and in the course of a few years accumulate a property with which they are perhaps content; they then migrate, and their places are supplied by others'.[4] During the rapid expansion in the early years of the industry, William Radcliffe claimed that 'any young man who was industrious and careful might... from his earnings as a weaver lay by sufficient to set him up as a manufacturer',[5] although he added that 'few of the great body of weavers had the courage to embark in the attempt'.

The early experience of David Whitehead, of the famous Rossendale textile family, suggests, however, that it was not as

[1] PP. 1840 (220) XXIV, p. 606; P. M. Giles, The economic and social development of Stockport 1815–36 (Manchester M.A. thesis, unpublished, 1950), p. 248; PP. 1833 (690) VI, Q. 9334; J. Holden, History of Todmorden (Manchester, 1912), p. 162.

[2] W. Radcliffe, The origin of the new system of manufacture called powerloom weaving (Stockport, 1828), p. 16; PP. 1803 (114) III, part 4, p. 112; J. H. Clapham, The early railway age (Cambridge, 1930), p. 185.

[3] The best account of the organization of an early handloom weaving concern will be found in the early chapters of George Unwin, Samuel Oldknow and the Arkwrights (Manchester, 1924). See also the same author's 'The transition to the factory system', English Historical Review, XXXVII (1922).

[4] PP. 1826/7 (237) V, Q. 2286.   [5] Radcliffe, op. cit. p. 10.

easy to set up as a manufacturer as Radcliffe implied. Whitehead and his brothers made their first effort to start as manufacturers at the end of the Napoleonic war, buying a small quantity of yarn and giving it out to friends to weave. They retained their own former occupations for the time being, a wise precaution, since their first effort was abortive as a result of the post-war slump. About 1819 they tried again, started a small spinning mill, and this time succeeded in establishing themselves. Even then, their business was modest for the first year or two; David Whitehead went to Manchester only once every two or three weeks, walking the whole distance on Monday afternoons, and staying overnight for the Tuesday market.[1]

Clearly, the requisites for success were some savings, good credit, experience and connexions in the trade, and a favourable economic climate. Even to set up as a master weaver with half-a-dozen looms in a shop at Bolton cost Jonathan Hitchin between £30 and £40 in 1799.[2] The people best able to branch out on their own as manufacturers were those whose previous work had been sufficiently well-paid to allow some saving and had given them extensive and useful contacts with reliable weavers, master spinners, and merchants; warpers, reed makers, or agents and putters-out in particular, were the groups most likely to furnish aspiring new entrepreneurs.[3] Frequent bankruptcy notices in the local press give a superficial impression that the risk of failure among these small manufacturers was quite high, and indeed George Smith, manager of a Manchester firm which employed 1,200 weavers in north Lancashire, told the 1833 select committee on manufactures that 'of 32 handloom calico manufacturers whom I knew personally in the trade from 1812 to 1826, 28 have failed', and went on to suggest that 'more than half of all the persons who have been engaged in that trade who have not added spinning to their business have failed during the time I have been in Manchester.'[4] It is probable that Smith was exaggerating,

---

[1] D. Whitehead, *Autobiography* (typescript edition from MSS in the Public Library, Rawtenstall, 1956), pp. 24, 29 and 30.   [2] *PP. 1835 (341)* XIII, Q. 2943.

[3] William Radcliffe himself began as putter-out for Samuel Oldknow. See George Unwin, 'The transition to the factory system', *English Historical Review*, XXXVII (1922), 217.

[4] *PP. 1833 (690)* VI, QQ. 9278 and 9281.

however; statistics collected by Burn show an annual average of fifteen 'bankruptcies in the cotton trade' in the first forty years of the nineteenth century, but are not broken down to indicate failures in the different branches of the industry.[1] But whatever the risks, the promise and the opportunity still attracted newcomers, since the cloth market was growing remarkably in the long run, however much its fortunes might fluctuate in the short term. The handloom manufacturer needed little fixed capital: a collection of loom accessories, chiefly healds and reeds for different kinds of cloth, to be loaned out to weavers as required; a warping mill and winding machinery to prepare the yarn ready for the weaver to fit in his loom, and a warehouse. It was very exceptional for the handloom manufacturer in the cotton industry to own the looms which the weavers operated in their cottages, with the result that there was no equivalent of the oppressive frame-renting system in the Midland hosiery industry.[2] The rest of a manufacturer's stock-in-trade comprised the supplies of warp and weft obtained from the spinner, the finished pieces awaiting sale or dispatch, and the personal connexion, built up over time, with a number of reputable weavers.[3] The effects of Thomas Parker, bankrupt in 1815, who combined spinning, weaving and farming at Arncliffe, north of Skipton, give some indication of what was involved in being a country manufacturer. They comprised:

carding engines with cards, drawing-fly, and spinning frames and throstles, winding machine, cotton-picker, warping-mills, bobbins, skips, cans, straps, lathe and tools, a large quantity of iron and brass, smiths' and joiners' implements, upwards of 200 calico warps, reeds, healds, etc., six valuable draught horses and gears, new waggon, two carts, cow, pigs, several lots of hay, etc., fourpost beds, feather beds and bedding, mahoganny tables, chairs, desk, etc., pianoforte, sofa, a clock, carpets, glasses, china, a glass, and a variety of kitchen utensils and brewing vessels.[4]

[1] R. Burn, *Statistics of the cotton trade* (London, 1847), table 25.
[2] Among the very few examples I have found, the property of one Joseph Bradley, bankrupt, of Ashbourne, Derbyshire included 'sixty-three looms in the hands of different weavers resident in the neighbourhood of Ashbourne' (*Manchester Mercury*, 23 Sept. 1800).
[3] When a weaving business was advertised for sale, the services of the weavers might be classed as part of the stock. For examples, see *Manchester Mercury*, 31 Dec. 1782; 17 July 1787; 11 March 1806.
[4] *Wheeler's Manchester Chronicle*, 11 March 1815.

III

The cotton handloom weaving industry is normally classed as an 'outwork' or 'domestic' industry; in other words, the manufacturing process was carried on by the workers in their own homes or workshops. Although this was undoubtedly true of the vast bulk of the weaving that went on, there was one interesting variant in the organization—the handloom weaving shed. It represented a half-way stage between true domestic industry and the modern power-driven weaving shed, and deserves a brief digression in view of the neglect which it has hitherto suffered in economic histories. Although it was never anything like the predominant form of organization in cotton weaving, it was not negligible, nor was it confined, as H. D. Fong suggested, to fancy goods only.[1] According to the historian of Rossendale, in the period 1815-30, when 'the trade of cotton weaving on the handloom was at its briskest, there were at the lowest computation thirty weaving shops, apart from the looms in dwelling houses, in the forest of Rossendale'.[2] The distinguishing feature of the sheds was that they employed a number of weavers on handlooms outside their own homes and families; they were substantially larger than the small shops of four or six 'pair of looms' run by a master weaver with journeymen and apprentices in some of the more specialized lines at Bolton or Paisley.[3] Isolated cases have been found with as many as 150 or 200 handlooms, quite a few with between 50 and 100, and a considerable number with 20 or more. Such sheds were to be found in town and country throughout the weaving area.[4]

Weavers in these handloom factories were in many respects in a situation very different from that of the wholly domestic

---

[1] H. D. Fong, *Triumph of factory system in England* (Tientsin, 1930), p. 45.

[2] T. Newbigging, *History of the forest of Rossendale* (London, 1868), p. 219.

[3] When contemporaries spoke of 'a pair of looms' they meant one loom; a comparable usage is spectacles or trousers. I am grateful to W. Spencer, Esq., of Colne, for drawing my attention to this usage.

[4] Among other places, evidence has been found of the existence of handloom sheds in Birmingham, Bristol, Liverpool, Chester, Manchester, Bolton, Blackburn, Ashton, Burnley, Clitheroe, Preston, Wigan, Caton (Lancaster), Cockermouth, Wigton, Dent, Sedburgh, Skipton, Eyam and Cromford (Derbyshire). Sale notices in the local press form the chief source of information here.

workers. They did not own the looms they operated, and they had to work regular hours under supervision—two factors which made them less independent than the domestic worker. On the other hand, their earnings were likely to be better, since they worked more methodically, and often had little preparatory work to perform for themselves.[1] This was not invariably the case, however, as they might have been recruited on special terms; a handloom shed might be worked by poor-law apprentices or, as in the case of a shed offered for sale in an unspecified place 40 miles from Manchester in 1806, by 'workpeople...hired for a term of years at low wages'.[2] Nor were the sheds managed only by private manufacturers; the overseers of both 'houses of correction' and 'houses of industry' often regarded the provision of a loom-shed, in which their respective charges might become self-supporting, as one of their chief duties.[3]

Bringing together hand workers into large workshops was by no means peculiar to cotton weaving in the industrial revolution. It seems to have occurred in the early days of spinning by hand-jennies and hand-mules, and it certainly developed in the Midland framework knitting industries[4]—to say nothing of the metal trades of the Black country or various sweated industries of London.[5] For both employers and workers, the handloom shed represented a transitional stage in the organization of cotton weaving between the true domestic system and the power-driven factory. It does not necessarily follow, however, that the handloom shed was a comparatively late development in cotton, or that it was a conscious imitation of the powerloom factory. With the coming of the dandyloom in the late 1820s, there was a probable increase in the number of such sheds, but there is some evidence from notices in the local newspapers for their existence in the 1780s and 1790s.[6] The majority of the cotton weavers were, however, organized

---

[1] See below, pp. 134-5.   [2] *Manchester Mercury*, 3 June 1806.
[3] See below, p. 43.
[4] E. G. Nelson, 'The putting-out system in the English framework knitting industry' *Journal of Economic and Business History*, II (1930), 484.
[5] For a discussion of the changing position of various artisan groups, particularly in London, at this time, see E. P. Thompson, *The making of the English working class* (London, 1963), pp. 234-68.
[6] See below, pp. 83-5, for the dandyloom.

on the traditional 'putting-out' system. They worked on their own looms in their own houses, using materials obtained from a manufacturer or his agent, from whom they received a wage according to the nature and amount of the work done. Under such a system the key figure was the man who actually 'put out' the work to the individual weaver. His status might vary enormously: the putter-out could be a manufacturer in his own right, making his own bargains with spinners to obtain yarn and with merchants to dispose of his cloth; he could be the owner of a spinning factory who had some of his own yarn worked up locally instead of selling it to other manufacturers at home or abroad; or he could simply be the agent or factor working on a commission basis or at a salary for one of the great Manchester merchanting houses.

At this period, a great deal of the work done in the countryside was performed on commission for the Manchester capitalists.[1] The local press contains several advertisements from those anxious to offer their services as agents, as for example:

TO THE MANUFACTURERS OF MANCHESTER

A respectable weaver in the neighbourhood of Gee Cross wishes to engage with some gentleman manufacturer in the quality of putter-out. From his situation and connexions he flatters himself that he should soon acquire a considerable number of muslin, cambric, calico, etc., weavers, if good work and liberal wages can be had.[2]

Some of the would-be agents were more specific, and no doubt enhanced their prospects of finding a position by stating the number of weavers at their disposal, and by offering security for any trust reposed in them. However, the emphasis in the early years of rapid expansion was sometimes in the opposite direction, with Manchester houses advertising for agents in the country in such terms as:

WANTED

A person in the country to put out calicoes to the weavers for a house in Manchester. One in the neighbourhood of Blackburn would be preferred.[3]

---

[1] Many of the smaller spinners also worked extensively on commission from Manchester in the early nineteenth century (S. Andrew, *Fifty years cotton trade* (Oldham, 1887), p. 2).
[2] *Manchester Mercury*, 17 June 1806.
[3] *Wheeler's Manchester Chronicle*, 21 May 1791.

The duties of a putter-out were not light. He had to know the weavers in his district, and to accept responsibility for the quality of the work they produced. He had to prevent the wastage or embezzlement of his employer's materials. And it was his job to see that an order was duly completed and dispatched at the proper time. Given the diversity of the work force, some of whom he might never meet and the rest of whom he would see at most once a week, his task of keeping them all up to the mark was a heavy one.

IV

At the base of the organization of the industry was the handloom weaver in his own home. Samuel Bamford thus described the house of his uncle, a Middleton weaver, in the 1790s: 'My uncle's domicile...consisted of one principal room called "the house"; on the same floor with this was a loomshop capable of containing four looms, and in the rear of the house on the same floor were a small kitchen and buttery. Over the house and loomshop were [bed] chambers...The whole of the rooms were lighted by windows of small square panes, framed in lead, in good condition, those in front being protected by shutters.'[1] The belief that the handloom weavers usually wove in damp and cheerless cellars below the street level generally appears to have been justified only in the bigger towns; cellars were obviously unsatisfactory places to work in—a freak thunderstorm in 1821 flooded most Blackburn weavers' cellars[2]—and in the country, where houses were less crowded together, it was usually possible to work above ground. The shop of most village weavers would be situated on either the ground or the upper floor, in the latter case being often reached by an outside staircase. Such shops, like those handloom sheds which occupied the whole top floor of a row of cottages, can still occasionally be identified in the villages of Rossendale and the Ribble valley, where handloom weaving survived longest.[3]

The head of the family would normally be responsible for the

[1] S. Bamford, *Early days* (London, 1849), pp. 98–9.
[2] *Manchester Mercury*, 1 May 1821.
[3] See below, p. 267.

36

execution of the work obtained from the putter-out, and the members of the household would be organized in an informal way by him to ensure its completion. Small children and old people would probably help in winding the weft for the more active members of the family who had looms of their own. A more formal type of workshop organization persisted in some of the skilled fancy branches of the trade where looms were more expensive and some expertise and training were required; master weaver, journeyman, and apprentice worked side by side, the first taking a percentage—perhaps a quarter[1]—of his journeyman's earnings to compensate for providing and maintaining a loom and other necessities of the workshop. But it is most likely that the average plain weaver's shop was manned by his family, not by outsiders who stood in a more formal relationship to the head of the household.[2]

The family's work would be suspended probably once a week for 'bearing-home day', when all the work finished since the last visit to the putter-out was taken back, and fresh materials obtained to be woven up. Sometimes a distance of up to eight or nine miles might have to be covered in each direction on these journeys to the warehouse, but this was exceptional.[3] The country weaver did not necessarily have to take his work in to the nearest town. William Varley, the diarist of the 1820s, lived five miles from Burnley, but his employer, although resident in Burnley, kept a warehouse in Higham, Varley's village; only once during the 1826 slump, when the manufacturer failed to turn up at his local warehouse because he had no new work to give out, did the Higham weavers have to carry their work to Burnley.[4] Likewise when David Whitehead began manufacturing in 1819, he had three different 'taking-in' points in Rossendale—Haslingden, Newchurch and Balladenbrook—which he attended on different days of the week.[5] The town weaver in Bolton or Blackburn, of

[1] G. D'Eichthal, 'Condition de la classe ouvriere en Angleterre en 1828', Revue Historique, LXXIX (1902), 69.
[2] For a further discussion of the role of the apprenticeship, see below, pp. 52–3.
[3] For examples of long distances, see A. P. Wadsworth and J. de L. Mann, The cotton trade and industrial Lancashire (Manchester, 1931), p. 394 n.
[4] W. Bennett, History of Burnley (Burnley, 1948), III, 386.
[5] Whitehead, op. cit. p. 37.

course, would have only a very short journey to make. It is very likely, therefore, that the long tramp in heavy clogs with a bag of cloth on one's shoulder is really a piece of picturesque, pre-industrial folklore. Occasionally, the visit to the warehouse might be tiring because it involved taking back an exceptionally heavy load; at Christmas, for example, it was customary to weave as much as possible in the last week before the holiday.[1] But usually, bearing-home day was a pleasant diversion from the usual routine, it gave a splendid opportunity for conviviality, and, above all, it was pay day.[2]

This system of industrial organization is sometimes extolled because of the 'independence' which the individual weaver enjoyed under it. But in what did the weaver's freedom consist? Economically, the weaver was 'free' in that he worked out the details of his own daily routine, and owned the loom which was his basic tool—the latter being a notable advantage over the framework knitter of the Midlands, since it meant that the hand-loom weaver could change more easily from one employer to another. Yet the mere ownership of tools does not make the weaver an 'independent manufacturer', any more than it makes the farm labourer who owns a spade an independent farmer. The weaver's freedom was considerably impaired by the fact that he did not own the materials from which the cloth was made, nor the more expensive parts of the loom, particularly the reed, of which the versatile weaver needed to use a variety, nor did he have any responsibility for marketing the cloth he produced. The cotton weaver, for all that he worked in his own home, was a wage-earner employed by a capitalist manufacturer. Whatever may have been the case in the Yorkshire woollen industry, there is no evidence that cotton weavers purchased their own raw materials, or were responsible for all the processes of manufacture,[3] or took their cloth to sell at the local market.

---

[1] A Preston family once took a grand total of 182 pieces back to the warehouse on Christ-Eve (*Manchester Guardian*, 10 Jan. 1829).

[2] For the conviviality, see the rather idealized reminiscences of S. Bamford, *Early days* (London, 1849), p. 117.

[3] A few of Samuel Oldknow's weavers were still spinning domestically in the 1780s (Weaving Ledger 1784–5, *Oldknow Papers*, English MSS 755, John Rylands Library, Manchester).

There were further practical limitations on even this modest freedom. The ability to change employers was liable to be impaired in country districts because there might be only one local man from whom it was convenient to get work or because the weaver could be tied to one particular master who let him a house or had made him some loan or advance. Moreover, when the cotton trade was facing its recurrent dilemma of excess capacity, and when work was scarce, the average handloom weaver would be more concerned to get any available work than to care who offered it to him. The basic nature of the labour force—numerous, scattered, and unskilled—further weakened the weaver's effective freedom, since concerted industrial action was extremely difficult to manage.[1]

Against all this, there were the prosperous times—not, admittedly, very common after the initial growth period of the late eighteenth century—when the demand for weavers greatly exceeded the current supply. And at all times, the handloom weaver was at liberty to work at his own pace and in the company of his own family. By comparison with the contemporary factory regimen, these were not negligible advantages. And when, in the next chapter, we consider who the handloom weavers actually were, it is factors of this kind which explain both why some workers were initially attracted into weaving and also why in some cases they were unwilling to leave it.

[1] See below, pp. 177–8.

CHAPTER 3

THE LABOUR FORCE

THE history of the cotton handloom weavers coincides almost exactly with the traditional time limits of the classic English industrial revolution. Before the 1770s, the cotton hand weavers as a body had not existed; by the late 1840s, they had effectively vanished. In three generations, the processes of economic change had first created and then destroyed a new type of labour.

The suffering which accompanied the displacement of these early casualties of the industrial revolution is a matter of common knowledge. But the preliminary process by which the great army of handloom weavers came into existence has been little studied. Yet it is an interesting story. Until the inventions of Hargreaves, Arkwright, and Crompton, the drawbacks inherent in the spinning process had made it extremely difficult to produce cotton yarn strong enough for a warp. Thus although cotton was increasingly used in textiles in the eighteenth century—1·4 million lb of raw cotton were imported in 1700; 2·4 million in 1760; and 6·9 million in 1780[1]—it had mainly been employed in producing mixed goods.[2] The most notable of these were fustians, extensively woven in Lancashire, where cotton weft was crossed with a linen warp.

All-cotton cloth was, therefore, the novel result of Arkwright's water-frame, which made strong warps possible. Indeed, until Arkwright secured a special Act of parliament in 1774,[3] such cloth, hitherto imported from the East Indies, was a prohibited commodity—Englishmen being required by law to wear only those textiles which were made at home. Once the new fabric could be made, its cheapness, adaptability and infinite variety immediately commended it to wide markets at home and abroad. To satisfy

[1] Figures from A. P. Wadsworth and J. de L. Mann, *The cotton trade and industrial Lancashire* (Manchester, 1931), appendix G.
[2] The chief exception were the cheap all-cotton stockings made in parts of the Midlands.
[3] 14 Geo. III, cap. 72.

this ever-growing demand, in the absence of a power-driven counterpart of the water-frame or mule, a new labour force of cotton hand weavers had to be created.

The recruitment of the new workers and their ancillaries— reed makers, warpers, loom builders and the like—took place on a scale and at a pace hitherto unknown in British economic history. Since the output of cloth grew continuously and rapidly from the 1770s, and since powerlooms were of no significance until the early 1820s, the number of weavers must have gone on increasing until the latter date. It is impossible to say exactly how fast the labour force grew, but various trade statistics give some indication: the quantity of raw cotton imported into the United Kingdom rose from just over 5 million lb in 1781 to over 150 million in 1820; the official value of cotton goods exported was £355,000 for both cloth and yarn in 1780, £5·4 million for cloth only in 1800, and £20·5 million in 1820;[1] finally, within the space of the decade 1801–3 to 1811–13 cotton's share in the national income is estimated to have risen from 5 to 7½ per cent.[2]

The recruitment of labour for the new industry must be seen, in the first instance, against the background of a sustained increase in the natural rate of growth of the population—an increase which seems to have begun in the country as a whole in the 1740s and which accelerated in the 1780s; and the latest detailed study suggests that this increase was even more marked in the north-west of England than in the country as a whole.[3] But this pheno-menon provides only a superficial explanation for the sudden appearance of a large new body of workers, for the increase in the number of cotton handloom weavers was out of all proportion to the increase in the total population, It is obvious, therefore, that the new trade attracted workers who had formerly followed other occupations. Where did they come from?

The Lancashire fustian weavers provided the obvious nucleus for the new labour force. For their mixed cotton goods had always been little more than a substitute for those real cottons which

---

[1] E. Baines, *History of the cotton manufacture* (London, 1835), pp. 347–9.
[2] P. Deane and W. A. Cole, *British economic growth, 1689–1959* (Cambridge, 1962), p. 163.
[3] *Ibid.* pp. 114–17.

technical shortcomings had previously made it impossible to manufacture. The changeover to cotton was both natural and easy.[1] But the demand for the new fabric was far too heavy to be met by the existing group of workers. As a result, many outsiders previously unconnected with weaving came to be employed in it. A great influx of weavers undoubtedly came from domestic spinners displaced by the new inventions. So slow was the old-fashioned single spinning wheel when compared with the handloom that Arthur Young in 1770 claimed that 'they reckon twenty spinners and two or three other hands to every weaver'.[2] Even if Young's ratio is high, it is still clear that the new spinning machines created considerable technological unemployment for many domestic outworkers. Fortunately, alternative but comparable work was available to them, in a way that it was not available later to the displaced domestic weavers. One of the first historians of the cotton industry wrote as follows of this phase: 'Carding, roving and spinning were now given up in the cottages, and the women and children formerly employed in those operations applied themselves to the loom. The invention of the mule, by enabling the spinners to make finer yarn than any the jenny or water-frame could produce, gave birth to the muslin manufacture and found employment for this additional number of weavers.'[3]

Workers directly displaced by those same changes which made possible the growth of cotton weaving—the fustian weavers and the domestic spinners—provided only one element among the new weavers, however. More numerous were those voluntarily drawn into the new trade from other occupations. It is worth considering the factors which attracted them to it.

From the outset, it is important to avoid the fallacy that cotton weaving was a skilled trade, or that the handloom weavers as a whole can be regarded as an 'aristocracy of labour' simply because, in the early years of expansion when weavers were in

---

[1] It is unclear how quickly fustian ceased to be in heavy demand and how soon the bulk of its makers disappeared; the term certainly continues in use well after 1800, and it would appear from frequent references in William Rowbottom's 'Annals of Oldham' that fustian weavers were still numerous in that area in the 1790s (Rowbottom's 'Diary' or 'Annals' was published in weekly instalments in *Oldham Standard*, 1887–8).

[2] A. Young, *Six months tour of Northern England* (London, 2nd edn, 1771), III, 164.

[3] R. Guest, *A compendious history of the cotton industry* (Manchester, 1823), p. 31.

short supply, good wages were paid. Except in the fancy branches, the qualifications required for weaving were not excessive. Plain weaving was easily learnt; three weeks were reckoned 'a sufficient length of time to teach a mere labourer, when committed for any offence to the New Bayley prison, to weave calico',[1] whilst of muslin weaving, a manufacturer once claimed that 'a lad of fourteen may acquire a sufficient knowledge of it in six weeks'.[2] So easy was weaving, indeed, that there was even an attempt (with what success it is not known) to teach it to children in the Liverpool school for the blind 'so as to enable them to maintain themselves when they leave the institution'.[3]

In addition, hand weaving was extensively taught as a useful trade to fall back on in extremities. Throughout the weaving districts, from Manchester and Liverpool down to the small country towns, pauper children in the workhouses learned to weave.[4] Some prisons shared with workhouses the function of teaching their inmates to weave in order to earn their keep; the good management of the Preston house of correction in 1819, for example, was attributed to the governor's zeal in setting the prisoners to work at the loom.[5]

The case of the minority of fancy weavers—usually reckoned at no more than a quarter of the whole weaving body[6]—was, of course, very different; their work called for dexterity and experience. In all circumstances, too, the weaving of good cloth, as opposed merely to getting to the end of a piece, called for special qualities. 'The weaver', wrote one authority, 'must be exclusively employed at one kind of fabric, never on any account changing his hand to any other description of work; and he must likewise be naturally well adapted for the particular kind of work to excell in it: he must have a nice perception of weight; great

---

[1] *Manchester Exchange Herald*, 22 Sept. 1818.
[2] *PP. 1834 (556)* x, Q. 165.
[3] *Manchester Mercury*, 20 Oct. 1818; for the Liverpool School for the Indigent Blind, see David Owen, *English philanthropy, 1660–1960* (Harvard, 1965), p. 119.
[4] See evidence of Alfred Power, assistant Poor Law commissioner, in *PP. 1837/8 (167)* xviii, part 1, QQ. 2849–58. Samuel Bamford's father managed the Manchester workhouse factory in the 1790s (S. Bamford, *Early days* (London, 1849), p. 51).
[5] *Manchester Mercury*, 18 May 1819.
[6] *PP. 1834 (556)* x, Q. 5552.

command over the muscular system; and sufficient energy to use his faculties in an effective manner.'[1]

Nor does the ease of learning to weave mean that it was necessarily light or pleasant work. Even Peter Gaskell, a sharp critic of the factory system, conceded that

the position in which the weaver sits is not the best for muscular exertion, having no firm support for his feet, which are alternately raised and depressed in working the treddles. He has thus to depend for a fulcrum chiefly on the muscles of his back, which are kept in constant and vigorous action, while one order of muscles is employed with little power of variation in moving the shuttle and beam. These processes when carried on for many successive hours are very wearying and the exertion required becomes after a while laborious.[2]

At the same time, the chief attraction of cotton weaving in the early years of good wages was that the weaver did not have to exert himself in order to earn a decent wage. As a disgruntled agriculturalist wrote, 'who will work for 1/6 or 2/- a day at a ditch, when he can get 3/6 or 5/- a day in cotton work and be drunk four days out of seven?'[3]

Good wages were not, however, the only attractive feature of handloom weaving. The tools of the trade were inexpensive, and, having acquired them, the weaver gained some measure of freedom, and perhaps also had the reasonable prospect of becoming master of his own loomshop. Although in the early years a new loom may have cost about £5,[4] by the 1820s the usual value was given at between 25s. and 40s., and sometimes even less.[5] Secondly, taking up the handloom did not necessarily involve moving house; there was no need, as there was in the case of factory spinning, to move either to some remote village where water-power was available or to some grimy mushroom town away from friends and family. Finally, in the best traditions of industrial outwork, handloom weaving was essentially a family trade; father, mother and children could all share in the work which, in so many cases, would be carried on in the home.

---

[1] G. White, *A practical treatise on weaving by hand and powerlooms* (Glasgow, 1846), p. 49.

[2] P. Gaskell, *The manufacturing population of England* (London, 1833), p. 35.

[3] J. Holt, *A general view of the agriculture of the county of Lancaster* (London, 1795), p. 213.

[4] T. Newbigging, *History of the forest of Rossendale* (London, 1868), p. 219; *PP 1826/7 (237)* v, Q. 813.   [5] *PP. 1833 (690)* vi, Q. 9431.

Given these advantages, it is not surprising that many previously employed in other trades saw a new opportunity in hand weaving, especially when prospective employers took pains to offer attractive terms. Sometimes the inducement would be strictly financial, as in the case of the Stockport manufacturers who advertised that

CALLICO WEAVERS

who can be well recommended will meet with as good warps as any in the kingdom, have full employment in weaving of common 7-8th callico at seven shillings an end and 9-8th ditto at nine shillings an end by applying to Messrs Joseph and John Dale at Stockport.[1]

Sometimes the appeal would be more subtle. A Liverpool manufacturer tried to attract weavers by promising that they would be 'protected from the impress' [i.e. the pressgang],[2] whilst weavers were enticed to Bamford, near Castleton in Derbyshire, by the offer of 'cow-keepings of four acres...of good land with a house and other conveniences which will be let at five guineas each by Hans Wintrop Mortimer, Esq., Lord of the Manor.'[3]

Agricultural labourers bulked large among those who responded to such invitations. Gaskell claimed that many who had hitherto combined weaving with farming now applied themselves chiefly, if not solely, to the loom, and that many labourers deserted the farms and took up weaving in the nearby villages.[4] Holt complained of the consequences for the farmers in his survey of Lancashire agriculture in 1795: 'the advance of wages and the preference given to manufacturing employment by labourers in general, where they may work by the piece and under cover, have induced many to forsake the spade for the shuttle, and have embarrassed the farmers by the scarcity of workmen, and of course advanced the price of labour.'[5]

[1] *Manchester Mercury*, 11 Dec. 1781.
[2] *Ibid.* 25 March 1782.   [3] *Ibid.* 30 July 1782.
[4] Gaskell, *op. cit.* pp. 35 and 46. General outdoor labourers—builders, road-makers, and the like—may also have been attracted to weaving in large numbers (E. W. Gilboy, *Wages in eighteenth-century England* (Harvard, 1934), p. 176).
[5] Holt, *op. cit.* p. 210. It will be appreciated that the great expansion of handloom weaving did not have the same dramatic consequences for agriculture as did the growth of the spinning factories in the towns, since the scattered pattern of settlement was not necessarily disrupted, and since part-time farm labouring and smallholding continued to be combined with cottage weaving (see below, pp. 58–60). Nevertheless a general

Such comment was, however, one-sided. Whatever the difficulties to the farmers, the appearance of a new form of industrial outwork was very welcome in reducing the under-employment which prevailed in some country districts. In the space of three weeks in the spring of 1791, *Wheeler's Manchester Chronicle* carried three notices of the sale of land which, in the sellers' opinion, was particularly suited for industrial development. The first of these, at Sandbach, Cheshire, claimed that 'the price of labour will be very moderate, as there is a numerous poor in the district unemployed, and no other works to create rivalship and enhance the price of labour'. The other two, at Burnsall, near Skipton, and Whaley Bridge, both asserted that 'children and up-grown persons are mostly in want of employment'.[1] Districts with an employment problem of this kind were obvious places for the cotton industry to take root in.

Another group of recruits came from the weavers who had formerly been employed on other fabrics, such as linen, wool, or sailcloth, but who now turned to cotton. The rapid development of a new and popular fabric considerably retarded the growth of the older-established textile industries. The woollen industry, whose output had probably been growing at a rate of 13 or 14 per cent per decade from the 1740s to the 1770s, expanded by only 6 per cent per decade in the last quarter of the century; the linen industry in the same period may even have contracted.[2] This slowing down is demonstrated in the former case by the extension

study of the effects of the spectacular rise of the cotton industry on Lancashire farming in the late eighteenth and early nineteenth centuries is urgently needed. The returns made by local clergy to the Home Office during the 'famine' of 1800 concerning the state of agriculture in their respective parishes would suggest that, even at that early date, the less urbanized areas relied on fairly distant sources for the greatest part of their consumption of arable goods: Haslingden, for instance, was said to be 'almost wholly dependent upon Yorkshire and Cheshire for meal, flour and potatoes'; whilst the incumbent of Burnley alleged that 'both flour and meal are brought to our market from the eastern and northern Ridings of Yorkshire chiefly by the Leeds and Liverpool canal'. It would appear that the local farmers were concentrating largely on profitable dairying to satisfy the growing demands of their immediate industrial neighbours (see the various returns in *HO. 42. 55*). Holt's claim that the shortage of agricultural labour following the rise of the cotton industry 'embarrassed' the farmers of Lancashire becomes less plausible when one remembers the very favourable demand situation which a growing industrial population offered.

[1] *Wheeler's Manchester Chronicle*, 19 and 26 March, 2 April 1791.
[2] Deane and Cole, *op. cit.* pp. 52-3.

46

of cotton weaving into some of the old woollen districts. Aikin's description of Lancashire in 1795 presents an excellent progress-report of the spread of cotton into Rossendale and north-east Lancashire. Of Colne, for example, he wrote: 'the trade formerly consisted in woollen and worsted goods, particularly shalloons, calamancoes, and tammies; but the cotton trade is of late introduced, the articles consisting chiefly of calicoes and dimities.'[1]

It was not, in fact, difficult to change about from fabric to fabric. Such changes may frequently have been made in parts of Yorkshire according to the relative prosperity of the cotton and woollen industries.[2] There was also considerable changing among the Warrington sailcloth weavers, whose work was in heaviest demand only in wartime. Many of these Warrington weavers gave up sailcloth for cotton at the end of the American war 'for the sake of more employment and better wages', but returned to sailcloth again at the outbreak of the French revolutionary war in 1792.[3] Similarly, in the late 1830s, the coming of the powerloom in cotton led many handloom weavers to change either to silks or to woollens.[4] The facility of changing from one type of cloth to another was a great advantage when new weavers were needed in the early days of the cotton industry.

The increasing precariousness of certain old-established industries other than textiles provided a further influx of new labour. The working out of some Derbyshire leadmines, for example, created an acute unemployment problem in several villages; Aikin mentioned Eyam, Bradwell and Castleton as places with declining populations in the 1790s.[5] That local landowners saw a suitable remedy in the introduction of cotton weaving is evident from the following advertisement:

TO COTTON MANUFACTURERS

Persons desirous of extending their business in any of those various branches in the cotton line where a large stream of water is not necessary may by

---

[1] J. Aikin, *A description of the country from 30 to 40 miles around Manchester* (London, 1795), p. 279. In Scotland, the earliest cotton weavers seem to have changed over from linen in the 1780s (G. M. Mitchell, 'English and Scottish cotton industries', *Scottish Historical Review*, XXII (1924–5), 102–4.
[2] *PP. 1812 (210)* III, p. 130.   [3] Aikin, *op. cit.* p. 303.
[4] See below, pp. 260–2.   [5] Aikin, *op. cit.* pp. 484 and 497–8.

immediate application to Mr Philip Sheldon...in Eyam, Derbyshire, receive particulars greatly to their advantage...Eyam is remarkably well situated for conveyance of carriage of any kind, and the number of hands ...might be greatly increased provided older persons could be employed in it, as the poorer sort of inhabitants, by the impaired state of the mines and bad payments, are driven to the utmost distress.[1]

Finally, the expanding labour force also collected some of the dregs, the runaways, and the outcasts of eighteenth-century society. According to the notices in the Manchester press, it was often assumed that runaway apprentices, whatever their trade, had chosen to hide themselves among the cotton workers of the ever-growing Lancashire metropolis. When the master of the Banbury (Oxfordshire) workhouse, a shag weaver by trade, absconded with one of his female charges and left behind a wife and family, the overseers who employed him inserted his description in the Manchester papers, an indication that they knew, or at least believed it likely, that he was seeking the safe anonymity of an expanding industrial area.[2]

As a result both of the considerable dependence of the early spinning mills on water-power and of the search for a whole host of handloom weavers, the history of the English cotton industry down to the end of the Napoleonic wars is one of geographical dispersal rather than of concentration. Thus the recruitment of the cotton weavers can be measured in terms of the advancing frontiers of the cotton area as well as of increasing numbers. Unlike factory spinning, whose location was determined by the availability of power supplies, the expansion of handloom weaving did not necessarily disrupt the existing pattern of settlement by causing massive migration from the farms and villages to a few advantageously sited towns. Some townward movement there undoubtedly was, but although the little country towns of south Lancashire grew markedly in the last decades of the eighteenth century, the expansion of cotton weaving in this period of rapid natural increase in numbers also witnessed a corresponding 'thickening' of population in the more remote rural hamlets and villages.

[1] *Wheeler's Manchester Chronicle*, 5 March 1791.
[2] *Manchester Mercury*, 2 Aug. 1796.

Aikin is the best chronicler of the process. Of Stalybridge, he claimed that 'the greatest part of this village…has been built in the last eighteen years'; at Middleton there had been an increase in the number of houses in the decade before 1795 from 'scarcely more than twenty' to 'between four and five hundred'; whilst the population even of Blackburn 'within the memory of man… was very inconsiderable to what it has lately been'.[1] In many cases, the rapid growth was attributed specifically to the introduction of cotton weaving. At Chapel-en-le-Frith, the people are 'chiefly supported by the manufacture of cotton, which has caused a great increase in population'; Tildesley, in 1780 a hamlet of two farms and eight or nine cottages, 'now contains 162 houses, a neat chapel, and 976 inhabitants who employ 325 looms in the cotton manufactories'; Darwen was 'formerly a small village, but is now a populous district manufacturing a large quantity of cotton goods'.[2] What Aikin said of Wigan might equally be applied throughout south Lancashire and the nearby parts of Cheshire and Derbyshire: 'the cotton manufactory, as in all other places, intrudes upon the old staple of the place.'[3] Its intrusion was demonstrated in town, village, and hamlet by the building of rows of weavers' cottages to house the new workers who flowed in from so many different sources.

II

Drawn from this wide range of sources, the great body of cotton handloom weavers grew continuously but probably spasmodically for four decades after 1780. It is difficult, however, to plot its growth statistically, or even to decide in what periods it increased most rapidly. The 1780s, following the successive inventions of the jenny, water-frame, and mule, clearly saw a more rapid expansion than William Radcliffe later recollected. Radcliffe, speaking specifically of the years 1770–88, argued that 'there was no increase of looms…but rather a decrease', and that the real increase came later:

[1] Aikin, *op. cit.* pp. 230, 243 and 270.
[2] *Ibid.* pp. 48, 203, 299 and 273.
[3] *Ibid.* p. 294.

49

the next fifteen years, viz. from 1788 to 1803, [he wrote], I will call the golden age of this great trade...The mule-twist now coming into the vogue for the warp as well as weft, added to the water-twist and common jenny-yarns, with an increasing demand for every fabric the loom could produce, put all hands in request of every age and description. The fabrics made from wool and linen vanished, while the old loomshops being insufficient, every lumber-room, even old barns, carthouses, and outbuildings of every description, were repaired, windows broke through the old blank walls, and all fitted up for loomshops.[1]

Radcliffe was wrong in denying an increase before 1788, however. Although it is true that the great expansion of muslin weaving began only then with the increasing use of the mule,[2] the coming of the water-frame and the jenny in the 1770s had given a great impetus to the weaving of coarse calicoes, particularly in the Blackburn region.[3] The import figures for raw cotton confirm this expansion of the early 1780s; the increase in imports between 1781 and 1790—about 25 million lb—was almost exactly the same as between 1791 and 1800; the former representing much the greater proportional increase.[4]

The many vicissitudes of the war period 1793–1814 greatly complicate the picture, because the cotton industry suffered frequent depressions as the chances of war interfered with trade. Yet it continued to expand in fits and starts, at a remarkable rate, with peaks of prosperity in 1802, 1805, and 1810.[5] With a significant proportion of the adult male population directly engaged in the war effort during these years, many of the recruits at this time were women and children. In 1799, a Wigan correspondent reported to the Home Office that 'the demand for manufactured goods is great, and were it possible to make one weaver into two they might be employed. Although numbers of our people are gone for soldiers and sailors there is still an increase of looms, for if a man enlists his wife turns weaver (for here the women are weavers

---

1 W. Radcliffe, *The origin of the new system of manufacture commonly called powerloom weaving* (Stockport, 1828), pp. 59–60.
2 Samuel Oldknow's muslin weaving business was at its height between 1789 and 1792. (G. Unwin, *Samuel Oldknow and the Arkwrights* (Manchester, 1924), p. 105.)
3 Baines, *op. cit.* pp. 333–4. Tradition in the Blackburn area gave 15 September 1776 as the date when the first-ever piece of calico was completed (*Blackburn Gazette*, 19 Sept. 1829).
4 Baines, *op. cit.* p. 347. The figures were: 1781, 5·2 million lb; 1790, 31·4 m. lb; 1800, 56 m. lb.
5 For the rapid expansion of 1810, see F. Crouzet, *L'économie britannique et le blocus continental* (Paris, 1958), II, pp. 503–10.

as well as the men) and instructs her children in the art of weaving; and I have heard many declare that they lived better since their husband enlisted than before'.[1] Of course, the frequency of industrial depressions as the fortunes of war fluctuated meant that the rate of growth was highly irregular, and indeed there were occasions when the supply of labour temporarily outran the demand, with disastrous effect on the weavers' standard of living.[2] But in spite of the unevenness, the growth of the cotton industry during the Napoleonic wars was so remarkable that it is difficult to imagine that it could have done much better over these twenty years, even if there had been peace and not war. For as Crouzet has shown, the war retarded the industrial development of Britain's continental rivals, made them dependent on her for many of their manufactured goods, and also gave Britain a virtual monopoly of that valuable Atlantic trade with the Americas for which the great powers had fought repeatedly during the eighteenth century.[3]

Again, despite the depressions of 1812 and the post-war years, it is quite clear that there was an increase in the number of cotton weavers in the decade 1810–20. For example, the number of pieces of handloom calico produced weekly in Blackburn is said to have increased from 27,000 to 40,000 between 1814 and 1824;[4] even if it is assumed that output per weaver rose over these years with the decline in piece-rates, it is unlikely that this increase would be as high as 50 per cent.[5] The alternative explanation is a significant increase in the number of workers, and the census figures lend some support to this view. In common with the country as a whole, Burnley, Accrington, Haslingden, Darwen, Blackburn, and Clitheroe—in other words, the centres of the north Lancashire calico trade—increased more rapidly in population between the censuses of 1811 and 1821 than at any other time in the first half of the nineteenth century.[6] Of all these places, only

---

[1] J. Singleton to Home Office, 27 May 1799 (*HO. 42. 47*). See also *PP. 1808* (177) II, p. 121.
[2] See below, pp. 100–3 and 107–8.
[3] See F. Crouzet, 'Wars, blockade, and economic change in Europe', *Journal of Economic History*, XXIV (1964).
[4] *Wheeler's Manchester Chronicle*, 3 Feb. 1827.   [5] See below, pp. 117–18.
[6] J. T. Danson and T. A. Welton, 'On the population of Lancashire and Cheshire, 1801–51', *Trans. Lancashire and Cheshire Historical Society*, X (1857–8), 10.

4-2

Blackburn could in any real sense be described as a 'factory town'. Apart from the rapid natural increase of population in the area, further explanations of the growing numbers might be found in the demobilization of soldiers and sailors after 1814, in the critical situation of British agriculture and the agricultural labourer after the war, and in Irish immigration. All these sources provided a continuing stream of recruits to a trade which, despite its ups and downs, still held many attractions at a time when the future of the powerloom remained problematical.

Formal apprenticeship could hardly be expected to survive in a trade which grew so rapidly, drew on so wide a range of recruits, and required such a small amount of skill. Many of the entrants were already adult, and did not serve a legal apprenticeship. As early as 1782, some of the Manchester weavers' societies tried to have the old seven-year laws enforced in order to restrict the numbers and maintain the quality of their fellow workers. Their efforts were, however, opposed by a manufacturers' 'committee for the protection and encouragement of trade', who offered to defend any whom the weavers' societies prosecuted; the manufacturers went so far as to refer to the new unapprenticed workers as 'perhaps the most ingenious and valuable' of the weavers.[1] Thus the pattern was early established of cotton weaving as an unskilled trade to which entry was completely free and unrestricted—a pattern which was to be an important factor in the weavers' sufferings.

On the other hand, apprenticeship was not entirely abandoned. Boys were still being apprenticed to individual cotton weavers or to the masters of loom shops in the late eighteenth and early nineteenth centuries. Orphans under the care of the Poor Law officials were particularly likely to be bound apprentice, and some loom shops may indeed have been manned entirely by labour of this kind. A Manchester advertisement of 1789, for example, offered for sale a factory of sixteen looms together with the labour of twelve apprentices.[2] Such cheap labour could have provided a strong commercial advantage to the manufacturer; in this particular case, the apprentices received wages of only 3s. a week.

---

[1] *Manchester Mercury*, 31 Dec. 1782.   [2] *Ibid.* 1 Dec. 1789.

Where apprenticeship did continue, it was often fairly informal, and its term might not necessarily be seven years.[1] The rapid expansion of the industry and the constant influx of new adult weavers were not, however, the only factors accounting for the limited survival of formal apprenticeship in cotton weaving. The lack of skill required in plain weaving made a long formal initiation into the 'mysteries' of the trade quite superfluous. Moreover, apprenticeship was irrelevant when a child was taught to weave at home; for in learning from his parents and in surrendering his earnings to the family pool until he reached maturity the child was in much the same position as if he had been legally bound to a master outside the family.[2]

With an ever-increasing demand for weavers, and with virtually free entry into the trade, the total number of cotton handloom weavers continued to grow until the early 1820s. There may have been some variations in the experience of individual districts, but over the country as a whole expansion must have gone on until there were a substantial number of powerlooms in use.[3] The slump of 1826, following the first large-scale adoption of power-looms, was probably the crucial factor in demonstrating that, without decisive assistance from the government, the handloom weavers could not expect an agreeable future. Thereafter, people continued to enter the trade only if they were particularly shiftless, or simply found it impossible to get alternative work; district by district, the number of weavers began to decline as new entrants stopped coming in, and the old weavers moved out or died.[4] It is fairly clear, however, that numbers were still increasing in the more remote districts in the early 1820s; as late as 1823, cotton weaving was said to have been only 'recently' introduced in the villages of Wensleydale to replace the knitting of stockings and caps, hitherto the staple domestic industry.[5]

---

[1] Examples have been found in the press of terms ranging from five years to eight or more.
[2] Formal apprenticeship seems to have declined sharply in other large-scale outwork industries in the early nineteenth century. For the case of the Midland framework knitters, see F. A. Wells, *The British hosiery trade* (London, 1935), p. 82. For a general discussion of the problem, see E. P. Thompson, *The making of the English working class* (London, 1963), pp. 252 *et seq.*   [3] See below, p. 89.
[4] See below, chapter 11, for the declining numbers.
[5] *Manchester Mercury*, 26 Aug. 1823.

The number of cotton handloom weavers, therefore, probably reached its peak in the mid-1820s. But is it impossible to say accurately how many weavers there were. The large area of the country over which they were dispersed and the large element of casual labour involved all add to the imprecision. Most contemporary estimates were purely conjectural. In 1795, Aikin calculated 350,000 workers in the whole cotton industry, or 240,000 if the spinners were excluded;[1] in 1803 the manufacturers of Glasgow claimed that cotton 'affords the means of subsistence to nearly a tenth part of the population of the island';[2] a Stockport spinner in 1812 spoke of 'so many hundred thousand weavers that I cannot calculate upon them';[3] Guest estimated at least 360,000 cotton weavers in the whole of Great Britain in the 1820s.[4] The most frequently quoted estimates belong to the period of the great select committees which dealt with the weavers' decline between 1830 and 1835. These varied from 200,000 to 250,000 for cotton weavers in Great Britain,[5] and from 240,000 to 280,000 for all types of weavers.[6]

Confusion has been caused because these last figures were often expressed in a roundabout manner. Contemporaries often spoke of people being 'dependent on the handloom' or 'supported by the handloom', by which they implied not only the actual weavers, but also their non-working dependants, both young and old, and possibly the ancillary workers—winders, warpers, loombuilders, heald and reed makers—too. Estimates of the numbers 'dependent on the handloom' in this wider sense in about 1830 ranged from half a million for cotton only[7] to 840,000 for all textiles,[8] the former based on an assumed ratio of $2\frac{1}{2}$ persons to each loom, the latter on a ratio of three persons. Some historians have mistakenly used these larger figures to represent the number of actual weavers.

---

[1] Aikin, *op. cit.* p. 179   [2] *Manchester Mercury,* 22 Feb. 1803.
[3] *PP. 1812 (210)* III, p. 269.   [4] Guest, *op. cit.* p. 33.
[5] *PP. 1833 (690)* VI, QQ. 9449 and 10171.
[6] *PP. 1830 (590)* X, p. 223 and *PP. 1834 (556)* X, Q. 5167.
[7] *PP. 1833 (690)* VI, Q. 9481.   [8] *PP. 1834 (556)* X, Q. 5169.

The frequent mention of a figure in the 200,000 to 250,000 range should not deceive us into thinking that it is necessarily correct. It could represent the parrot-like repetition of a general impression derived from some common source, such as a contemporary pamphlet. The basis of these various calculations was rarely stated. The estimate by George Smith, a manufacturer— 200,000 cotton weavers in England and Scotland—looks most plausible because it was said to be based on the quantity of yarn spun; but Smith did not divulge how he had used his data to reach this conclusion.[1] Since in England, at any rate, no census, official or otherwise, was ever taken of the number of handloom weavers, all these figures must be treated with caution.

Scotland furnishes an exception to these warnings about the doubtful accuracy of the available figures. Here, the general agreement as to the total number of handloom weavers—usually set at about 50,000 in the 1830s—is confirmed by two surveys, the first taken by the weavers' leaders at the time of the 1834 select committee and the other compiled by assistant commissioner Symons for the royal commission of 1837. The former gave a total of 'between 49,000 and 50,000',[2] the latter of 51,060. Both referred to all types of textiles, but cotton weavers were nine-tenths of the total in the second survey.[3]

Rather more reliable information is available about the number of weavers in particular places at certain dates. There are, for example, several estimates in the parliamentary papers of the numbers in Bolton, and these agree quite well with an independent statistical survey of the town undertaken by Dr James Black, of the Royal College of Physicians, in 1837. They suggest figures of the order of 400 and 1,000 respectively in the 'fancy' lines of bed-quilt and counterpane weaving, and a total of 7,000–9,000 ordinary weavers when the trade was at its height, this figure falling to under 5,000 by 1837.[4] In the division of Bolton, including eight or nine of the surrounding townships as well as the town itself,

[1] PP. 1833 (690) VI, Q. 9450.   [2] PP. 1834 (556) X, Q. 1937.
[3] PP. 1841 (296) X, p. 283.
[4] PP. 1833 (690) VI, QQ. 11920 and 11924; PP. 1834 (556) X, Q. 5058; J. Black, 'Summary of statistics of Bolton, Lancashire', Trans. Provincial Medical and Surgical Association (1837).

there were said to be a total of 23,500 weavers in 1817, when the magistrates ordered a local enumeration to be taken.[1]

If there were still between 8,000 and 10,000 weavers in Bolton itself around 1830, this was a substantial element in a population which then totalled 40,000. But it looks as if the proportion in some of the smaller towns and villages was even higher: four-fifths of the parish of Wilmslow were 'dependent on the hand-loom' in 1827, according to their rector;[2] at Irlams-o-th-Height, a small village near Manchester, 169 out of 389 'persons in receipt of wages' in 1835 were handloom weavers.[3] The heaviest con-centration of handloom weavers, however, was undoubtedly in north-east Lancashire, where perhaps nearly two-fifths of the entire population was weaving calico in the 1820s. A survey of Darwen in 1826 revealed 897 weavers in employment and 1,985 unable to get work—2,882 in all—out of a total population of 7,283.[4] Figures for some of the small villages around Burnley suggest that half of their inhabitants engaged at least inter-mittently in weaving; in 1826, again, Old Laund Booth contained 440 inhabitants and 219 looms, Goldshaw Booth had 769 inhabi-tants and 387 looms, and the neighbouring townships of Barley and Roughlee had respectively 737 and 1,009 inhabitants and 345 and 429 looms.[5] If two-fifths had been the average proportion of the whole hundred of Blackburn, then on the basis of the 1831 census there would have been a total of between 60,000 and 70,000 handloom weavers in the area.[6]

One particularly significant fact indicated by the few available local figures is the small number of handloom weavers still remaining in Manchester and the towns nearest to it by the mid-

[1] *PP. 1833 (690)* VI, Q. 11783.   [2] *PP. 1826/7 (237)* V, Q. 443.
[3] B. Heywood, Survey of Irlams-o-th-Height, MS, 1835 (*Papers of Manchester Statistical Society*, Manchester Central Library).
[4] Enclosure in J. T. Hindle and R. Noble (Blackburn J. P.s) to Peel, 27 April 1826 (*HO. 40. 19*).
[5] Memorial of Burnley magistrates to the King, 4 May 1826 (*Ibid.*).
[6] George Smith (*PP. 1833 (690)* VI, Q. 9384) estimated 30,000 weavers in the remotest part of the hundred of Blackburn beyond Burnley and in the adjoining part of the West Riding. Not all country villages in the cotton area necessarily had a high proportion of weavers, however. At Alderley, a few miles from Wilmslow, in 1836 there were only 33 in a population of 1,325 (E. Stanley, 'Statistical report on the parish of Alderley', *Papers of Manchester Statistical Society* (London, 1838)).

1830s. This is not, of course, really surprising since these towns were at that period the centres of both factory spinning and powerloom weaving; yet so far it has escaped comment. Detailed surveys by the Manchester Statistical Society of 170,000 persons in Manchester and Salford revealed only 3,192 hand weavers, compared with 3,842 power weavers, in 1836; only 275 out of 14,322 persons in Bury, where there were over a thousand power weavers; and only 371 out of 41,882 persons in Ashton, Stalybridge, and Duckinfield, where there were 3,463 power weavers.[1] These figures cannot, of course, be regarded as absolutely accurate, and may underestimate the total, since not all those questioned in the survey actually stated their occupation. Even so, they show conclusively that, as a proportion of the total population, the handloom weavers were of little importance in and around Manchester by the 1830s.[2]

With the aid of these and other local figures—though none can be accepted as wholly accurate—it is possible to make a rough-and-ready calculation to decide whether the usual estimates of 200,000 to 250,000 cotton handloom weavers seem plausible. If there were nearly 50,000 in Scotland; over 60,000 in north-east Lancashire; 23,000 in the Bolton district; 13,000 in the Preston district;[3] and 5,000 families dependent on the handloom in the Carlisle region;[4] then, with an unknown number in the Manchester region at the height of the trade, together with the country weavers in the outlying areas of Derbyshire, Cheshire and the West Riding, it would seem that figures of the order of 200,000 to 250,000 will not represent an over-estimate of the total number of handloom weavers when the labour force was at its peak.

[1] *The condition of the working classes in an extensive manufacturing district, 1834–6* (Report of the Manchester Statistical Society (London, 1838), table 5). The figures are for weavers of all fabrics. By the 1830s the remaining Manchester weavers seem to have been concentrated in east Manchester and especially in Miles Platting. See D. Winstanley, *A schoolmaster's notebook* (ed. E. and T. Kelly, Chetham Society, Manchester, 1957), pp. 7–11, 117–22.

[2] Many of them in any case were weaving silk, not cotton. See below, p. 260.

[3] *PP. 1834 (556)* x, Q. 5867.   [4] *PP. 1826/7 (550)* v, Q. 2831.

IV

It is in many ways very misleading to compare the vast body of cotton weavers with either the factory workers or the skilled urban craftsmen who also flourished in the late eighteenth and early nineteenth centuries. Unlike these other groups, the domestic outworkers in large and relatively unskilled industries formed an element in the labour force which has no modern counterpart. Many handloom weavers would have found the concept of following one occupation full-time an alien one. Industrial outwork served largely to occupy part of the family for part of the time, and this tradition remained a basic feature of cotton weaving in the industrial revolution.

Thus handloom weaving was frequently combined with other jobs, in many cases with agricultural work. 'Younger men' reported commissioner Hickson 'are rarely persons having no other resources than the loom. They calculate upon field-work in harvest-time; upon the produce of their potato settings; in some districts upon fishing; and upon occasional employment in various capacities.'[1] The combination of weaving and farming was old-established on both sides of the Pennines.[2] Its implications can be gathered from this typical sale notice of 1791:

TO BE LET

A farm situate at Royston, near Oldham...called the Poultry House Farm; consisting of an exceeding good farm house with room for six pair of looms, a spinning frame of 100 spindles—large and convenient Barn, Cowhouse, and outbuildings, and about fourteen acres and a quarter of meadow, arable and pasture of Lancashire measure.

N.B. The tenant of the above premises in the last year kept one horse, four cows, one calf, and plowed three acres for corn.[3]

In Rossendale in the early years of the nineteenth century, young David Whitehead, then a fustian weaver, described his

[1] *PP. 1840 (639)* XXIV, p. 649.
[2] A somewhat idealized picture of the old farming–weaving way of life can be found in the writings of Samuel Bamford, particularly *The dialect of South Lancashire* (Manchester, 1850), introduction.
[3] *Wheeler's Manchester Chronicle*, 5 March 1791.

work as being 'to milk morning and night and weave fustian the rest of the day'.[1]

In addition to the weaving that might go on on a large farm, many of the country weavers were smallholders. William Varley, of Higham, near Burnley, whose diary and account book for the 1820s survive, was probably typical of this class; he kept a pig and a few hens on a patch of land near his cottage, and grew fruit and vegetables.[2] Agriculturalists were divided in their attitudes to the smallholder. Holt in the 1790s commended the Lancashire weavers for their interest in horticulture,[3] whereas R. W. Dickson, twenty years later, was very scornful of their primitive potato-growing and hen-keeping methods. 'Whatever they perform' he wrote '... is commonly done in the worst and most irregular manner, and they seldom attend at all to any improvements...Nothing can be more prejudicial to the interests of the landed proprietors or more injurious to the community than the practice of annexing land as small farms to cottages designed for weaving and other mechanical labourers.'[4]

Finally, even the landless weavers would be pressed into field-work in the country districts at harvest-time. It was regarded as natural that the total output of cloth would fall in the summer months for this reason, and the busiest weaving seasons were, in fact, spring and autumn. At the beginning of the summer of 1827, with the cotton trade still suffering from the aftermath of the previous year's depression, the *Manchester Chronicle*, for example, predicted that 'as the hay and harvest seasons will *of course* [my italics] take off a great number of hands from their usual occupation at the loom, the quantity of cloth produced from the hand-loom will decrease weekly until the end of August or beginning of September'.[5] This kind of casual farm labour continued to occupy some of the handloom weavers throughout our period in both Scotland[6] and England, and Clapham's suggestion that the

[1] David Whitehead, *Autobiography* (typescript ed. from the MSS in Rawtenstall Public Library, 1956), p. 3.
[2] The diary is printed as an appendix in W. Bennett, *History of Burnley* (Burnley, 1948), III.
[3] Holt, *op. cit.* p. 81.
[4] R. W. Dickson, *A general view of the agriculture of Lancashire* (London, 1815), p. 107.
[5] *Wheeler's Manchester Chronicle*, 9 June 1827.
[6] For Scotland, see W. H. Marwick, 'The cotton industry and the industrial revolution in Scotland', *Scottish History Review*, XXI (1923-4), 213.

'farmer-weaver' was 'half-mythical' by 1830 is wide of the mark.[1] For it was in precisely those country districts where the farmer-weaver combination existed that cotton handloom weaving survived longest.[2] Weaving was not a part-time job in the country only. Many urban workers also took to the loom when their own trade was depressed or suffering its usual slack season. Builders' labourers, often unemployed in bad weather, and struggling small shopkeepers, appear to have eked out a living by weaving in hard times. Thus at Great Harwood, a large weaving village near Blackburn, there were in 1826 persons variously described as 'mason and weaver', 'joiner and weaver', 'collier and weaver', 'shoemaker and weaver' and even 'weaver and calico-printer'.[3] So common was it for workers in other trades to turn occasionally to handloom weaving that it was claimed in 1824 that 'there is hardly a man in Lancashire or Yorkshire who cannot turn his hand, if necessary, to weaving'.[4]

Not all the handloom weavers, of course, came into this casual category, and there were certain men to whom hand weaving was a full-time occupation. Prominent among them were the more highly-skilled and frequently well-paid fancy weavers at Bolton or Paisley; the heads of households in overcrowded country villages where there was relatively little part-time farm work and no other form of industrial employment;[5] and the workers in handloom sheds.[6] In all these cases there were a number of adult men whose sole employment was weaving cotton.

As against them, however, the casual element becomes even greater when the place of women and children in the labour force is considered. Adult men were, after all, only a fraction of the industrial workers of the early nineteenth century. As early as 1808,

[1] J. H. Clapham, *The early railway age* (Cambridge, 1930), p. 552.
[2] See below, pp. 266-7.
[3] *Great Harwood parish papers*, Lancashire County Record Office, PR. 163.
[4] *PP. 1824 (51)* v, p. 543.
[5] In the 1830s, Peter Dixons of Carlisle employed 3,571 handloom weavers, two-thirds of them scattered over country districts in the north of England, and the rest in the nearby parts of Scotland and Northern Ireland. Above half of them—2,200—were adult men (*PP. 1840 (220)* XXIV, p. 606).
[6] At Cockermouth in the 1830s, most of the hand weaving was done in sheds. Of the 353 looms in the town, 216 were worked by 'adult males' (*ibid.* p. 604).

half the total number of weavers were said to be women and children,[1] and by 1833, men were estimated as 'but a small proportion' of the calico weavers in the Burnley–Colne–Skipton area.[2] Out of the 1,963 looms in the Carlisle district in the late 1830s, 813, or more than two-fifths, were worked by children.[3] The prominent place in the labour force occupied by women and children at once disproves any theory that the handloom weavers in the cotton industry originally represented a group of skilled full-time craftsmen who suddenly tumbled from a prosperity fully-warranted by their craft status to a position of abject poverty. The real importance of cotton handloom weaving in the industrial revolution was not that it provided skilled work for men— although, as has been observed, it did so in certain cases—but that it furnished the kind of by-occupation for the aged, the unmarried sisters and daughters, and the growing children in a family who in many cases might previously have found comparable work in domestic spinning. For these people, weaving was the best way of making some contribution to the family income; but instead of following it as a full-time trade, they wove only when time and inclination suited, or necessity compelled them, to make such a contribution.

It is easier to understand why many handloom weavers earned low wages when we realize that they regarded weaving as no more than a casual employment. Their earnings from weaving were a useful—indeed in most cases a necessary— supplement to other income. Thus there was much hand weaving by women in the Derbyshire lead-mining villages, and a witness reported in 1833 that the people were 'much better off than where no weaving existed and where they were entirely dependent on the precarious occupation of mining'.[4] In Scotland, too, it was customary to set very young children weaving for the small earnings they might make before they were old enough to be apprenticed formally to whatever trade they might be destined for life.[5] A detailed example of the extent to which plain cotton hand

[1] PP. 1808 (177) II, p. 107.   [2] PP. 1833 (690) VI, Q. 9385.
[3] PP. 1840 (220) XXIV, p. 604.   [4] PP. 1833 (690) VI, Q. 11359.
[5] PP. 1834 (556) X, Q. 3058.

weaving was essentially the by-occupation of the 'junior' members of a family—in age and in status—can be seen at Great Harwood, near Blackburn.[1] Here the local clergyman kept a register of the state of the poor during the slump of 1826. The entries relating to Lowertown, the most populous part of the township, are particularly revealing. Seventy-five families, consisting of 393 people, are listed; forty-one of the heads of those families were weavers, the rest following other trades. Yet the total number of looms in the seventy-five families was 177, which meant that three-quarters of the looms were operated by junior members of the family. In all but two cases, each family had at least one loom, and the average was more than two. Even where the head of the family was not himself a weaver, the number of looms might still be above the average if the family was large. The complete register covers more than 250 families, or about two-thirds of the whole population of Great Harwood, and scarcely a dozen were without looms.

Women and children had, of course, also woven before the industrial revolution. Arthur Young in 1770 found women and children weaving in nearly half of the branches of the Manchester check and fustian trades, and at Kendal he reported the weavers to be 'chiefly women'.[2] One has only to go back to Defoe, too, to see what little substance there was in Gaskell's claims that in the 'golden age' of domestic industry children did not begin work as young as they did both under the factory system and in the last unhappy days of handloom weaving.[3] What probably happened in the early nineteenth century was that the proportion of women and children steadily increased, and that they had to apply themselves with greater constancy to their weaving. The reasons for this are obvious enough: the heavy demand in a growing industry for labour of a kind which, in many cases, women and children could perform as competently as men; the tendency for women to

---

[1] The details about Great Harwood are from the *Great Harwood parish papers* in the Lancashire Record Office (PR. 163). The various surveys taken by Ann Ecroyd (see below, p. 240) of the poor in Great and Little Marsden (now Nelson, Lancashire) show a similar average of between two and three looms in each weaving family (*Farrer MSS*, D. 96, Manchester Central Library).

[2] Young, *op. cit.* pp. 187–90 and 134.   [3] Gaskell, *op. cit.* p. 19.

replace men during the war period;[1] the need for some form of domestic by-occupation to enable all the members of a family to help supplement the family income; the demand for male labour in other trades in a rapidly-growing industrial area; and finally the declining piece-rates, which made it necessary to work both harder and longer. By the 1830s, the situation had been reached where a manufacturer could regard it as 'a common case' for a child of eight to be actually running his own handloom in the Colne district.[2] It could hardly be argued that such a child was better off than if he had been working in a factory.

As always, women and children represented an element in the labour force which would work longer for less money than would the adult men. In the last lean years, it was, therefore, inevitable that handloom weaving would find most of its workers from among these groups. Women and children needed some form of work to enable them to supplement the family income, and in many cases weaving was the only work available. There was, however, another group of workers who would accept the low wages which handloom weaving involved in the end—the Irish, who often disliked the discipline of more organized forms of work, and also accepted a low standard of living. Their place in the labour force requires a brief consideration.

The Irish immigration into the industrial parts of England and Scotland, including the textile districts around Glasgow and Manchester, has been studied by Professor Redford, and its causes need not detain us.[3] The overcrowding in Irish agriculture and the decay of Irish weaving caused a steady stream of immigrants into the cotton regions, many of whom were either already weavers or, given the ease of learning to weave, able to qualify as such if they wished. This basic fact is undeniable, but its effects should not be exaggerated, for it certainly did not result in the Irish becoming the dominant element among the cotton weavers. Most of the confusion on this point arises from the claim of commissioner Hickson in 1838 that 'one half, or perhaps the majority of weavers of plain fabrics, even in this country, are

---

[1] See above, p. 50.   [2] *PP. 1833 (690)* VI, Q. 10071.
[3] A. Redford, *Labour migration in England, 1800–50* (Manchester, 2nd ed. 1964), chapters 8 and 9.

Irish or persons descended from Irish parents',[1] and on a similar claim in 1833, when the Irish were said to be at least one-third of the weavers in Glasgow.[2]

Disregarding the fact that all Hickson's observations were the result of a brief tour of investigation in an industry and a district with which, on his own admission, he had no previous acquaintance, there is plenty of evidence to throw strong doubts on his views. The most important piece is the census of 1841, which first recorded countries of origin, and revealed that there were 105,916 Irish in Lancashire.[3] The fact that almost half of them were in Liverpool and a further 34,000 in Manchester immediately disproves any theory of something approaching a majority of Irishmen among the weavers, since there was never more than a negligible amount of weaving in Liverpool, and by the 1830s there was little in Manchester, either.[4] Now, it may be true, as Dr J. P. Kay claimed in 1832, that the Irish formed a majority of such weavers as still remained in Manchester;[5] a survey of 10,000 families, 40 per cent of them Irish, in the four poorest districts of Manchester—Ancoats, Newtown, Deansgate and Portland Street—revealed 627 families of English handloom weavers and 924 families of Irish in 1842.[6] But in practically every other cotton town, the Irish formed only a small proportion of the population; only seventy-five out of 3,000 heads of families in Bury were Irish in 1836;[7] they were 'very few' in Oldham and Blackburn;[8] and in the more remote small towns and country districts they were negligible.[9] Since it was in these last areas that handloom weavers survived longest and in the greatest numbers,[10] there seems no reason for supposing that the Irish ever constituted a very large element in the total labour force. Once this is accepted, the secondary thesis of Professor Redford, that 'as the English and Scotch handloom weavers

[1] PP. 1840 (639) XXIV, p. 693.   [2] PP. 1833 (690) VI, Q. 11720.
[3] Redford, op. cit. p. 155.   [4] See above, p. 57.
[5] J. P. Kay, The moral and physical condition of the working classes employed in the cotton manufacture in Manchester (Manchester, 1832), p. 44.
[6] J. Adshead, Distress in Manchester (London, 1842), p. 12.
[7] Manchester Statistical Society Survey, The condition of the working classes in an extensive manufacturing district, 1834-6 (London, 1838), table 7.
[8] PP. 1833 (690) VI, Q. 11170 and PP. 1826/7 (237) V, Q. 2011.
[9] Ibid. Q. 2270.
[10] See below, pp. 266-7.

left the trade or died out their places were taken by low-grade Irish labour at starvation rates of wages', becomes untenable;[1] whilst Dr Read's statement that 'soon after this date [1820] most of the English weavers seem to have given up, but many of the Irish struggled on for almost another twenty years'[2]—although possibly true of Manchester—bears little relationship to what actually happened in the labour force as a whole.

The ultimate decline of handloom weaving, then, should only partly be seen as the displacement of a group of skilled craftsmen by new machinery. More importantly, it represented the disappearance of a domestic by-occupation at a time when it was still necessary for every able member of a working man's family to help the family economy by working. The theory that Irish immigrants replaced English weavers tends to suggest that the trade suffered a high degree of labour mobility, but this is in fact the reverse of the truth; mobility *into* an expanding industry was easy enough, but mobility *out* was very difficult until some new source of employment had emerged which would be suitable for the great mass of unskilled and casual workers who formed the bulk of the cotton handloom weavers. In the last resort, much of the suffering of the handloom weavers was to stem from the fact that comparable alternative occupations, into which they might be absorbed as their economic position worsened, did not exist on a sufficiently large scale; for many of the old weavers were either living in small and remote places where work was relatively scarce, or were so habituated to the idea of casual work that the prospect of factory employment was quite repugnant to them. Alongside technical change, the 'industrial revolution' of the early nineteenth century involved on the one hand a redistribution of population even within the old manufacturing districts, and on the other increasing specialization and organization in the deployment of labour. All three developments were ultimately inimical to the continued existence of a large body of handloom weavers such as had been created in the first stages of industrialization.

[1] Redford, *op. cit.* p. 42. In any case, the heaviest Irish immigration was in the 1840s, by which time the cotton handloom weavers were dwindling rapidly.

[2] D. Read, *Press and people, 1790–1850* (London, 1961), p. 6.

CHAPTER 4

THE COMING OF THE POWERLOOM

THE unimproved handloom was one of the most ancient and simple of man's inventions. The materials used in its construction were easily obtained, and the mechanical principles on which it worked were primitive. In the mid-eighteenth century, all the cloth produced in England, with the exception of certain articles in the small-ware trade, was woven on a wooden loom consisting of four uprights joined together by crosspieces at top and bottom to form the framework of a box. A wooden roller or beam was placed between the pair of uprights at either end of the frame. The warp thread was let off from the first of these beams, and the newly woven cloth was taken up on to the second.

The basic operation of weaving consists in sending the shuttle which contains the weft thread from one side of the loom to the other through the threads of the warp, and in driving the weft threads closely together to form even cloth. To achieve this, two devices were added to the simple superstructure of the loom. The first of these, the healds, were operated by means of foot-treadles which raised and lowered the alternate warp threads between each passage of the shuttle and created the 'shed' through which the shuttle moved. The second was the lathe, which hung pendulum-like from the top of the loom above the cloth beam. It both provided the bed along which the shuttle ran, and also enabled the weaver to beat each weft thread against the edge, or 'fell', of the cloth already woven. The art of weaving had thus three elementary motions: the use of the foot-treadles to operate the healds; the propulsion of the shuttle; and the swinging of the lathe backwards and forwards to beat together the weft threads.

But the handloom weaver's work did not end there. Before the actual weaving could begin, he had first to wind the warp on to its beam and pass its individual threads through the healds and the reed (that part of the lathe which beat up the weft), after which

66

they were fixed to the cloth beam. The weaving of fancy and patterned goods, where more than two sets of healds were employed, made this a complex and tedious business. This done, the weaver had to dress the warp threads with flour-and-water paste so as to strengthen them to withstand the friction and tension to which they would be subjected in the loom. Again this was a slow and irksome task, as it was only possible to dress at any one time that length of warp which lay between the two beams. According to James Butterworth, an ex-weaver, one third of the hand worker's time was taken up in dressing, for, having woven one such length, the weaver had to stop in order to prepare the next section, and could not resume until the new dressing was dry.[1] The elementary process of working healds, shuttle, and lathe was liable to still further interruption when, as inevitably happened, threads broke; when more warp had to be let off or more cloth wound on to its respective beam; or when the 'temples', which kept the cloth extended to its proper width, had to be moved forward.

Taking all these factors together, handloom weaving was not only monotonous but also, in view of the many distractions from the basic weaving processes, slow. Even so, it was far more speedy and efficient than was hand spinning before the famous inventions of the 1760s and 1770s. Until the spinning process had been improved, there was little impetus towards any further development of the handloom—a factor which helps to explain the slow adoption in many places of Kay's fly-shuttle, which was the chief eighteenth-century innovation in weaving.

Arkwright's water-frame, marking the beginning of the transfer of spinning to power-driven factories, inspired the first essay at improving the cumbersome process of hand weaving. The first man to experiment with the possibility of running a loom by mechanical power—Edmund Cartwright—described in an often-quoted passage the factors which prompted him to pursue the subject:[2]

[1] J. Butterworth, *The antiquities. . . and a complete history of the trade of Manchester* (Manchester, 1822), p. 109. See also B. Woodcroft, *Brief biographies of inventors of machinery for the manufacture of textile fabrics* (London, 1863), p. 32.
[2] Letter of Cartwright, quoted in *Encyclopedia Britannica* (9th edn, Edinburgh, 1877), VI, 500, article 'Cotton'.

Happening to be at Matlock in the summer of 1784, I fell in company with some gentlemen of Manchester, when the conversation turned on Arkwright's spinning machinery. One of the company observed, that as soon as Arkwright's patent expired, so many mills would be erected and so much cotton spun, that hands never could be found to weave it. To this observation I replied, that Arkwright must then set his wits to work and invent a weaving mill. This brought on a conversation on the subject, in which the Manchester gentlemen unanimously agreed that the thing was impracticable; and, in defence of their opinion, they adduced arguments which I certainly was incompetent to answer, or even to comprehend, being totally ignorant of the subject, having never at that time seen a person weave. I contraverted, however, the impracticability of the thing, by remarking that there had lately been exhibited in London an automaton figure which played at chess.

Intellectual curiosity was thus behind the first attempts of the Rev. Dr Cartwright to apply mechanical power to the basic operations of the loom and so supersede the manual energy of the weaver. The extent to which Cartwright at first regarded this as largely an academic exercise can be measured from the fact that it was not until after he had taken out his first patent in April 1785 that he took the trouble to find out how the simple handloom actually worked by watching a weaver in his shop.[1]

In fact, Cartwright's efforts in the 1780s were premature, in that the problem which the powerloom was to solve—the lack of weavers to work up all the yarn produced by the new spinning machines—had not then seriously arisen. By 1800, however, the slowness of hand weaving relative to improved spinning had been emphasized by the development of a large-scale export of cotton yarn to Europe. This was viewed with alarm by such manufacturers as William Radcliffe because of the encouragement it would allegedly give to foreign weavers, who would soon be making all their own cloth, instead of importing British.[2] Since, according to Radcliffe, 'we employed every person in cotton weaving who could be induced to learn the trade',[3] the only way to ensure that all the English-spun yarn was woven at home seemed to be to improve the weaving process. Those who defended

---

[1] *Ibid.*

[2] See Radcliffe's evidence to s. c. on Dr Cartwright's weaving machine, *PP. 1808 (179)* II, p. 141.

[3] W. Radcliffe, *The origin of the new system of manufacture commonly called powerloom weaving* (Stockport, 1828), p. 12.

the export of yarn used a similar argument. An anonymous correspondent of the *Manchester Mercury*, writing at the turn of the century under the title 'Twenty-two queries to the manufacturers', asked 'Would it not be more essentially useful, and, of course, more profitable, for you to imitate rather than oppress the spinner, by turning your thoughts upon the introduction of machinery in weaving so as to reduce the price of labour, increase the number of hands employed, and overcome your continental opponents in like manner as the spinners have done?'[1]

Of course, Radcliffe's fears in 1800 had little foundation. In the first place, cotton weaving did not find it difficult, at a time of rapidly growing population, to go on winning new recruits for the first two decades of the nineteenth century; and indeed, there were many occasions during the unsettled wartime period when there was an excess, not a shortage, of handloom weavers.[2] It could in fact be maintained that, whereas a labour shortage at a time of modest population increase and in an occupation where productivity was notoriously low provided the main stimulus in the search for new spinning techniques in the third quarter of the eighteenth century, a relative abundance of labour during a period of unprecedentedly rapid population growth between 1780 and 1820 served in part to deter the adoption of the powerloom, especially when it is remembered that this was an industry where, in comparison with hand spinning, productivity was high, and where, for much of the time, marketing conditions were hazardous and unpredictable, and labour requirements correspondingly variable. Secondly, there were sound economic arguments for Britain exporting yarn at this period; looking at the figures for cloth exports, there is no evidence that overseas markets were declining *in toto*, and in providing cotton yarns to satisfy a new foreign demand Britain was merely maximizing her comparative advantages.[3]

[1] *Manchester Mercury*, 6 May 1800.
[2] See above, pp. 50–1 and below, pp. 100–3.
[3] The case *against* banning the export of yarn was most ably put in *A letter to the inhabitants of Manchester on the exportation of cotton twist*, (Manchester, 1800) by 'Mercator'. *Inter alia*, he argued (pp. 15–16) that 'the depression of our trade is not owing to the exportation of cotton twist, but to causes which operate equally on other manufactures, I mean the natural consequences of the war and the various effects and changes thereby pro-

The first impetus to improved weaving came, nevertheless, from this alleged inefficiency of the old handloom when compared with the new spinning machinery. But the efforts to speed up the weaving process at this period did not necessarily imply a desire to work healds, shuttle and lathe entirely by non-manual power, or to house large numbers of looms in factories. The handloom itself could be improved upon, either by removing from the weaver's responsibility the time-consuming preparatory processes of warping and dressing, or by performing the basic motions of throwing the shuttle or winding-on the cloth beam more efficiently.

In the first years of the nineteenth century, there appears to have been at least as much interest in improving the handloom as in developing a powerloom, and probably more prospect of success. After all, Kay's fly-shuttle had shown how a relatively simple device could greatly increase the speed of weaving. It had enabled the weaver to throw the shuttle entirely with one hand and swing the lathe with the other, a development of such significance that 'it is probable that no division of labour between the two hands of one operative ever produced results equal to those obtained by this invention'.[1] It was, in fact, the inefficiency of weaving after the 1770s which prompted the universal adoption of the fly-shuttle, which had previously been confined to limited areas.[2]

Thus there were many attempts about 1800 both to improve the handloom and to develop a powerloom. In 1803, for example, the *Manchester Mercury* observed that 'a very commendable emulation appears to have obtained for improving the weaving manufacture of this Kingdom, and in consequence a variety of looms, upon new and improved constructions, have been exhibited for public

duced', and that 'if the spinning business should sink to the low state to which a prohibition of the exportation of twist or even a tax would infallibly reduce it, few people engaged in that trade would escape ruin. Their machinery or buildings would be worth little or nothing and all the property engaged in them would be lost to them and to the nation. Thousands of poor wretches would become burdens to their parishes, or depend for their existence on the casual assistance of the charitable, or compelled by necessity, support a miserable existence by the perpetration of crimes.'
[1] Woodcroft, *op. cit.* p. 2.
[2] The fly-shuttle seems to have been little used in Scotland before the 1790s. See below, p. 132.

approbation'.[1] Those who stuck to the handloom seem to have directed their attention to two main problems—an automatic device for taking up cloth on the beam, and a time-saving method of dressing the warp. Both problems were solved by the experiments of William Radcliffe.

Much of our knowledge of Radcliffe comes from the autobiography written in his embittered old age. But if the blatant self-justification can be overlooked, it is clear that he had a very shrewd appraisal of the problems facing the weaving industry at the beginning of the century. First of all, he discovered in 1802 'a simple motion attaching the lathe to the cloth beam which, by only two small wheels, regularly takes up the cloth.'[2] The loom incorporating this device was later known as 'the dandy-loom'.[3] Secondly, in the following year he patented in the name of his assistant Thomas Johnson a dressing machine; this wound and dressed the warp, which was then delivered to the weaver ready for the loom. These inventions enabled the weaver henceforth to spend his time actually weaving.[4] What Radcliffe did not do, although there has been some confusion on this point (caused probably by the misleading title of his autobiography), was to invent a powerloom. He was not, however, hostile to powerlooms, and clearly regarded them as being just as satisfactory a solution to the yarn problem as was the improved handloom. For in 1808 he told the parliamentary committee investigating Cartwright's claim for compensation for his efforts that 'the manufacture of the [surplus] cotton yarns in Great Britain would more than counterbalance the diminution of labour by the general use of Dr Cartwright's machine'.[5]

The yarn problem and the inefficiency of the old-fashioned weaving process were not the only spurs to invention, however. Other advantages were anticipated, especially in a loom where healds, shuttle, and lathe were power-driven. In the first place, such a machine might well improve the quality of the cloth, since a mechanical lathe could surely beat up the weft much more

---

[1] *Manchester Mercury*, 22 Feb. 1803. For specific examples of improvements, see *ibid.* 5 Jan. 1802 and 1 Feb. 1803.
[2] Radcliffe, *op. cit.* p. 30.   [3] See below, p. 84.
[4] Woodcroft, *op. cit.* p. 32.   [5] *PP. 1808 (179)* II, pp. 140–1.

regularly than could the human hand. Indeed, it was claimed in 1808 that powerloom calico might be sold at twopence a yard more than handloom calico because of its superior quality.[1]

Secondly, the cost of production would be cut. For, as Charles Babbage the mathematician wrote in 1832, 'the first object of every person who attempts to make any article of consumption is, or ought to be, to produce it in a perfect form; but in order to secure to himself the greatest and most permanent profit, he must endeavour by every means in his power to render the new luxury or want which he has created cheap to those who consume it'.[2] The direct saving of labour charges in the early years was relatively unimportant, however, since this saving had to be set against the high initial outlay on a machine which still had imperfections. Indeed, John Makin, a Bolton manufacturer, told the 1834 select committee on the weavers that the real advantage of the power-loom was that it enabled a manufacturer to predict with greater confidence when an order could be completed, and that it gave him greater control over the materials of manufacture, thus cutting down the danger of losses from embezzlement to which handloom manufacturers felt particularly exposed.[3]

Another advantage of powerlooms in factories was that they could be operated by low-paid women and children; although these, it should be remembered, had long been an important element among the handloom weavers, and the advantage was therefore somewhat limited. It was a matter of general comment by contemporaries that the earliest powerloom weavers were women and girls,[4] and the Bradford woollen weavers went so far as to argue in 1834 that 'the great object in all such improvements' was 'to adapt the machinery to the youngest class of workers'.[5]

---

[1] *Ibid.* p. 139. This claim should not, at this date, be taken too seriously. See below, pp. 87–8.

[2] C. Babbage, *On the economy of machinery and manufactures* (London, 1832), p. 98.

[3] *PP. 1834 (556)* X, Q. 5204. In the *Blackburn Mail*, 14 July 1824, a correspondent signing himself 'a weaver of the old school' urged that the present scale of embezzlement made the powerloom essential. 'It is high time', he wrote '...that we should have a change either to powerlooms or to [hand] loom shops and factories, when at least one sixth part of the production of cotton goods in this town is effected by this dishonest means'. See below, pp. 124–5.

[4] See, for example, a French observer, G. D'Eichthal, 'Condition de la classe ouvriere en Angleterre', *Revue Historique*, LXXIX (Paris, 1902), 70.

[5] *Agricultural and Industrial Magazine*, I (1834–5), 250.

More important, perhaps, was the fact that such workers were more tractable than adult men; during the Rochdale woollen weavers' strike of 1828, the *Manchester Guardian* actually threatened that 'a direct consequence of the contest...will be a great extension in the use of powerlooms, for which several manufacturers have already given considerable orders'.[1]

Such were the advantages which manufacturers might expect of the powerloom. Many contemporaries also held that the weaver would benefit considerably from its introduction. Andrew Ure, the most fanatical public defender of the factory system in the 1830s, argued that '...in the factory, every member of the loom is so adjusted that the driving force leaves the attendant nearly nothing at all to do, certainly no muscular fatigue to sustain, while it procures for him good, unfailing wages besides a healthy workshop gratis'.[2] Although one-sided, all these points had a good deal of validity: hand weaving was both fatiguing and monotonous, and, when carried on in the home, it was under conditions which contributed nothing either to industrial efficiency or to domestic comfort. Furthermore, a manufacturer who had invested in machinery was likely to be more anxious to keep his workers in full employment than was a handloom manufacturer, for whom the problem of valuable capital standing idle did not arise.

II

Given these apparent advantages to both manufacturer and weaver, and the alleged deficiencies of unimproved weaving by the 1790s, it is at first sight surprising that the development of the powerloom should have been so slow, and its adoption on so small a scale for many years. Yet this is the case with many inventions; as Cooke Taylor observed in 1844, 'the slowness with which they are adopted is nearly the most wondrous thing about them'.[3] After patenting his second loom Dr Cartwright built the first English powerloom shed at Doncaster in 1787. It contained

---

[1] *Manchester Guardian*, 16 Feb. 1828. The argument was probably stronger in woollens than in cotton, but not negligible in the latter.
[2] A. Ure, *The philosophy of manufactures* (London, 1835), p. 7.
[3] W. Cooke Taylor, *Factories and the factory system* (London, 1844), p. 16.

twenty looms, eighteen of them weaving cotton, and before a steam-engine was installed in 1789 the machinery was driven by a bull.[1] By 1793, however, the shed had been abandoned. Grimshaw's factory at Manchester, containing twenty-four of Cartwright's patent looms, had an even shorter life. Opened in 1790, it was burnt down two years later by irate handloom weavers.[2] It does not appear that any more of Cartwright's looms were licensed for use before the end of the eighteenth century, although there were a few independent experiments with powerlooms in Scotland in the 1790s.[3]

Although a number of new looms were patented between 1800 and 1815, the total in operation at the end of the French war was still very small. The first advertisement for the sale of powerlooms in the *Manchester Mercury* appears to be on 21 January 1806, and the first notice of a weaving mill for sale was on 25 March of the same year, when the Westhoughton factory of Messrs Parkes, with its 118 patent looms, came on the market. It is an indication of the general lack of enthusiasm for the powerloom at this stage that the mill (whose owners had gone bankrupt—in itself an ominous sign) was still unsold two years later.[4] William Radcliffe told the committee which considered Cartwright's claims for compensation in 1808 that he knew of '28 or 30' mills where there was some power weaving, but they were clearly very small.[5] For the committee had been set up precisely because the powerloom had not been widely adopted since Cartwright had begun his experiments.

Only with the return of peace and prosperity at the end of the Napoleonic wars do advertisements for either looms or sheds become more frequent in the local press, and even in 1814 a leading Manchester spinner could still maintain that the only important development in the weaving process in the past half-century had been the universal adoption of the fly-shuttle.[6] He did, however,

---

[1] Woodcroft, *op. cit.* p. 23.   [2] *PP. 1808 (179)* II, p. 138. See below, p. 198.

[3] W. H. Marwick, 'The cotton industry and the industrial revolution in Scotland', *Scottish Historical Review*, XXI (1923–4), 213.

[4] The same notice appeared regularly in the press until January 1808.

[5] *PP. 1808 (179)* II, p. 143.

[6] J. Kennedy, 'Observations on the rise and progress of the cotton trade in Great Britain' (1815), in *Miscellaneous papers on subjects connected with the manufacture of Lancashire* (printed privately, Manchester, 1849), p. 6.

add that 'several improvements in the construction of powerlooms had lately been brought forward', although he concluded that 'their real value can be determined only by time and experience'.[1] Not until the 1820s did people begin to speak as if the powerloom had come to stay and to assume that it would ultimately be responsible for all the cotton weaving of Great Britain. Thus in 1822 James Butterworth wrote 'every day brings forth new discoveries, and it is not difficult to see by what has already been achieved and from the general spirit of improvement that is now abroad that we are placed far beyond the reach of competition in the manufacture of every species of cotton goods'.[2]

After the slump of 1826, it was generally recognized that the triumph of the powerloom was now inevitable. In June of that year, the *Blackburn Mail* called for the early adoption of the 'room and power system', whereby small manufacturers could rent a room within a large factory and fill it with their own machinery, as the best means of achieving the imperative changeover from hand to power weaving.[3] The clergymen, landowners, philanthropists, and weavers who appeared before the emigration committee of 1826–7 were almost unanimous in predicting the eventual disappearance of the handloom,[4] and J. R. McCulloch, the economist, not only concurred in this opinion, but warmly welcomed the prospect of such a manifestation of 'progress'. In an article in the *Edinburgh Review* in 1827 he wrote:

We have not indeed the slightest doubt that weaving by machinery is destined, and at no distant period, entirely to supersede weaving by the hand. There are no limits to the powers and resources of genius: the various processes carried on in the weaving mills will be constantly receiving new improvements; and the race of weavers—a race that has always been proverbial for poverty and want of forethought—will be changed to machine makers, a business which requires a better education and is, in many respects, better calculated to raise the character and improve the habits of those engaged in it.[5]

Undoubtedly the destruction of Grimshaw's factory at Manchester in 1792 furnished a partial reason for the reluctance of

---

[1] *Ibid.* p. 20.　　[2] Butterworth, *op. cit.* p. 104.　　[3] *Blackburn Mail*, 28 June 1826.
[4] See below, p. 157 for the emigration committee, and chapter 11, *passim*, for the decline of handloom weaving after 1826.
[5] J. R. McCulloch, 'The rise, progress, present state, and prospects of the British cotton manufacture', *Edinburgh Review*, XLVI (1827), 17–18.

entrepreneurs to develop the powerloom. As those responsible for the fire put it, 'we have sworn together to destroy your factory, if we dye for it, and to have your lifes for ruining our trade'.[1] There was some apprehension among manufacturers that the handloom weavers might take a similar vengeance on other attempts to use the new machines. William Radcliffe claimed that there would have been 10,000 of Cartwright's looms at work within ten years of the establishment of the Doncaster shed, had it not been for the deterrent effect of the 1792 incident,[2] whilst as late as 1842, Cooke Taylor could still attribute the absence of industries other than coalmining from the Westhoughton area to the damaging effect of the loombreaking which had taken place there thirty years before.[3]

Yet these fears must not be exaggerated. For the entrepreneurs' reluctance to invest in an imperfect piece of machinery was far more potent than the weavers' concern that their trade would be destroyed. This reluctance can be traced at many points in the history of modern British industry: in cotton alone (normally regarded as a pace-maker in adopting new ideas) there are several examples even in the nineteenth century of the long time-lag between original invention and universal adoption. Apart from the powerloom, the case of the self-acting mule could be cited to illustrate the effects of uncertainty as to technical reliability.[4] In the early nineteenth century, there must have been many who, like the Manchester men Cartwright encountered at Matlock, believed that an efficient powerloom would never be built; old Samuel Greg of Styal was one. His opposition delayed the introduction of powerlooms there until 1835, the year after his death.[5]

Indeed, for many years it looked as if these pessimists were right. The machine-tool industry was in its infancy, and the early

[1] PP. 1808 (179) II, p. 138. Popular ballads, expressing the general dislike of powerlooms, were printed and sold in Manchester after the fire at Grimshaw's (J. Harland, Ballads and songs of Lancashire (London, 1865), pp. 273-5).

[2] PP. 1808 (179) II, p. 142.

[3] W. Cooke Taylor, Notes of a tour in the manufacturing districts of Lancashire (London, 1842), pp. 167-9. For the events of 1812, see below, pp. 198-9.

[4] The self-acting mule, invented in the 1820s, did not triumph until the 1860s (S. Andrew, Fifty years cotton trade (Oldham, 1887), pp. 2 and 5).

[5] F. Collier, The family economy of the workers in the cotton industry, 1784–1833 (Manchester, 1964), p. 39.

makers of textile machinery simply lacked the technical know-ledge and expertise to construct so complex a machine as the powerloom. Discussing Cartwright's experiments, one recent historian has concluded that 'considering the primitive state of engineering technique at the time, it is not surprising that the loom would not work economically'.[1] Much of the early factory spinning machinery was made of wood, often in workshops attached to the individual mills, and cast-iron machinery built by specialist machine-makers became common only after 1800.[2] Thus the difficulty of solving certain technical problems constituted the biggest barrier to the rapid adoption of the powerloom.

It was not too difficult to co-ordinate the three basic movements of the loom—the actions of the healds, the shuttle, and the lathe—and to drive them from a single source of power.[3] Cartwright's second patent of 1786 had, in fact, solved these problems by inverting the lathe so that it swung from the bottom of the loom, not from the top, and by propelling the shuttle with springs. But other complications proved very troublesome. It was, in the first place, necessary to remove from the weaver's province such distracting and delaying operations as warping and dressing. Cartwright tried to incorporate devices into his second patent which would automatically dress the warp in the loom, but they were cumbersome. It was not until the invention of William Radcliffe's dressing machine in 1803, which made possible the complete preparation of the warp outside the loom, that it became no longer necessary for the powerloom to include such complex arrangements as Cartwright had envisaged.[4]

---

[1] J. de L. Mann, 'The textile industry: machinery for cotton, flax and wool, 1760–1850', in C. Singer, E. J. Holmyard, A. R. Hall and T. I. Williams (eds.), *The history of technology*, vol. IV, *The industrial revolution* (Oxford, 1958), p. 300.

[2] *Ibid.* pp. 282–3. It is interesting to note that Richard Roberts, who made important contributions to the improvement of the powerloom in the 1820s (see below, p. 79) had worked for two years before setting up on his own in Manchester in 1814 for the great Maudslay, from whose workshop most of the leading machine-makers of the early nineteenth century graduated (*Ibid.* pp. 288 and 428–9).

[3] The technical details in the following paragraphs are chiefly derived from A. Barlow, *History and principles of weaving by hand and by power* (London, 1878); R. Marsden, *Cotton weaving. Its development, principles and practice* (London, 1895); G. White, *A practical treatise on weaving by hand and powerlooms* (Glasgow, 1846); from which further details can be obtained.

[4] Woodcroft, *op. cit.* p. 32.

Even then, three major difficulties remained. Once the actual weaving movements were impelled by non-human power, the weaver's attention became much more cursory and he might no longer notice faults which, on a handloom, would at once have made him stop weaving. The powerloom needed an automatic device to stop the machine whenever the weft broke or became exhausted, or the shuttle came to rest in the middle of the warp. Secondly, an automatic 'temple' was required to keep the newly-woven cloth extended to its proper width and to counteract its natural tendency to shrivel up at the edges; in the handloom this was done by means of a set of pins at each side of the cloth beam, which the weaver altered manually as new cloth was woven. Finally there was the problem of altering the speed of the cloth beam, since its circumference grew as the amount of cloth on it increased. This necessitated its moving more slowly, while conversely the warp beam, which was becoming lighter, had to move more quickly.

Not until all these problems had been overcome would cautious manufacturers regard the powerloom as a worthwhile investment. And it was only in 1841, with the patenting of the roller-temple and the weft-stop motion by Kenworthy and Bullough of Blackburn, that a powerloom came into use which closely resembled the traditional non-automatic Lancashire loom, the staple of the cotton industry in its late nineteenth-century heyday.[1] The half-century between Edmund Cartwright and Kenworthy and Bullough was a time of piecemeal improvements, half-solutions, and compromises as machine-makers painfully acquired by trial and error the experience to build a compact and fully reliable machine.[2] That the powerloom was by no means perfected in the early 1820s is evident from Guest's words:

Invention is progressive, every improvement that is made is the foundation of another, and as the attention of hundreds of skillful mechanics and manufacturers is now turned to the improvement of the steamloom, it is probable that

[1] Marsden, *op. cit.* p. 95.
[2] The crudeness of much of the early machinery was also a problem in America. In one instance, the powerloom weavers were unable to earn a living wage on a piece-rate system because of the excessive time taken up in repairing mechanical faults, and had to be paid a time-rate (C. F. Ware, *Early New England cotton industry* (New York, 1931), pp. 72–3).

its application will become as general and its efficiency as great in weaving, as the jenny, water-frame and mule are in spinning, and that it will, in this country, at least, entirely supersede the handloom.[1]

Within this half-century, three types of loom stand out as having been more satisfactory than the rest in solving the technical problems. The first was that patented in 1803 by William Horrocks of Stockport, who, *inter alia*, borrowed the 'taking-up' device for the cloth beam from Radcliffe's dandyloom.[2] Most of the looms built over the next twenty years were based on it to some extent, and there was little significant development until 1822, when Sharp and Roberts patented a much improved form of the Horrocks loom. Its chief virtues were a superior take-up and let-off device for the beams, and a better method of applying power to the healds.[3] This loom was widely used, and, according to Ellison, 'marked the real starting point of modern powerloom weaving'.[4] The third major development, William Dickinson's 'Blackburn loom' of 1828, was significant for its 'over-picking system', a basic element in the plain Lancashire loom, whereby the shuttle was moved by two picking-sticks which represented the arms of the old handloom weaver. It does not appear to have been patented, but it was extensively used for plain cloth, and 'in its original and improved forms, probably ten times as many have been made as any other', wrote Marsden in 1895.[5]

Manufacturers were naturally reluctant to invest in an imperfect machine which might constantly be breaking down and might rapidly become outmoded. With the price of a loom running from £8 to £13, according to size, in the 1820s, setting up a weaving shed was a costly business, since the entrepreneur had also to provide a building, a steam-engine, and the machinery needed in the preparatory processes.[6]

Imperfect machinery also depreciated rapidly in value. In 1831,

---

[1] R. Guest, *A compendious history of the cotton manufacture* (Manchester, 1823), p. 48.
[2] Radcliffe, *op. cit.* p. 27.   [3] Marsden, *op. cit.* p. 73.
[4] T. Ellison, *The cotton trade of Great Britain* (London, 1886), p. 36.
[5] Marsden, *op. cit.* p. 89.
[6] The estimated prices of powerlooms are from *PP. 1824 (51)* v, pp. 309 and 383. As an example of the value of a whole factory, a Glasgow mill containing a 50 h.p. engine, 10,000 mule spindles, and 245 powerlooms was offered for sale in 1817 'at the very low upset price of £16,000' (*Manchester Mercury*, 6 May 1817).

Joshua Milne, an Oldham manufacturer, sold for £255 looms which had cost £1,400 when new in 1826; yet the improved looms with which he replaced them cost only five-eighths the original price of the old ones. In only five years, the powerloom had increased considerably in efficiency, and been reduced substantially in price.[1] Obsolete machinery remained a hazard in the 1840s. In Rossendale, according to David Whitehead, the 1848 slump lowered power weavers' wages. This caused great hardship to those who worked at the old ratio of two looms per weaver. However, Whiteheads, having introduced improved looms, were able to go on to a three-loom system, so that the fall in piece-rates did not affect their weavers adversely.[2]

Rapid rates of depreciation were not the only serious bar to early and heavy investment in powerlooms. The old master manufacturers in the hand weaving industry (those on commission from Manchester merchants rather than the spinners who also put out), were hardly likely to be able to raise the capital needed for the heavy initial outlay on buildings, power and machines. This certainly delayed the introduction of the powerloom in north-east Lancashire. In 1838, a projected joint-stock company to build spinning and weaving mills which would provide new work for the handloom weavers of Marsden, near Colne, failed to raise the £7,000 necessary for the buildings and the engines.[3]

But in the early nineteenth century lack of capital was not the only inhibiting factor. The small manufacturer had little incentive to adopt new methods, when the chief losses of the old system fell on the weavers. A small man had suffered little during a recession, provided he had not worked too much on credit, as he had had no machinery standing idle. Since, after the early 1820s, hand weaving was so poorly paid, and since, as the rector of Wilmslow put it, the competition between hand and power was to some extent 'maintained out of the poor rates' by the doles given to weavers with families,[4] the handloom manufacturer could still

[1] PP. 1833 (690) VI, QQ. 10961–2 and 11008.
[2] David Whitehead, *Autobiography* (typescript edn from MS in the Public Library, Rawtenstall, 1956), p. 94.
[3] W. Bennett, *History of Marsden and Nelson* (Nelson, 1957), pp. 196–7.
[4] PP. 1826/7 (237) V, Q. 428.

make some kind of living even after many of the technical problems of the powerloom had been solved.

This point has been elaborated still further by H. J. Habakkuk, who maintains that the universal adoption of the powerloom was delayed, even after its technical superiority was assured, simply because handloom labour was so cheap and plentiful; faced with falling piece-rates, the handloom weavers simply increased their output, and when they did so the relative cost advantages of the powerloom declined, so that entrepreneurs had less incentive to invest in the newer machine. As a result, it became worthwhile to take up the powerloom only when a vast increase in output was called for at the height of a boom, or when further technical improvements lowered the costs of powerloom production.[1] And indeed, there are isolated cases on record of manufacturers who, on account of the cheapness of handloom weaving, actually abandoned their powerlooms and reverted to the old system.[2] However, this argument should not be carried too far, since the force of Habakkuk's reasoning is weakened by his assumption (following Ellison's figures) that the number of handloom weavers hardly declined at all before 1830 and fell only slowly thereafter;[3] whereas it will be seen below that the disappearance of the cotton handloom weavers began earlier, and was effected more quickly, than has usually been supposed.[4] To some extent it is true, as Habakkuk has argued, that 'if Labour had been scarce in England, the domestic system would have contracted more rapidly than it did';[5] but the fact remains that, in a thriving and expanding industrial area such as Lancashire was in the second quarter of the nineteenth century, an abundance of alternative employment opportunities did cause the domestic system to decline rather rapidly.

[1] H. J. Habakkuk, *American and British technology in the nineteenth century* (Cambridge, 1962), pp. 147–50.

[2] See, for example, *Manchester Guardian*, 16 Jan. and 27 March 1830, and S. Clarke, *Clitheroe in the old coaching days* (Clitheroe, 1897), p. 43.

[3] Habakkuk, *op. cit.* p. 147, where it is accepted that the number of handlooms declined from 240,000 to 225,000 between 1820 and 1829, and where it is maintained that 'it was not until the 1850's that the English [cotton] industry went over more or less entirely to a powerloom basis'.

[4] See below, pp. 267–8   [5] Habakkuk, *op. cit.* p. 150.

To sum up: the cotton-weaving industry was not much affected by technological change until the 1820s mainly because, in the relatively primitive state of machine-making, it was simply not possible to produce an efficient machine at a cost which a manufacturer would be prepared to incur in order to enjoy the powerloom's expected advantages. To a lesser extent, this technological factor was reinforced by the absence of a shortage-of-labour situation, which might otherwise have prevented the massive extension of the old system; for population was growing rapidly after 1780, and in any case the general commercial uncertainty created by a long war and its immediate aftermath made for very violent short-term fluctuations in labour demand, in spite of the long-term tendency for that demand to increase. Under conditions which differed so much from those which had prompted the improvements in spinning techniques in the third quarter of the eighteenth century, it is not surprising that there was little incentive to give too much thought to the possible advantages of a new, costly, complex, and unreliable machine. Thirdly, it is just possible that fear of violent reactions against the new machines by the numerous hand-workers who had a vested interest in the continuation of the existing system acted as a further deterrent. This last should not be taken too seriously, however: as soon as the main technical problems had been solved, and stable peacetime conditions offered the prospect of large-scale and permanent market expansion from the 1820s, manufacturers did not hesitate. Even the cheapness of handloom weaving and the weak bargaining position of its workers could not long prevent the large-scale adoption of the new machine and the speedy displacement, except in a few specialized branches of the trade and in particular localities, of the old system and those who had laboured under it.[1] In W. E. G. Salter's terminology, by the 1820s, the powerloom had established itself as the 'best practice technique' in many branches of cotton weaving, and it would be only a matter of time before the handloom establishments closed their doors and abandoned their increasingly obsolete methods.[2]

[1] See below, pp. 89–91 and pp. 267–8.
[2] W. E. G. Salter, *Productivity and technical change* (2nd edn, Cambridge, 1966), esp. chapters 3 and 4.

III

The advantages which the powerloom proved in fact to possess were not necessarily those which the early inventors and entrepreneurs had anticipated, and it is difficult to make a comparison between the relative efficiency of the handloom and the powerloom during the period from the 1820s to the 1840s, when the two types of manufacturing co-existed. Part of the difficulty arises from the introduction in some districts of improved handlooms in an effort to bolster up the old trade during these years of decline. These attempts to help the handloom survive took several forms. According to Newbigging, the nineteenth-century historian of Rossendale, some of the weavers developed a so-called 'dandyloom', whereby one weaver could operate two looms by sitting between them; indeed one enterprising weaver, John Hargreaves of Dean, actually managed 'by an ingenious application of cords, pulleys and levers' to work four handlooms at once, a practice which he abandoned only when his employers stopped 'putting-out'.[1] As early as January 1824, William Rowbottom, the Oldham annalist, recorded in his diary: 'A deal of cloth is wove two in a breadth, and when wove the two pieces are cut up the middle and then the weaver has two pieces to carry home. There is some who weave three in a breadth.'[2] A loom of this kind was also in use around Colne in 1834; eighteen calico pieces were once woven on such a 'double loom' in a week.[3] But it is unlikely that this form of improved handloom was ever widely used, and when most contemporaries spoke of a 'dandyloom' they meant something rather different.

The most widely-used form of superior handloom was probably that developed by William Radcliffe to work in conjunction with his dressing machine.[4] It had a light iron frame instead of the usual

---

[1] T. Newbigging, *History of the forest of Rossendale* (London, 1868), p. 250.

[2] *Oldham Standard*, 17 Nov. 1888.

[3] For the 'double loom' in Colne, see *Manchester Guardian*, 8 Feb. and 8 Nov. 1834; 25 March 1835. Another abortive project of the early 1830s was the 'pendulum loom'. Richard Oastler saw it as a possible means of saving domestic weaving, and extolled its advantages in one of his public letters to the Duke of Wellington (J. T. Ward, *The factory movement* (London, 1962), p. 98).

[4] See above p. 71.

cumbersome wooden one, and was called the dandyloom 'on account of its neatness and compactness'.[1] The effect of this particular improvement seems to have been to increase the weaver's output by as much as 50 per cent.[2] A manufacturer who described a 'dandy-shop' to the select committee on the weavers expressed surprise at the great speed at which the looms worked, and was of the opinion that it must be 'a very exciting arduous sort of labour'.[3]

Such improvements, however, could have only short-term effects in propping up a dying trade. According to one practical expert on weaving, the dandyloom, in whatever form, 'effects almost all that can be done for the handloom as to motion' and could not, unlike the powerloom, be further improved upon.[4] Furthermore, its use was never widespread. It certainly came into fashion after the slump of 1826, and it was still spreading in Bolton in the early 1830s.[5] Yet John Fielden, the Todmorden manufacturer and M.P., who knew the Lancashire weaving districts at first hand, had apparently never seen one at work.[6] Its use was also shortlived; according to a statement by a prominent radical reed-maker, George Dewhurst, at Blackburn in 1838, all the dandy-looms there 'had been given up within the last four years... because they were found inconvenient'.[7] Technical difficulties partly accounted for this, for the dandyloom was used only on plain, coarse goods, the first to be hit by direct powerloom competition. It could not work effectively on fine goods, because the action of the automatic take-up device disturbed the free movement of the lathe, and reduced the weaver's power to regulate the force with which the weft thread was driven against the fell of the cloth.[8]

The inability of the dandyloom to stave off the ultimate collapse

---

[1] W. A. Abram, *History of Blackburn* (Blackburn, 1877), pp. 231–2.
[2] According to Major T. Moody's evidence to the s.c. on emigration (*PP. 1826/7 (237)* v, Q. 361) an adult man would weave 144 yards of cloth on a dandyloom in a week. Usual estimates for a good weaver on an ordinary loom never exceeded 100 yards.
[3] *PP. 1834 (556)* x, Q. 5043.   [4] White, *op. cit.* pp. 128–9.
[5] *PP. 1834 (556)* x, Q. 5042.   [6] *PP. 1835 (341)* XIII, Q. 9.
[7] *Blackburn Standard*, 1 Aug. 1838. The dandyloom was still in use in Wigan in 1841 (*Manchester Guardian*, 14 Aug. 1841).
[8] White, *op. cit.* p. 129.

of handloom weaving went deeper than this, however. The dandy-loom was almost invariably worked in large shops, although William Radcliffe's original intention may well have been to rent out his new looms to the weavers in their cottages.[1] Thus there was no appreciable difference to the weaver between working in a powerloom factory and in a dandy-shop, for the latter was simply a factory without power. For that reason, the dandyloom was largely an irrelevance, for it involved the surrender of what might be regarded as the 'best' features of the old system—employment in the home for the whole family, ownership of the tools, and freedom to plan the working day—in favour of most of the attributes of powerloom weaving.

The improved handloom thus did little to retard the adoption of the powerloom, of whose comparative advantages there is plenty of evidence, albeit sometimes contradictory. It was usually reckoned in the 1820s and 1830s that a powerloom produced three or four times as much cloth as a handloom,[2] but there were other estimates even more favourable to the newer machine: an experienced Belfast manufacturer, for example, claimed in 1835 that Martins and Co. of Killeleigh produced as much calico on 200 powerlooms as they had done with 1,500 handlooms.[3] An exact ratio cannot, however, be obtained, in view of the many variables involved; a man working full-time at the handloom would produce much more cloth than would a woman or child weaving casually, just as a primitive powerloom would put up a much worse performance than would the latest improved model. Indeed the difference in output between an active dandyloom weaver and a girl operating one rather obsolete powerloom may

[1] Radcliffe, *op. cit.* p. 30.
[2] See John Maxwell's statement in *3rd Series Hansard*, vol. XXIII, col. 1095; R. Guest, *A compendious history of the cotton manufacture* (Manchester, 1823), p. 47; PP. *1834 (556)* X, Q. 982, and PP. *1826/7 (237)* v, QQ. 167–8. In view of the vagueness and contradiction of the different estimates (which may well stem largely from the fact that the efficiency of all the power looms in use at any one time would vary greatly according to the age of the different machines), it would be unwise to put too much trust in calculations (such as those in Habakkuk, *op. cit.* p. 147 n. 1) which, on the basis of these estimates, attempt to solve the important but tricky problem of the total amounts of cloth produced by hand and power respectively at different dates.
[3] PP. *1835 (341)* XIII, Q. 1288. Twelve years earlier, Guest had claimed that 200 powerlooms would produce 700 pieces of shirting in a week—a task which would require 875 handlooms (Guest, *op. cit.* p. 47).

have been very slight.[1] Where the powerloom really scored in these early days was not simply in its greater speed, but rather in being constantly at work, in being suitable for docile workers to supervise, in ultimately permitting one weaver to manage two looms, and in reducing embezzlement.

Comparisons are also misleading because of the much larger number of auxiliary workers involved in a powerloom shed. As the *Manchester Chronicle* pointed out in 1826, even if it were true that a weaver with two powerlooms could produce as much cloth as seven handlooms, it did not follow that six-sevenths of the old weaving force would become redundant under the new system.

Suppose 1,000 pieces of cloth per week be wanted, [it argued]; to produce this by the handloom would require 4 warpers, 2 sizers, 42 winders (generally girls or old women) and 250 weavers—in all, 298 persons; to produce the same quantity in the same time by the powerloom would require 3 warpers, 17 dressers etc., 9 overlookers, mechanics, etc., 6 measurers and pickers and 134 weavers, in all, 169 persons, exclusive of colliers, carters, engineers, and machine-makers, whose employment would necessarily be increased by the use of the powerloom.[2]

This calculation is not without its dubious points. The number of handloom weavers is certainly too low, since many of the women and children would not make four pieces a week; and the number of powerloom weavers is much too high, although it must be remembered that some of them might have a young child as assistant or 'tenter'. Against this, however, must be set the large number of winders for the hand weavers, who constituted an extremely casual kind of labour—the very oldest and the very youngest—whose corresponding numbers in a power weaver's household would be unable to find employment; whilst conversely, the many auxiliary workers in a weaving shed would actually be adult men working full-time. Thus it is unlikely that, as regards output per worker, the difference between hand weaving and the yet-unperfected power weaving—although considerable—was quite as great as many of the contemporary estimates at first sight suggest.

[1] Richard Needham, an experienced Bolton weaver, claimed that the dandyloom could produce as much as a powerloom (*PP. 1834 (556)* x, Q. 5492).
[2] *Wheeler's Manchester Chronicle*, 15 July 1826.

One important factor in the slow adoption of the powerloom was its inability in the early years, contrary to expectation, to weave certain types of cloth, which continued to be better made by hand. Even in the 1830s, according to Edward Baines, there were only three kinds of cotton cloth predominantly woven by power: stout printing calicoes, coarse domestic calicoes, and shirtings, all of them being carried on in Manchester and the towns to the east of it.[1] In all other branches of the cotton industry —common calicoes, muslins, velvets, stripes, checks, ginghams, quiltings, and fancy goods generally—the handloom either retained a virtual monopoly, or at least accounted for the greater part of the goods produced.

Only gradually, as technical imperfections were overcome, was the powerloom able to take over in the more skilled branches. In the 1830s it was frequently held that hand- and powerloom rarely came into direct competition, but that each produced distinct types of cloth,[2] and as late as 1842, Cooke Taylor could still be surprised to find that 'power has not yet been applied to the manufacture of a great variety of fabrics on which the handloom weavers are employed'.[3] However the lack of direct competition from the powerloom did not necessarily make the fancy weaver much better off than the plain weaver who had to encounter such competition. For there was a good deal of indirect competition, as cheap printed powerloom cloths became an increasingly popular substitute for the hitherto more expensive fancy and figured goods after the excise on printed cotton was repealed in 1830.[4]

Thus where there was direct competition, with hand- and powerloom producing exactly the same types of cloth, the wages of the hand weavers were not necessarily lower than those of some weavers who did not compete directly with the factory; John Fielden, who made by hand between two and three thousand pieces weekly of a cloth also produced by power, claimed that his

---

[1] E. Baines, *History of the cotton manufacture* (London, 1835), p. 418.
[2] Compare the statements of Kirkman Finlay, manufacturer (*PP. 1833 (690)* VI, Q. 1198); John Makin, manufacturer (*PP. 1834 (556)* X, Q. 4894); and Phillip Halliwell, weaver (*ibid.* Q. 5727), which agree on this point.
[3] W. Cooke Taylor, *Notes of a tour in the manufacturing districts* (London, 1842), p. 71.
[4] See below, p. 110.

weavers were earning more than many of the weavers in the fancy trade at Bolton, on which the powerloom had not yet encroached.[1] Furthermore, as the powerloom increasingly took over in the plain lines, many who clung to the handloom from choice, not from necessity, merely transferred to different or more specialized fabrics, where they swelled the numbers competing for work in lines which in many cases were being hit by falling demand.[2]

IV

Having considered the various factors which influenced the adoption of the powerloom in the cotton industry, our remaining problem is to examine its growing use both chronologically and geographically. There was no official census of the number of powerlooms at work until 1835, when a special parliamentary return from the newly-appointed factory inspectors revealed that there were 109,319 cotton powerlooms in the United Kingdom, 61,176 of them in Lancashire.[3] Before 1835, the available figures are estimates only. Those given by Edward Baines and Thomas Ellison are the most frequently quoted:

TABLE I. *Estimated numbers of powerlooms, 1813–33*[4]

	1813	1820	1829	1833
England	—	12,150	45,500	85,000
Scotland	—	2,000	10,000	15,000
TOTAL	2,400	14,150	55,500	100,000

Given the inefficiency of the powerloom before the Sharp and Roberts patent of 1822; the heavy outlay involved in setting up a factory; and the disturbing effects of the last years of the war and

[1] *PP. 1835 (341)* XIII, Q. 18. [2] See below, pp. 105 and 111.
[3] *PP. 1836 (24)* XLV. The return had some gaps, and the real total was therefore larger than that given above.
[4] Sources of the table: Ellison, *op. cit.* p. 35, and Baines, *op. cit.* p. 235. For other contemporary estimates in the 1820s, Guest (*op. cit.* p. 47) reckoned 'not less than 10,000' powerlooms in Great Britain in 1823, and *Manchester Guardian*, 23 Feb. 1828, produced a figure of 58,000 currently at work in the United Kingdom.

of the post-war depression, these figures, although not exact, provide a credible general picture of the powerloom's rate of progress.

Since the powerloom had made a negligible impact on the cotton industry before 1820, it was between 1820 and 1850 that the industry was transformed from one in which the powerloom was a little-tried experiment to one where the handloom, formerly the rule, was very much the exception, and fast disappearing. The increase in powerlooms came in a series of brief but intensive bursts which coincided with periods of expansion in the economy generally—1823–5; 1833–6; 1843–5; and the end of the 1840s. Between these phases had been a number of recessions, particularly intense in 1826, 1829, 1837, 1841–2 and 1847, in which its extension had been retarded, if not halted.

There can be no doubt that the powerloom first came to be used on a large scale in the cotton industry in the 1820s. Its new significance is demonstrated by the greatest outbreak of loom-breaking in our period (in 1826), and by the general realization, already noted, after the slump of that year, that the powerloom had come to stay.[1] In the summer of 1824, the *Manchester Mercury* reported that 'in no branch [of industry] is there a greater demand for labour than in the manufacture of machinery for spinning and weaving. As an inducement to take orders, the machine-makers are readily supplied with payment in advance, and most of them are under engagements which it will take them many months to complete'.[2] A year later, there were said to be at least thirty powerloom sheds 'in full operation' in and around Glasgow, and a further twenty in process of starting up.[3] By the end of 1825, however, this advance had been halted; the machine-makers were turning off their men, and not until the 1830s was progress resumed on a comparable scale.[4]

[1] For the loom-breaking, see below, pp. 199–203.
[2] *Manchester Mercury*, 13 July 1824.   [3] *Ibid.* 13 Sept. 1825.
[4] *Ibid.* 15 Nov. 1825. R. C. O. Matthews, *A study in trade-cycle history* (Cambridge, 1954), pp. 129–33, argues that the continued investment in powerlooms over the period 1826–33 was the work of spinning masters who hoped to make up on their powerlooms for their losses on spinning. Most of the evidence for this theory comes from individual witnesses at the 1833 s.c. on manufactures, commerce and shipping. It is of only limited value, however, in explaining why the first powerlooms were set up by spinners. The spinners—having power supplies, experienced mechanics and factory buildings

Evidence of the extension of power weaving in the 1830s and 1840s can best be gleaned from the reports of factory inspectors. Thus Mr Rickards, reporting on the north-western district for the half-year ending February 1836, wrote: 'New mills are erecting in various parts of the country, and many old ones being at the same time enlarged or improved, more and more hands will consequently be wanted.'[1] During the boom of the mid 1840s, Leonard Horner noted that between January 1844 and April 1845 there had been 220 cases of new investment in factories within his district, 51 of them representing completely new mills. At least 8,542 powerlooms had been set up in them, but Horner was 'satisfied that this is far short of the real increase'.[2] In October 1845, he spoke of a 'vast increase' in the number of powerlooms, and reported that his district, which according to the 1836 return had 63,861 powerlooms, now had 142,949.[3] By 1850, there were almost exactly a quarter of a million cotton powerlooms at work in the United Kingdom, about 175,000 of them being in Lancashire.[4]

The biggest hold-up to the extension of powerloom weaving probably came in the protracted recession which the cotton industry experienced (not always, of course, with equal severity) between 1837 and 1842, and which provided the general background for the activities of both Chartists and anti-Corn Law Leaguers. The unfavourable conditions acted as a drastic deterrent from establishing new mills, or buying up old ones.[5] Even in June 1842, Horner was still lamenting that 'the great and general depression of trade continues unabated, nor have I been able to learn that any well-grounded hopes of a speedy revival are entertained by the best-informed and least desponding among the millowners'.[6]

The distribution of the earliest powerlooms created a particularly acute problem for some of the handloom weavers. Whether carried on in small sheds or in cottages, handloom weaving was

already to hand—would inevitably take up power weaving as soon as the powerloom became technically satisfactory. It must not be forgotten that many of the great spinners already employed handloom weavers, and that by investing in powerlooms they were merely modernizing their weaving section, not embarking on a new branch of industry.

[1] *PP. 1836 (78)* XLV, p. 165. [2] *PP. 1845 (639)* XXV, p. 449.
[3] *PP. 1846 (681)* XX, p. 567. [4] *PP. 1850 (745)* XLII, pp. 456–7 and 470.
[5] *PP. 1841 (31)* XXII, pp. 342–3, contains specific examples of the difficulty of selling mills.
[6] *PP. 1842 (410)* XXII, p. 466.

essentially an industry of the villages and the hamlets. Its siting was not, as was the case with power weaving, affected by the need to be near a source of power, whether water or steam.[1] It was natural, however, that the first entrepreneurs to embark on power-looms should be those already having access to a form of mechanical power. Thus in the 1820s most of the cotton powerlooms were to be found in south Lancashire and Cheshire, where factory-spinning was already concentrated. Indeed, the two branches of the industry were most commonly carried on side-by-side in the same mills.[2] The master spinners of the Manchester area already had the experience of dealing with machinery, the buildings in which to house looms, and the power with which to drive them—advantages conspicuously lacking to the manufacturers in the traditional handweaving areas of Bolton and north-east Lancashire. The earliest powerlooms were located outside the old weaving districts for this reason.

It was in Manchester and its eastern neighbours—Middleton, Hyde, Stalybridge and Stockport—that the great expansion of the 1820s took place. Guest had alleged an increase from fourteen mills and about 2,000 looms to thirty-two mills and 5,732 looms in the Manchester region between 1818 and 1821,[3] whilst as early as 1824, Thomas Ashton, a leading Hyde industrialist, could state that 'there is no handweaving in our neighbourhood in consequence of powerlooms'.[4] Yet at the same date there do not appear to have been any powerlooms at all in Bolton, and ten years later there were still less than 1,500 there.[5] Burnley was another late starter in acquiring powerlooms; in 1835, according to the parliamentary return published the following year, it had ten small mills with only 1,165 looms between them.[6] The last

---

[1] By the time the powerloom became of any importance in the 1820s the waterwheel had largely given place to the steam-engine. Thus there were never many powerlooms driven by water—in fact, contemporaries spoke of 'steamlooms' rather than of 'powerlooms'. In 1850, in English mills engaged in cotton weaving only, there was 2,840 h.p. of steam power and 370 h.p. of water; while in the combined spinning–weaving factories, the figures were 37,368 and 3,170 h.p. respectively (*PP. 1850 (745)* XLII, pp. 456–7).

[2] The best account of these 'double mills' is in A. J. Taylor, 'Concentration and specialization in the Lancashire cotton industry, 1825–1850', *Economic History Review*, I (1949), 114–22.

[3] Guest, *op. cit.* p. 47.   [4] *PP. 1824 (51)* V, p. 302.   [5] *PP. 1834 (556)* QQ. 5333 and 5627.

[6] *PP. 1836 (24)* XLV, pp. 146–9. Assistant Poor Law commissioner Henderson attributed Burnley's backwardness to the losses suffered by the failure of the local bank in 1826 (*PP. 1834 (44)* XXVIII, p. 923).

places to take up the powerloom, however, were the straggling manufacturing villages or market towns which had sprung from obscurity earlier in the century with the rapid expansion of hand weaving. The huge parish of Whalley contained only thirty-two cotton-weaving mills in 1835 (ten of them in Burnley), and only 4,737 looms—an average of less than 150 looms per shed. Darwen, Haslingden, Oswaldtwistle, Colne, Clitheroe and Marsden had only two mills each, and Accrington and Padiham had only one.[1]

By comparison with these slow-moving places, there were in 1835 over 3,200 looms in Blackburn; over 4,000 each in Ashton and Stockport; nearly 9,000 in Bury parish; and over 15,000 in Manchester parish. The average size of individual mills in these places was also considerably larger than in north-east Lancashire— 250 looms per mill in Manchester, nearly 300 in Blackburn, and nearly 400 in Ashton and Stockport.[2] Almost all these latter establishments were 'double mills' where spinning had long been carried on, and where the entrepreneurs found it much easier to embark on large-scale power weaving. The 'double mill' continued to dominate the cotton industry long after handloom weaving had ceased to be of any account. For in 1850, there were in the whole of England 184,816 powerlooms weaving cotton in double mills (143,690 of them in Lancashire), compared with only 36,544 (31,875 in Lancashire) in sheds devoted to weaving only.[3]

The great boom in 'weaving only' establishments in the Preston–Colne area did not come until the second half of the century, and it is still difficult to explain convincingly why the trend towards concentration and combination in south Lancashire came to be reversed and why by 1900 there was a clear distinction between the predominantly spinning towns of the south and the largely weaving towns of the north-east. Improved transport, with the completion of the railway network in the late 1840s, may have done something to revive the former hand weaving centres as factory weaving towns;[4] but probably the most important factor in the long run was the great increase in the grey-cloth market in

---

[1] *PP. 1836 (24)* XLV, pp. 146–9.   [2] *Ibid. loc. cit.*
[3] *PP. 1850 (745)* XLII, pp. 456–7.   [4] Taylor, *op. cit.* p. 122.

the Far East—a market which could well be supplied by small firms requiring little capital equipment. It was precisely this kind of firm which had the best chance of developing in the former hand weaving districts.[1]

V

Thus the peculiar way in which the powerloom was taken up in the cotton industry was bound to aggravate the situation of the handloom weavers and add to the painfulness of the transition to the factory. Largely for technical reasons, its general adoption was slow in coming, and for commercial reasons it was spasmodic. Furthermore, because of the way the industry was organized, the first powerlooms were set up outside the former major weaving areas. Again, it was a feature of the newer system that it demanded chiefly the labour of women and girls, with the result that some of the adult hand weavers may have found difficulty in 'moving with the times' and abandoning their cottage workshops in favour of the factory. It was such factors as these, just as much as any 'reluctance' on the weavers' part to leave their old trade, which helped to keep the handlooms going in some districts long after the ultimate triumph of power had been generally foreseen.

[1] The best attempt to explain the eventual division between the spinning and weaving towns in Lancashire is J. Jewkes, 'The localization of the cotton industry' (*Economic History*, II (1930), 91–106). But the subject is by no means exhausted.

CHAPTER 5

WAGES: (I) THE PIECE-RATE

HISTORIANS still debate whether, in the account-book of the English industrial revolution, the debit or the credit pages should contain the greater number of entries. But on one point they are unanimous: the deterioration in the material condition of the handloom weavers and similar groups of domestic workers in large and relatively unskilled trades was one of the least happy consequences of the economic developments of the period 1780–1850. The traditional picture of a decline in living standards is supported by a mass of evidence. The parliamentary inquiries of the early 1830s abound in comparisons between the weavers' prosperity in the last years of the eighteenth century and their recent miseries. A Bolton manufacturer in 1834 reflected thus on the status of a weaver in this vanished 'golden age': 'it was the trade of a gentleman; they brought home their work in top boots and ruffled shirts; they had a cane and took a coach in some instances, and appeared as well as officers of the first degree when they appeared alone.'[1] An old Glasgow weaver, looking back from the same year, remembered that in his youth 'it was quite common for a handloom weaver to lay in as much meal, potatoes, cheese and butter in harvest as would serve till spring, and coals were laid in in larger quantities, and very commonly handloom weavers salted meat at Martinmas for winter'.[2] It was recollected, too, that in those good old days the diligent weavers of Chorlton, near Manchester, had saved enough money to build themselves substantial houses with large gardens.[3]

Against these hazy but satisfying memories of high wages, fine clothing, good food, and comfortable housing were set the stark realities of the 1830s—periodic unemployment, low earnings, patched clothes, bare and cheerless cottages, and a monotonous

---

[1] *PP. 1834 (556)* x, Q. 5342.   [2] *Ibid.* Q. 858.
[3] *PP. 1843 (402)* VII, Q. 1121.

and insufficient diet of oatmeal and potatoes. 'Since I can re-collect', John Makin told the 1834 select committee on the weavers,[1] 'almost every weaver that I knew had a chest of drawers in his house, and a clock and chairs, and bedsteads and candle-sticks, and even pictures, articles of luxury; and now I find that those have disappeared.' As early as 1824, it was said in Bolton that the weavers were 'so ill-clothed that they are not able to attend divine service...they are ashamed to turn out'.[2] A report on the upper George's Road district of Manchester in the slump of 1842 ran: 'The greatest distress abounds in this district. It is not confined to any one class of labourers exclusively, but appears to be most felt among the poor handloom weavers, as their earnings do not afford more than two meals a day when labouring fourteen hours a day; so when they are out of work two or three weeks to-gether, as they often have been lately, they are literally starving.'[3]

With the decline in material comfort went a decline in social status. A letter from 'A Weaver' of Bury to the *Manchester Observer* at the time of the weavers' strike of 1818 complained that

we are shunned by the remainder of society and branded as rogues because we are unable to pay our way. For this reason a man of good moral character, should he be a weaver, is repulsed by the object of his affections as beneath her notice, not being able to provide for the wants of a family, and perhaps is supplanted by some profligate wretch who is accepted because he can earn four times the amount of a weaver with the same labour. For this reason, if we apply to the shopkeeper, tailor, shoemaker, or any other tradesman for a little credit, we are told that we are unworthy of it, and to trust us would be dangerous... In short, so it is with all whom we have to deal with; even the partner of our cares can scarce refrain from falling in with the general contempt which is poured upon us, until we are become weary of our very existence. Really, Mr Editor, [it concluded], such a degradation is insupportable to the mind of an independent man...[4]

Since this lament was uttered even before the powerloom was in use to any significant extent, it suggests that handloom weaving ceased to be 'the trade of a gentleman' at a very early date.

---

[1] *PP. 1834 (556)* x, Q. 4910.   [2] *PP. 1824 (51)* v, p. 397.

[3] J. Adshead, *Distress in Manchester* (London, 1842), p. 33. On one occasion at Preston during the same depression, the week's wages bill of 200 weavers was said to be less than £9 (*Manchester Guardian*, 8 Dec. 1841).

[4] *Manchester Observer*, 22 Aug. 1818.

There is no need to dwell on the weavers' physical and mental sufferings after the stage had been reached where earnings were normally so low as to buy little more than a bare subsistence diet. Connoisseurs of human misery can find plenty to savour in the contemporary parliamentary reports and eye-witnesses' accounts such as Cooke Taylor's *Notes of a tour in the manufacturing districts* (1842). The basic fact of a decline in the money earnings of hand-loom weavers more drastic than the decline in the cost of living cannot be controverted. What can be subjected to closer examination, however, is the cause, the rapidity, and the extent of that decline.

The whole question of wages and the standard of living during the industrial revolution bristles with problems which arise from the limitations of the available evidence, and any conclusions, no matter how tentative or qualified, are likely to be disputed. The inherent difficulties are well-known: wage series are often piece-rates rather than actual individual earnings; and cost-of-living indices are frequently based on wholesale prices, and include items unlikely to figure prominently in a working-class budget. None-theless, the change in the standard of living is a crucial question in the history of the cotton handloom weavers, and some attempt, however limited, must be made to examine it. The ensuing chapters may appear inconclusive; but it would be misleading to attempt to infer too much from the very defective evidence which now survives.

II

Since the piece-rate system is the only possible method of payment for industrial outwork, the easiest way to approach the subject is to study the change in the money-rate paid for weaving one piece of cotton cloth over the whole period of the industrial revolution. The existence of a number of series of piece-rates, chiefly in the parliamentary papers, makes it possible to examine the long-term trends in considerable detail.

Even if accurate, these piece-rate series must be handled with caution. It is impossible to be sure that any particular set of figures is representative, since rates of pay, even for the same types of

cloth, differed from one place to another. In 1824, Ashton-under-Lyne rates were said to be higher than Bolton rates, and ten years later the weaving prices for various types of checks were from 30 to 50 per cent higher at Bolton than at Blackburn.[1] The difference between the piece-rates being offered by Glasgow and Carlisle manufacturers in the late 1830s was sufficient for the Carlisle weavers to send a deputation to Scotland to see whether any Glasgow employer might be induced to put out work in the Border country.[2]

Such regional variations are not unexpected. A larger supply of labour with fewer employment opportunities usually means that wages diminish as one moves from the centre of a manufacturing area towards its fringes. Arthur Young and others noticed this phenomenon with regard to London in the late eighteenth century,[3] and it was true of the cotton area centred on Manchester in the nineteenth. A Shrewsbury manufacturer, anxious to dispose of a handloom shed at the onset of a trade depression in 1815, stressed that 'a manufacturer or a good weaver who could get plenty of work might do very well, as the difference between the wages given in Manchester and [the wages given] in the neighbourhood ...is very considerable'.[4]

Piece-rates create other difficulties. As the cotton trade was notoriously liable to rapid short-term fluctuations of prosperity and depression, the rates paid for weaving might alter considerably within a short period. The weaving price for a piece of 80-reed cambric, a yard and a half wide, at Stockport was 19s. in June 1805; by the end of the year it had fallen to 15s., and another twelve months later it stood at 11s. 6d.; in June 1807, however, it was back to 14s.[5] Similarly, in the eighteen months of boom and slump from the middle of 1813 to the beginning of 1815, the piece-rate for a 60-reed cambric at Bolton first rose from 21s. to 32s. 6d., and then sank back to 20s.[6] Variations of such magnitude,

---

[1] PP. 1824 (51) v, p. 398, and PP. 1834 (556) x, p. 502.
[2] Carlisle Journal, 30 June 1838.
[3] E. Gilboy, Wages in eighteenth-century England (Harvard, 1934), p. 39.
[4] Wheeler's Manchester Chronicle, 28 Jan. 1815.
[5] PP. 1824 (51) v, p. 419.
[6] R. Guest, A compendious history of the cotton manufacture (Manchester, 1823), p. 35.

often in the space of a calendar year, create two problems. In the first place, there might be a difference of 10–15 per cent at any given time between the piece-rates offered by individual manufacturers even in the same town and for the same type of cloth, since the adjustments of price were rarely simultaneous.[1] Secondly, most of the available series simply give one figure for each calendar year, which represents the average of the whole year; disparities between different sets of figures often, therefore, reflect the degrees of care which the various compilers bestowed on working out the average. Thirdly, there was always something of a tendency for workers, anxious to emphasize their distress, to produce lower figures than did the manufacturers.[2]

Among the series of piece-rates which survive, there are two distinct groups which have been taken as the basis of the present analysis. Each group is particularly useful, since it contains several independent series of rates over fairly long periods for the same qualities of cloth and the same districts. Although these series do not usually agree exactly as to the weaving price in any one year, their fundamental agreement on the extent of fluctuations over a period of years is impressive. The first group of piece-rates is for a fine muslin cloth—described in technical terms as a 60-reed cambric a yard and a half wide—which was extensively woven in Bolton, the English centre for quality cottons.[3] There are four independent sets of figures which between them give comprehensive coverage over the period 1795–1820. The second group of figures is for plain calico, which involved less skill, a lower piece-rate, and more rapid weaving than in the case of fine muslin. Plain coarse cloth of this sort was extensively woven in the towns and villages of the region bounded by Skipton on the north, Todmorden on the east, Bury on the south, and Preston on the west.

---

[1] PP. 1833 (690) VI, Q. 11854; PP. 1834 (556) X, Q. 4390 and pp. 205–6.
[2] See below, p. 127.
[3] The sources for the 60-reed cambric muslin are:
  (a) Evidence of W. Gifford and R. Ellison, Bolton weavers, to s.c. artisans and machinery (PP. 1824 (51) V, p. 392).
  (b) Evidence of R. Needham and W. Pilling, Bolton weavers, to s.c. manufactures, commerce and shipping (PP. 1833 (690) VI, p. 703).
  (c) Evidence of J. Honeyford, Bolton weaver, to s.c. petitions of cotton manufacturers and weavers (PP. 1808 (177) II, p. 120).
  (d) Guest, op. cit. p. 35.

TABLE 2. *The piece-rate for muslin weaving at Bolton, 1795–1820*[1]

Date	Average piece-rate s. d.	Index (1805 = 100)	Date	Average piece-rate s. d.	Index (1805 = 100)
1795	34 0	136	1808	14 0	56
1796	36 0	144	1809	18 0	72
1797	31 0	124	1810	20 6	82
1798	29 0	116	1811	14 0	56
1799	27 0	108	1812	15 0	60
1800	27 6	110	1813	21 0	84
1801	27 0	108	1814	23 0	92
1802	31 6	126	1815	14 0	56
1803	24 0	96	1816	12 0	48
1804	23 0	92	1817	10 6	42
1805	25 0	100	1818	11 0	44
1806	22 6	90	1819	10 0	40
1807	18 6	74	1820	10 0	40

Five sets of figures are available here, all provided by local manufacturers, and they cover the period from the end of the Napoleonic war to the early 1840s.[2]

The long-term movement of the piece-rate for fine muslin weaving, as indicated by table 2, was certainly sharply downward between the 1790s and the end of the post-war depression. The decline was not, however, smooth and continuous, for it was interrupted by significant rises from time to time. These violent fluctuations largely reflected the varying fortunes of an industry

[1] For the sources of this table, see p. 98, n. 3, and for the details of the wage series on which it is based, see appendix 1.
[2] The sources of the figures for plain calico are:
   (a) Speech of John Fielden, M.P., 7 March 1833 (*3rd Series Hansard,* vol. 16, col. 365).
   (b) Evidence of J. Grimshaw to s.c. manufactures, commerce and shipping (*PP. 1833 (690)* VI, Q. 10120).
   (c) and (d) Two sets of figures (relating to slightly different types of cloth) given by G. Smith to the same committee (*Ibid.* Q. 9390 and Q. 9400).
   (e) Statement of W. Ecroyd at 'grand meeting of deputies' of the cotton trade summoned by the anti-Corn Law League in Manchester, December 1841 (*Manchester Guardian,* 18 Dec. 1841).
   These series are given in full in appendix 1.

and a nation having to face a war fought with economic as well as military weapons. When markets were cut off, or when food was scarce and expensive at home, the demand for cloth would fall off, and the weavers had to compete for a limited amount of work. Conversely, when conditions in the home and export markets improved, the demand for goods was so great that labour had to be attracted into weaving by high wages.

There had of course been fluctuations in the piece-rates even before the French war. But in the early 1790s most branches of the cotton industry were in their infancy. New fabrics were still being developed, and cottons enjoyed very much the status of novel luxuries for which the demand exceeded the supply. High piece-rates were inevitable under such circumstances, but they were bound to tumble when the market settled down, when the novelty wore thin, and when the supply of labour came to equal or even to exceed the demand. As early as 1803, a Bolton manufacturer, discussing the new fancy lines developed a few years earlier and offered to the market at exorbitant prices, admitted that 'there was a great deal of money got by them to the weaver, more than what is decent to mention'.[1]

If the freak nature of these early piece-rates is admitted, then a gradual decline from the 1790s was only to be expected. Unfortunately, the process was exaggerated by the economic fluctuations of the war period, in which rapid declines in periods of depression alternated with rises in prosperous times.[2] Thus the natural fall from the abnormal peak of the early 1790s was intensified in the 'bad years' around the turn of the century but was reversed at the return of peace in 1802. On the resumption of the war, decline began again, but it was halted for a short time in 1805. However, it was with the imposition of Napoleon's connental system after the Berlin decree of 21 Nov. 1806 that the position of the English cotton industry became very serious indeed. Of all British industries, it was the most exposed to fluctuations in international trade, since its raw material came from America and

---

[1] PP. 1803 (114) III, part 4, p. 59.
[2] Other series of piece-rates during and just after the war behave in precisely the same way as the Bolton 60-reed cambric in table 2. See PP. 1808 (177) II, pp. 116, 122–3; PP. 1824 (51) V, p. 419; and PP. 1833 (690) VI, p. 705.

its finished product was widely marketed both there and on the continent. When an attempt was made to close the European market, and when relations with America became strained as a result of the British reaction to Napoleon's economic measures, cotton was bound to suffer.

Yet even in these critical years 1806–13 the story is not simply one of uninterrupted decline, with the shortage of work, the erratic supplies of raw cotton, and the increasingly restricted and competitive markets causing continual reductions in the piece-rate.[1] The fall was certainly startling over the three years 1805–8—from an index figure of 100 to one of 56—and the weavers' reaction was first to press for a minimum wage bill and second, when this failed, to stage a major strike.[2] There was, however, a marked recovery in the latter part of 1808. The Spanish rebellion opened the Iberian and south American markets, and Napoleon's preoccupation with the Peninsula led to a relaxing of the 'system' on the part of those northern European rulers who had imposed it only with great reluctance. As a result, in Crouzet's words, the cotton industry experienced 'une véritable période de boom qui porta sa production à un niveau record, et...elle connut une activité et une prospérité bien supérieures à celles des autres industries'.[3] When a serious depression recurred in 1812, manufacturers looked back on 1810 as 'the best year we ever had'.[4] One cotton spinner recalled: 'I had a very great demand for my yarn; it was sold every week as it was spun, and taken from the mill; my people were all desirous of working longer hours, and worked seven days, and some part of the year seven days and a half, per week.'[5] The effect of the prosperity of 1809–10 on the weavers was reflected in a rise in piece-rates which, though it did not reach the 1805 level, was still remarkable.

For a time, the discontent of 1808 faded away, but worse was to come. The economic situation again became critical in the latter part of 1810: a grain shortage, a sudden fall in import prices, the

---

[1] A detailed account of the effects of the 'continental system' is in F. Crouzet, L'économie britannique et le blocus continental (2 vols. Paris, 1958).

[2] See below, p. 154 and pp. 189–92.

[3] Crouzet, op. cit. p. 510.   [4] PP. 1812 (231) III, p. 229.

[5] Ibid. p. 264.

blighting of trade prospects in south America, and the reinforce-
ment of the continental system after Napoleon's victory over the
Austrians all combined to produce a financial crisis at home and
to cut off vital markets for cotton products abroad. The recently
swollen industry found itself in the usual predicament of having
too many workers and too little work. A wage fall was the result;
the index figure of 1811 was only two-thirds what it had been in
1810, and little more than half the 1805 figure. Witnesses at the
1812 committee on the working of the Orders in Council were
unanimous in regarding working-class distress as the most acute
they had ever known.[1] Under such circumstances the political discontent, the food riots, and the loom-breaking which took place
in Lancashire were hardly unexpected.[2]

The boom at the close of the continental war in 1813–14 was
the last period on which the handloom weavers subsequently
looked back as one of real prosperity. Nonetheless, it was the outcome of freak conditions which could hardly be expected to last.
The end of the war released the accumulated demand for cottons
at home and abroad, whilst the relative scarcity of raw cotton
during the Anglo-American war of 1812–14 meant that this increased demand coincided with a diminished supply. In 1811, of a
total 174,000 bags of cotton wool imported into Liverpool, 97,000
came from the southern United States; in 1813 and 1814, only
18,000 and 42,000 bags respectively came to Liverpool from that
quarter.[3] The shortage was less acute than in the more famous
'cotton famine' fifty years later, since England at this stage was
much less dependent on America for her supply; nevertheless, the
average annual consumption of raw cotton between 1812 and 1815
was less than two-thirds of that consumed in the bumper year
1810,[4] and according to T. S. Ashton's table of price-relatives
(1829 = 100), raw cotton prices were 281 in 1812; 454 in 1813;
497 in 1814; 389 in 1815; falling to 173 in 1820: at a time when
general commodity prices moved as follows: 173 in 1812; 197 in

---

[1] *PP. 1812 (231)* III, pp. 205 and 219. [2] See below, p. 198 and pp. 208–10.
[3] Printed enclosure, headed 'Imports of cotton wool into Liverpool', in W. R. Hay to
H. Hobhouse, 1 Aug. 1818 (*HO. 42. 179*).
[4] B. R. Mitchell and P. Deane, *Abstract of British historical statistics* (Cambridge, 1962),
p. 179.

1813; 211 in 1814; 177 in 1815; and 132 in 1820.[1] Part of the high profit yielded by this situation was passed on to the weaver, who probably enjoyed it in the usual way by working less hard; in so doing he avoided the immediate threat of an excess supply of labour at a time when work was relatively scarce, but he encouraged it in the long run because his high wages attracted newcomers to the trade. Thus once a new horde of recruits had entered the industry and the normal supply of raw cotton had been restored, the familiar process of wage reductions began again when market conditions at home and abroad deteriorated in 1815. By 1816, the piece-rate was lower than at any time during the war, and, except for the short-lived gains after the 1818 strike, it continued to fall until the end of the decade.

The movement of piece-rates over the period 1806–20 epitomizes the problems which the handloom weavers had to face in the years before the powerloom came into use, as it ultimately did in the 1820s. The real trouble was that the weavers were ensnared in an industry which depended entirely for its raw materials, and largely for its markets, on foreigners, and as such their trade was liable to be disrupted by forces beyond the control of themselves or their employers. When markets were buoyant and raw materials scarce, as in 1813–14, piece-rates were very high; when markets were buoyant and raw materials plentiful (as in 1810) they were moderately high; but when markets collapsed and raw materials were easily obtainable (as in 1806–7 or 1815–17) they slumped drastically. Essentially the supply of labour in the industry lacked the flexibility to respond adequately to the varying demand situation which the frequent changes created.

Furthermore, the wage reductions in this first phase were all the more serious because they took place in a period of general inflation. The famous Silberling price index is no longer regarded as wholly reliable, but at least it indicates the sort of sharp increase in prices which took place during the war. From a base of 100 in 1790, Silberling found that the index figure was 130 in 1795; 170 in 1800; 154 in 1805; 176 in 1810; and 187 in 1813. Even after the

[1] T. S. Ashton, 'Some statistics of the industrial revolution', in E. M. Carus-Wilson (ed.), *Essays in economic history* (London, 1962), III, 249.

war, the figures are 150 in 1815; 132 in 1820; and only in 1822, for the one year, is the level of 1790 again recorded.[1] Under such circumstances, the fall in handloom weavers' real wages over the period as a whole would be even more drastic than the movement of piece-rates would indicate.

However, as the immediate post-war depression lifted and prices fell in the early 1820s to something like the levels that had obtained in the early 1790s, it looked for a year or two as if the cotton weavers might again enjoy relative prosperity. Turning to table 3— covering a period when, incidentally, the Silberling index was generally steady at levels a little above those prevailing in 1790 —we find that the weaving price for calico remained fairly stable over the years 1819–22.[2] In money terms, the piece-rates of 1820 and 1821 certainly appear low when compared with 1814. Yet the unusual quiet of these years, by contrast with, say, 1816–17, strongly suggests that even the 'poor starving handloom weavers' were not discontented with their lot as late as the early 1820s. One indication of the comparative prosperity of these years is the prominent and honourable part the cotton handloom weavers played in the trade processions and festivities of the Preston Guild in 1822.[3]

By 1826, however, all this had ended. Between 1821 and 1826, there had been a staggering drop in the piece-rate from 3s. 2d. to 1s. 4½d. The effects of such a change at a time when food prices were rising again can be imagined.[4] Two factors were responsible: technological change, in the form of an increasingly large number of powerlooms, was beginning to be felt at last in cotton weaving;[5] and in 1826, when much the sharpest fall was registered, England experienced her first modern peace-time financial crisis and industrial depression. The former meant an ever-diminishing field in which the handloom could remain a viable method of production; the latter meant a sharp contraction in the demand

---

[1] J. H. Clapham, *The early railway age* (Cambridge, 1930), p. 602.
[2] See below, p. 130, for the prosperity of William Varley's family in the early 1820s, and also appendix 2.
[3] *Manchester Mercury*, 10 Sept. 1822.
[4] See appendix 2 for details of food price movements in the post-war period.
[5] See above, p. 89.

TABLE 3. *The piece-rate for calico weaving in north-east Lancashire, 1814–41*[1]

Date	Average piece-rate s. d.	Index (1815 = 100)	Date	Average piece-rate s. d.	Index (1815 = 100)
1814	6 9	162	1828	1 9½	43
1815	4 2¼	100	1829	1 2	28
1816	2 10¾	70	1830	1 5½	35
1817	2 10¾	70	1831	1 7¾	39
1818	3 7½	87	1832	1 4¾	33
1819	2 10½	69	1833	1 5½	35
1820	2 10¾	70	1834	1 9⅜	43
1821	3 2	76	1835	1 9¾	44
1822	2 8¼	64	1836	1 8⅜	41
1823	2 5¼	58	1837	1 2¾	29
1824	2 2½	53	1838	1 3⅜	31
1825	2 4	56	1839	1 3¾	32
1826	1 4½	33	1840	1 3	30
1827	1 8	40	1841	1 1⅞	28

for cloth and consequently a very much reduced amount of work immediately available for the weavers.

The year 1826 was the real turning point in the history of the cotton weavers. After the slump, their piece-rates never recovered significantly; the increasing use of the powerloom, coupled with recurrent industrial depressions, made it impossible that they should do so. Those weavers who kept to the kinds of cloth also woven by power became a true Marxian 'reserve army of labour', for whom there was a strong demand only in prosperous times to supplement the work being done in the factories; those who turned to the more specialized fabrics to which power had not been applied merely added to the numbers competing for a very limited quantity of work. Thus the decline in fancy weavers' wages from

[1] For the sources, see above, p. 99, and also appendix 1. The index after 1833 is based on only one set of figures.

the early 1820s was almost as sharp as the decline in plain cloth rates, although there was no direct competition from the power-loom. The Bolton 60-reed cambric, which was paid at the rate of 10s. per piece in 1820, fell sharply in 1826 and again in 1829, when it stood at 5s. 6d.[1]

Although there was no major recovery in either plain or fancy piece-rates after 1826, the times were not uniformly hard thereafter. With the recovery of trade late in 1827, hand weavers were again in demand, and piece-rates rose; in order to find workers, one Bolton manufacturer went round the town 'beating up with drum and fife for weavers of silk and cotton fabrics'.[2] From the late 1820s to the early 1840s, a clear pattern emerges, with low piece-rates in the bad years—1829, 1832, 1837 and 1841—followed by increases when trade recovered, and more weavers were needed. Since the periods of greatest industrial activity coincided with low food prices, the handloom weavers' condition, although not prosperous, can hardly have been poverty-stricken. Thus there was relative prosperity in 1834–5; at Bolton, the advance in piece-rates in those years averaged 20 per cent,[3] and a prominent Manchester weaver, Edward Curran, recalled of the year 1835 that 'we expected, from the sudden change that then took place, that our condition was likely to be improved, because our food got cheaper and our wages increased'.[4] There was a similar improvement in the years 1843–4; factory-inspector Leonard Horner reported a 30 per cent increase in handloom weavers' piece-rates within twelve months of the end of the 1842 depression.[5] Even after 1826, therefore, extreme poverty was likely to be periodic, not permanent.

III

Even so, and disregarding for the moment the questions of real wages and of the standard of living, the decline in money wage rates for handloom weaving between the 1790s and the 1830s was

[1] PP. 1833 (690) VI, Q. 11738. See above, pp. 87–8, for an explanation of this unusual phenomenon.
[2] Manchester Guardian, 17 Feb. 1828. [3] Ibid. 18 Dec. 1841.
[4] Ibid. 21 Aug. 1841. [5] PP. 1844 (583) XXVIII, p. 576.

spectacular, and it is worth considering in some detail why it happened. Essentially, the cotton handloom weavers were unable to resist the reductions which their employers decided (for whatever reasons) to make. The cause of the weavers' weakness was simple, and, as has already been suggested, had, in the early years, little connexion with the course of technical change. There was, as the royal commission on the weavers discovered in 1841, a lack of balance between the supply of labour and the demand for it. Both had been generally increasing, since over the long term the cotton industry expanded rapidly in the early nineteenth century; but the supply had been unable to respond with sufficient flexibility to the wild variations of demand, since it was difficult for those who had joined the labour force in a boom period to find alternative work in the ensuing slump. Movement *into* the industry, then, was easy, but movement *out*, at any rate until the great expansion of all kinds of factory work in the cotton districts from the 1820s, slow; and once inside, the handloom weaver was trapped in a dead-end job where his material well-being might improve temporarily in a boom, but where in a slump he and his family, relatively defenceless against their employer, had to bear the brunt of the suffering. A war situation made the whole problem worse, because the transition from boom to slump came with terrifying frequency and suddenness. At a time when population growth was rapid, labour mobility low, and the range of employment opportunities limited, it is inconceivable that any labour force could have had the flexibility to respond successfully to such violent fluctuations. In so far as the weavers did respond to the changing situation, their habits of work probably only tended to make things worse: for they artificially enhanced the scarcity of labour in the early stages of a boom by, individually, working less hard when the piece-rates were rising, which meant that too many new recruits were attracted into the trade; and they artificially enhanced the excess of labour during a slump by a willingness to take in more work to make up for a falling piece-rate.

Thus, as early as 1811, a French observer noted: 'The fact is, there are too many labourers, and the only remedy is for a less number of young men to take to the loom and a greater number

to shoulder the musket and go on board ship;'[1] whilst in the same year, a Glasgow weaver claimed that the labour force was twice as large as the current demand for its services.[2] Under such circumstances, when work was scarce and the weaver was faced with either taking work at a reduced rate or being unemployed, it is obvious where his decision would fall. As a result the course of piece-rates was inexorably downward.

After about 1820, however, the nature of the weavers' problems was fundamentally altered. The coming of the powerloom served in part to intensify the traditional competition for work among the weavers. Installing several thousand powerlooms had a similar effect to recruiting another horde of handloom weavers: it increased the cotton industry's weaving capacity, with the result that, when markets were restricted in periods of slump, there would again be too many weavers chasing too little work. There were two important differences, however: after the 1820s the powerloom was increasingly a more effective and less costly means of production than the handloom; and the entrepreneur who had invested heavily in power but who still employed some hand workers would prefer to employ his costly powerlooms rather than his handlooms in a depression. Both factors worked to the detriment of the handloom weavers.

The nature of the demand for cloth and the defective marketing structure of the industry together account for cotton's very variable labour requirements. In the early nineteenth century, the English cotton industry depended on selling what was, at that time, a vast quantity of manufactured goods in markets which were widely scattered and not always physically very accessible, and to customers whose consuming power was low at the best of times and whose demand for cotton clothing was likely to be fairly elastic. In some of these markets, it encountered the competition of native manufacturers, many of whom might actually be working up yarns spun in England. As a result, the cotton industry experienced periods of intense competition among the many manufacturers anxious to dispose of their goods.

[1] L. Simond, *Journal of a tour and residence in Great Britain* (2 vols. Edinburgh, 1815), II, 215.   [2] *PP. 1810/11 (232)* II, p. 394.

The peculiar structure of the industry, with its many small masters dependent on getting commission work from great Manchester merchants, was frequently alleged to make these periodic bouts of 'cut-throat competition' exceptionally severe. Complaints against such competition were voiced as early as 1808,[1] but the theme became particularly common at the time of the great select committees of the early 1830s.[2] Richard Oastler, for example, stigmatized it as 'the slaughterhouse system of trade', but characteristically tried to shift the blame from the small, struggling, but honest master to the rapacious merchant capitalist, who alone seemed to profit by it.[3] Richard Needham, the veteran Bolton weaver, described the main features of the pernicious 'system' to the 1833 committee on manufactures: 'the small manufacturers go to Manchester three times a week to sell their goods and if they cannot sell them in the morning they will sell them in the evening at any price, and then they reduce wages'.[4] William Varley's diary for the 1820s provides supporting evidence, for it abounds in complaints about the 'diabolical example' of one John Moore, a Burnley manufacturer, who was always the first to cut his piece-rates and the last to make any small increase.[5] Once one master had lowered his piece-rates the rest usually had to follow suit, and the weavers, being badly organized for industrial action against their employers, could do little to resist. Hence the chief objective of the various wage-fixing schemes constantly advocated by the weavers and some of the more sympathetic manufacturers was to prevent the small struggling manufacturer from reducing his rates below those offered by the rest of the trade.[6]

Just as the coming of the powerloom intensified the competition for work between weaver and weaver, it also increased the 'cut-throat' competition among employers. The *Manchester Guardian* commented after the 1826 depression:

As there cannot at one time be two prices for the same articles in the same market, it is obvious that handloom manufacturers can only pay such a rate for

[1] *PP. 1808 (177)* II, pp. 102, 112, and 119.
[2] For examples, *PP. 1834 (556)* X, QQ. 781, 2052–6.
[3] *Ibid.* Q. 3788.   [4] *PP. 1833 (690)* VI, Q. 11837.
[5] W. Bennett, *History of Burnley* (4 vols. Burnley, 1947–9), III, appendix I *passim*.
[6] See below, pp. 168–73.

weaving as will enable them to sell the articles they manufacture on the same terms as similar ones made by powerlooms are disposed of. The rate of handloom weaving will always, therefore, except perhaps in some fine and peculiar sorts of goods, be kept low by that of powerloom weaving.[1]

Whether directly or indirectly, the handloom manufacturer now competed to dispose of his goods with the powerloom manufacturer; but the latter was in much the stronger position, and it was only by ruthless reductions in the piece-rate when hard-pressed that the struggling handloom manufacturer could cut his costs and survive.

One should, however, beware of putting all the blame for the reduction in piece-rates on either the near-bankrupt manufacturer or the rapacious merchant. The plain fact was that, between the 1780s and the 1820s, cotton cloth passed from the luxury class into the category of goods in common consumption; by 1834, said a manufacturer, the price of cloth had 'become low to a proverb, and despicable on that account'.[2] This momentous change resulted, first, from the potentially very large market for cheap clothing, and second, from the particular suitability of the cotton industry to supply the same. This latter factor calls for a brief examination.

Many elements, apart from the course of piece-rates in weaving, were contributing to make cotton goods cheaper to produce during the first half of the nineteenth century. Other technical developments—such as the replacement of jennies and water-frames by steam-driven mules and self-actors, and of block printing by cylinder printing—played their part. Developments on the supply side in America were also responsible for a sharp drop in the price of raw cotton wool—from $19\frac{1}{2}$ pence per pound in 1815 to $8\frac{1}{2}$ pence in 1824, according to John Fielden.[3] Finally, government fiscal policy helped: the abolition in 1830 of the duty of $3\frac{1}{2}$ pence per yard on printed cotton in the home market was a substantial gift to the domestic consumer. It was also, incidentally, a very serious blow to the weavers of fancy and patterned goods; popular taste was not prepared to pay the wider differential

---

[1] *Manchester Guardian*, 21 April 1827. [2] *PP. 1834 (556)* x, Q. 4930.
[3] *3rd Series Hansard*, vol. 17, cols. 1297–8.

between the cheap, power-woven printed cloths and the hand-made figured goods, whose price fell as a result.[1]

The precarious nature of the handloom weavers' position after the early 1820s can be measured from the massive reduction in the market price of grey cotton cloth which resulted from the combination of factors mentioned above. Two sets of figures for the market price of calico—one provided by James Grimshaw, a manufacturer from the Colne district, and the other by John Fielden in a Commons debate—agree in showing that a piece which would sell for 18s. in 1815 would rarely rise above 6s. after 1826; this fall was in almost exactly the same proportions as the decline in the piece-rate.[2] So drastic a drop in the selling price of cloth hit the handloom manufacturers' profits just as it did the weavers' wages. With their own position thus weakened, it is hardly surprising that some employers were inclined to sympathize with their weavers in the latter's attempts to halt the decline in piece-rates.[3]

IV

Although these basic factors in the decline of the piece-rates for cotton weaving seem obvious enough today, yet contemporaries were inclined to cite other causes on occasions. Some of the suggestions were pure fantasy; an anonymous contributor to the *Manchester Mercury*, for instance, complained of '...the great influx of Jews into this country, who have nearly taken the manufactory out of our hands and caused such great competition in the [export] market, which competition we are obliged to meet by making our goods of inferior material, or reducing the wages of the poor weaver'.[4] The bulk of these alternative explanations, however, concerned aspects of fiscal policy which, since they lay within the province of government, might be the legitimate objects of reform. The chief specific targets were the 1815 Corn Law, the repeal of the income tax, and the return to a convertible

---

[1] The repeal of the duty on printed cloth was bitterly resented by the Bolton weavers in the 1830s (*PP. 1833 (690)* VI, Q. 11770 and *PP. 1834 (556)* X, Q. 5196). Muslins were said to be the least profitable branch of the cotton trade in 1834 (*ibid.* Q. 5230). See above, pp. 87–8 and 105–6.

[2] *PP. 1833 (690)* VI, p. 611; *3rd Series Hansard*, vol. 17, cols. 1295–6.

[3] See below, pp. 153 and 171–2.   [4] *Manchester Mercury*, 28 Nov. 1820.

currency after 'Peel's Act' of 1819; but in more general terms the high cost of living, high taxation, and an ill-devised commercial policy were regarded as being responsible for much of the poverty, unemployment, and distress.

The high cost of living was, of course, a popular argument used by Corn Law repealers from the 1820s onwards, and this is not the place to demonstrate the weaknesses of their case.[1] It should be pointed out, however, that many of the handloom weavers themselves did not accept the free-traders' arguments. When two Glasgow weavers were asked for their views on the Corn Laws, they replied:

The general opinion of the weavers is that it would benefit the trade by enabling the countries from which we received the corn to take part of our manufactures; but when we recollect that machinery [i.e. powerlooms] will be just increased in proportion as the demand for manufactures is increased, we are quite certain that hand weaving cannot, under the present circumstances, afford a living, even were that [i.e. repeal of the Corn Laws] to be obtained.[2]

The Bradford woollen weavers were likewise sceptical of trusting everything to free trade; they argued that there was no guarantee that other nations would allow Britain to become 'the workshop and manufactory of the world'.[3]

Thus the theory that they were poor because the Corn Laws raised the cost of living and restricted international trade was not always accepted by the handloom weavers. Such laws might aggravate, but did not cause their distress. This was also the case with many of the other aspects of government policy which came in for criticism. The taxes imposed on the various stages of manufacture—on the import of raw cotton and on printed cloth—were held, for example, to raise the price of goods and limit their sale. But the reasoning of the Glasgow weavers held good here, just as it did in the case of the Corn Laws: if there was any increase in the demand for cloth after the early 1820s, it would be met by the use of additional powerlooms. Similarly, there were those who, like William Radcliffe, maintained that, whilst the government

---

[1] See D. Walker-Smith, *The protectionist case in the 1840s* (Oxford, 1933), and M. Blaug, 'The empirical content of Ricardian economics', *Journal of Political Economy*, LXIV (1956).

[2] *PP. 1826/7 (237)* v, Q. 84.

[3] G. P. Scrope, *Political economy versus the handloom weavers* (Bradford, 1835), p. 11.

hampered the cotton trade in some directions, it failed to protect it in others, notably by allowing cotton yarn to be exported and woven abroad, to the detriment of the English weavers.[1] Again, however, the solution was obvious: to recapture and extend the foreign markets, the weaving industry must cheapen its methods of production by adopting the latest and most efficient techniques. In every case, the answer lay in the powerloom once its technical reliability had been established.

It is not easy to assess the effects on a working-class budget of the abandonment of income tax in 1816 or of the deflation which followed the return to gold three years later. Radicals such as Cobbett and Fielden made great play of the fact that, as a result, the bulk of the public revenue was derived from indirect taxation, which fell hardest on the working classes, and was spent in paying the interest on a national debt which had been contracted during a period of wartime inflation.[2] Had there been no wartime inflation or had there been a greater measure of direct taxation after the war, no doubt the handloom weavers' wages would have gone further; yet it was not only the handloom weavers who were affected by the government's fiscal policy, which had similar repercussions throughout the economy. Taxation was a general, not a local, grievance, and its amendment would have done nothing in itself to remove the basic disparity between the labour supply and the labour demand which was the essential local cause of the handloom weavers' troubles. There was little that any government might do to regulate the demand for labour in any particular trade, and there were only two ways of controlling its supply: severe and effective restriction on entry into the trade, and the complete prohibition of new inventions likely to upset the labour market. In the circumstances of the early nineteenth century, when the state lacked knowledge, experience, and administrative machinery, such a policy of paternalism would have been neither practical nor wise.

---

[1] For Radcliffe, see above, pp. 68–9 and 71. For the campaign of 1816–17, see below, p. 156. Arguments against yarn exports were less frequently employed after 1820, although an old-fashioned weaver like Richard Needham could still use them in the 1830s (PP. 1833 (690) VI, Q. 11848).

[2] For Cobbett and Fielden's views, see, for example, 3rd Series Hansard, vol. 16, cols. 353–369 and vol. 17, cols. 1277–1315.

CHAPTER 6

WAGES: (II) EARNINGS AND THE STANDARD OF LIVING

UNFORTUNATELY, a detailed knowledge of the course of piece-rates in cotton weaving during the industrial revolution is not sufficient to enable us to form any definite conclusions about the weavers' standard of living over the same period. For it is very difficult to convert these piece-rates into actual earnings. Yet since we know so little about real earnings, it is worthwhile making some attempt to establish a relationship. Even in the 1830s commissioner Hickson found it difficult to get hard facts, although he and other investigators heard a good many estimates of what a 'good weaver' or the 'average weaver' ought to be earning. Hickson wrote: 'The object of the weaver being to procure government interference in his favour, he has no disposition to weaken his case of hardship and distress by stating the whole of his resources; and he will withold the knowledge of every fact tending to show that he has sometimes the command of other means of alleviating his sufferings than appear to the inquirer.'[1]

Although the piece-rate should be able to help us make up for this deficiency, in practice its value is limited. Since earnings in a piece-rate industry are strictly proportional to output, the piece-rate can be useful only if we can be sure that output did not differ greatly either from one worker to another or over time. Yet neither assumption can be made about cotton weaving, where output varied enormously.[2] As a result, it is difficult to see much value in wage statistics based on the assumption that each worker would be producing so many pieces at such a price. When a Manchester merchant, Thomas Whitelegg, was pressed to estimate the average weaver's earnings in 1816, he replied 'it is so various, it is impossible to answer'.[3]

The causes of this variety are obvious enough. Handloom

---

[1] PP. 1840 (639) XXIV, p. 648.   [2] See below, p. 133.   [3] PP. 1816 (397) III, p. 391.

weavers' earnings would differ according to the type of cloth woven, the locality, the worker's age and ability, the efficiency of his tools, and the industriousness of each individual. Thus the weaver of fancy cloth in the early days might earn up to twice as much as the weaver of calico, since his work required greater skill and had luxury value.[1] As has been observed in the previous chapter, piece-rates varied from place to place. Then again, the amount of work weavers had the strength or the will to perform varied greatly: in 1834 a Perth weaver estimated that, whereas a youth might make 5s. 9d. a week and an active adult man about 3s. a week more, an old man would be unlikely to earn much more than the youth.[2] Finally, the industriousness of the individual depended very largely on the nature of his family obligations and on the standard of living which he sought to maintain.

Since it was variety of earnings which mattered so much in handloom weaving, a set of average wage figures derived from the piece-rate is of limited value. Nonetheless, there were a considerable number of estimates of speeds of working which might be used to give a general indication of the trend of money earnings. It was usually reckoned that a piece of muslin 24 yards long, such as the 60-reed Bolton, would be a good week's work for an active weaver, and that four pieces of calico of the same length could be finished in the same time.[3] Women and children, it was generally agreed, could not produce so much. The 1,200 north Lancashire calico weavers employed by James Massey and Sons produced a total of 97,688 pieces of cloth in the first six months of 1833, an average of just over three pieces each per week.[4] Since they were said to be 'principally women and children', it seems reasonable to expect that an active adult man could produce an average of at least four pieces.

On this basis, multiplying the piece-rates given in the previous chapter by a factor of 4, our average male calico weaver would be earning 16s. a week in 1815; 11s. 6d. in 1820; 9s. in 1825; and rather less than 6s. in 1830. Such a calculation, however, ignores the likelihood that, as piece-rates fell, output per weaver tended

---

[1] PP. 1803 (114) III, part 4, p. 93.   [2] PP. 1834 (556) X, Q. 3026.
[3] PP. 1833 (690) VI, Q. 11757 and p. 609.   [4] Ibid. QQ. 9340 and 9343.

to rise, and from certain recorded cases of 'expeditious weaving' it would appear that the really industrious could produce more than four pieces a week. In 1798, a Preston weaver undertook for a wager to produce four pieces of muslin in a week, and completed his task in just over five days.[1] Furthermore, even at the age of 60, David Whitehead's mother, a hard-working Methodist, could still manage six pieces of calico per week, an achievement in which her son evidently took great pride.[2]

The first real problem, then, is to decide whether, as piece-rates fell over the long term, there was a general tendency for output per weaver to rise, and if so, how great an increase took place. According to traditional accounts of the early weavers' proverbial laziness and the stories of their long working days in the last years, some such general increase seems plausible. After all, William Thom maintained that in the 'golden age', 'four days did the weaver work—for then four days was a week as far as working went, and such a week to a skillful workman brought forty shillings. Sunday, Monday, and Tuesday were, of course, jubilee'.[3] The slackness in the early part of the week was allegedly made up by working late on Friday in order to have the piece ready for the warehouse by Saturday. Conversely, by the 1830s, the weavers were often supposed to work much harder—14 or 16 hours a day in a six-day week. Nevertheless, this did not necessarily mean a proportional increase in output. John Makin, a Bolton manufacturer, argued that the weavers had become so depressed and listless in the 1830s that, even if they spent the greater part of their waking time about the loom, they wove intensively for only a short space.[4] The formidable Dr Ure, anxious to emphasize the inefficiency of handloom weaving, claimed that the 1,800 weavers who produced 2,000 pieces of cloth weekly for a Manchester house could have woven 9,000 pieces if they had really applied themselves.[5] He attributed their low average performance to the

---

[1] *Manchester Mercury*, 6 Feb. 1798.
[2] D. Whitehead, *Autobiography* (typescript edn from the MS in the Public Library, Rawtenstall, 1956), p. 29.
[3] W. Thom, *Rhymes and recollections of a handloom weaver* (2nd edn, London, 1845), p. 9.
[4] PP. *1834* (556) x, QQ. 5254 and 5256.
[5] A. Ure, *The philosophy of manufactures* (London, 1835), p. 333.

need to punctuate the monotony of their work by frequent pauses.[1] Clearly, there were always physical limits to the worker's output at a task so dull and uncomfortable as handloom weaving, even when he was willing and able to devote his whole time and energy to it. Some increase in output very probably occurred as a response to a sharp drop in the piece-rate, but, given that many of the women and children's output was at all times limited by their physical shortcomings and by their essentially casual, part-time, attitude to work, it is unlikely to have been very marked, except perhaps in the case of such adult men as had been fairly lazy in the years of high piece-rates. H. J. Habakkuk has suggested a general increase in output per weaver in the 1820s of 25 or 30 per cent.[2] Although this cannot be regarded as proven, since the figures both for the size of the labour force and for the relative efficiency of hand- and powerloom on which his calculation is based are suspect,[3] it is probably a plausible guess as to the sort of increase which a reasonable weaver might have been able to attain.

However, the long-term increase in output is only a small part of the problem of converting piece-rates into actual earnings. For it seems likely that much shorter-term fluctuations in output in fact took place. Assuming that work was plentiful, or in other words that a weaver could take away as much work as he was prepared to have, and assuming also that general price levels (and in particular food prices) were stable or falling, then it is not unreasonable to suggest that in the short run a weaver would produce slightly more cloth if his piece-rate fell, and slightly less if his piece-rate rose; such a short-term variation in output, however difficult to calculate, is no less plausible than the supposition of a long-term increase in output. At any rate, contemporaries continued to believe that the weavers characteristically behaved in this way even in the last years of the trade; as late as 1828, the *Manchester Guardian* upbraided the handloom weavers for their refusal to work a six-day week now that piece-rates had recovered again somewhat from the recent slump, and urged upon them the

---

[1] *Ibid.* p. 7.
[2] H. J. Habakkuk, *British and American technology in the nineteenth century* (Cambridge, 1962), p. 147 n.
[3] See above, pp. 81 and 85 n. 2.

necessity of doing as much work as possible now that weaving prices were high, so as to save against the inevitable future when work would be scarce and wages low.[1]

If this supposition is correct, then in order to construct a worthwhile index of earnings from the known piece-rates we would need to have a ratio which changed, according to the quantity of work currently available and the short-term movement of prices in general and piece-rates in particular, not only from year to year, but from month to month, and even from week to week. Since the detailed information from which to construct so delicate a ratio does not exist, it would appear to be impossible to speak about changes in output with sufficient certainty to use the piece-rates to estimate actual earnings, except in a very vague and general sense.

In the light of these comments, how much reliance ought we to place on the best-known estimates of handloom weavers' earnings, those of G. H. Wood?[2] Wood, of course, recognized that his figures were merely tentative guesses based on slender evidence; but as with all sets of historians' statistics, once set down in print they have since acquired a degree of authority which is perhaps undeserved.[3] It is true that Wood appears to have collated all the available long-run series; but a number of these are not real earnings, and more of the series in fact relate to Scotland than to England; whilst at no point in his account does he indicate that he considered the problem of changes in output when relying to a large extent on piece-rate figures. The result is a series of figures which, although bringing out the long-term decline clearly enough, fails to indicate the sharp short-term variations in actual earnings. Thus, during the war period after 1805, the picture it presents is one of continuous decline broken only by the recovery of 1813–14, and the difference, for example, between the prosperity and calm of 1809–10 and the poverty and despair of 1811–12 is not very apparent. But this failing becomes particularly serious in the later

---

[1] *Manchester Guardian*, 12 April 1828.
[2] G. H. Wood, *History of wages in the cotton trade during the past hundred years* (London, 1910), pp. 106–13. His summary table, reprinted in appendix 3, below, appears on p. 112.
[3] See above, p. 12.

years: neither the prosperity of the early 1820s and the recoveries of 1827–8 or 1834–6, nor the severe depressions of 1826, 1829 or 1837, emerge with the prominence which they probably ought to do. In the case of the handloom weavers' earnings, the mystical view held by many economic historians that any set of figures, however bad, is better than none at all, should be abandoned.

II

Even if gross earnings could be estimated from the piece-rates, they could still be misleading, since they were liable to important deductions before a realistic net figure can be obtained. In the first place, wages were not necessarily paid in coin of the realm. In the 1780s, there were complaints that the working classes of Manchester generally received their wages in 'base copper half-pence' whose value was much depreciated.[1] Furthermore, the truck system and its variants, such as the tied cottage owned by the employer, were just as likely to affect handloom weavers as other workers. Even in the 1820s, for example, there is evidence from such different places as Westhoughton, Bolton, and Rochdale of weavers being paid partly in goods or having deductions made from their earnings in lieu of rent.[2]

Earnings could also be reduced by fines imposed on the weaver by the manufacturer for shoddy workmanship. The fact that a Cotton Arbitration Act was called for in 1800 is sufficient proof of the frequency with which disputes arose on this score; when the weaver took back a piece which the manufacturer regarded as unsatisfactory, there would inevitably be a quarrel, with the manufacturer alleging inefficiency on the weaver's part, and the latter attempting to pass off the blame on inferior materials.[3] Fines or

---

[1] *Manchester Mercury*, 29 March 1788.

[2] See, for example, *Wheeler's Manchester Chronicle*, 20 Jan. 1827; *PP. 1824 (51)* v, p. 398; *PP. 1826/7 (237)* v, QQ. 2083–5.

[3] For examples of the types of disagreement which arose, see *PP. 1803 (114)* III, part 4, *passim*. The more generous manufacturers were also willing to make allowances when their workers had to contend with faulty materials; it is clear from the Oldknow papers that in the 1780s and 1790s Samuel Oldknow would allow up to 10s. a piece in such circumstances. One should beware of treating these fines as an example of the rapacity

'abatements' continued to be a grievance in the 1830s. A Lanark weaver produced for the 1834 select committee a weaving ticket which bore detailed instructions as to how a particular piece of work had to be executed: among other things it specified that, 'if not finished in four weeks, 2s. will be deducted for each week longer kept. No bad work will be accepted...Sour dressing must not be used, under the penalty of 2s. 6d. per piece...If the colours of this web [i.e. warp] are hurt, or the white sullied by starching or otherwise, 10s. 6d. will be stopped'.[1] At Carlisle in the 1830s, some of the manufacturers adopted an opposite approach: their tickets read 'one shilling extra for work if approved'.[2] It is well known that the early factory lords used pecuniary fines to punish late-coming, inattention, or gross personal conduct among their workers.[3] According to William Thom, who had worked in one, similar rules were applied in handloom factories.[4]

A more important set of deductions resulted from working expenses which today would be borne by the manufacturer as part of his overall costs, but which in this form of industrial organization fell upon the weaver.[5] The main items were three: provision of implements and tools, particularly the periodic replacement or repair of healds and shuttles, and the purchase of flour and brushes for warp-dressing; the lighting and heating of the workshop, as required; and the payments which a weaver had to make to his assistants—particularly his winders, or, if he were a fancy weaver, his drawboy who worked the complex sets of healds.

It is difficult to estimate how large a sum all these expenses involved. Contemporaries frequently claimed that the working

and heartlessness of the manufacturers; provided they were not abused, they were essential to ensuring good workmanship. Far from appropriating these fines, Dixons, the leading Carlisle manufacturers, actually distributed the proceeds in pensions to the local poor and aged (*Carlisle Journal*, 30 June 1838).

[1] *PP. 1834 (556)* x, p. 205.
[2] *Carlisle Journal*, 23 June 1838.
[3] See S. Pollard, 'Factory discipline in the industrial revolution', *Economic History Review*, XVI (1964), 261–2.
[4] Thom, *op. cit.* p. 12.
[5] The deduction of working expenses does not appear to have applied to weavers in the large handloom sheds. Attempts to charge loom-rent and make deductions for repairs to tools caused strikes among the Manchester factory handloom weavers in 1829 (*Manchester Guardian*, 25 July and 21 Nov. 1829).

costs took away threepence out of every shilling of gross earnings;[1] but no one stated convincingly how this convenient round figure was arrived at, and it seems fair to conclude that it overstated the necessary deductions. In the first place, the cost of tools was not excessive: the actual loom itself would last for thirty years.[2] Only the healds and shuttle needed regular replacement. William Varley, the Higham calico weaver, purchased a set of healds each for himself and his wife for 7s. 8d. in January 1820, and does not appear to have replaced them for more than two years; he also bought only four shuttles, at a cost of 1s. 3d. or 1s. 4d. each, over the period December 1819 to autumn 1822 which his surviving account-book covers. Flour probably constituted the most expensive item; Varley bought an average of 30 lb a month at prices which ranged from 6s. to 4s., but we cannot tell how much of this was used for warp-dressing and how much for other household purposes.[3] Even this expense was not apparently exorbitant, however; in the 1830s, the Bolton weavers tried to pass the expense of warp-dressing back to their employers, but they estimated the annual saving from such a move to be no more than 10s. per weaver.[4]

Secondly, it does not seem reasonable to make too much allowance for the cost of lighting and heating as a purely working expense, since some part of it would have been incurred as a necessary item of household expenditure, if weaving had not been carried on in the home.[5] Finally, it is true that payments to assistants might be heavy, particularly in fancy weaving, where the services of a strong drawboy of 15 or 16 might cost up to 5s. a week;[6] but in most families, winding and other subsidiary pro-

---

[1] *PP. 1803 (114)* III, part 4, p. 14; *PP. 1808 (177)* II, p. 120; *PP. 1833 (690)* VI, Q. 11748; and *PP. 1840 (220)* XXIV, p. 607.　　　　[2] *PP. 1833 (690)* VI, Q. 11697.

[3] *Household accounts of W. Varley, 1819–22* (transcript in Burnley Central Reference Library, by W. Bennett).

[4] *Manchester Guardian*, 9 April 1831; 5 Oct. 1833; 25 June 1836.

[5] Nevertheless, the merchants and manufacturers of Manchester, when objecting in 1819 to the government's proposed duty on inland coal, advanced the argument that 'the proposed burthen would be severely felt by the cotton weavers, whose work is performed at home and who are obliged at their own expense to keep up fires in summer as well as in winter for dressing their warps and other operations of their employment: and to augment their privations by the duty in question would be abhorrent to the dictates of humanity and wholly inconsistent with the soundest maxims of national policy' (*Manchester Mercury*, 9 March 1819).

[6] *PP. 1833 (690)* XI, Q. 11287.

cesses were performed gratis by the oldest or very youngest members of the family, who would otherwise be unemployed, since they were unfit for weaving. An actual wage payment, deducted from the weaver's own earnings, would be made only if the winding had to be done outside the family. Altogether, it seems unlikely that working expenses accounted for so high a proportion of the weaver's gross earnings as 25 per cent; and it does not indicate a lack of sympathy for the weavers' sufferings to point out that, as Hickson argued, it was always in their interests to make their net earnings seem as low as possible.

There is one final problem in attempting to work out earnings from the piece-rates. How far was the weaver's output affected by such factors as unemployment or underemployment over which he had no control? In any system of unsupervised outwork, there is inevitably a large amount of voluntary unemployment since the individual worker decides how much work it is necessary—indeed, possible—for him to do. But how far was it the weaver's own decision as to how much work he did? How far did it depend on the amount of work which the manufacturer had available? Most economic historians would agree with Professor Ashton that in the eighteenth century much industrial outwork was seasonal and that 'the normal condition of most domestic producers was one of underemployment'.[1] Some seasonal underemployment, particularly in the summer, may have occurred in cotton weaving, since the chief weaving 'seasons' were autumn and spring. However, since many of the country weavers took to farm labour in the summer, in normal years a reduction in the amount of weaving available in certain months did not have disastrous effects.[2]

In view of the generally rapid expansion of the cotton industry during the industrial revolution, seasonal underemployment of the eighteenth-century variety was probably less important than the cyclical unemployment which accompanied periodic slumps and depressions. In good years, a cotton weaver could probably have as much work as he was willing to take, but with the onset of a trade recession, he might be 'stinted' or rationed to a limited

[1] T. S. Ashton, *An economic history of England: the eighteenth century* (London, 1955), pp. 202–3. [2] See above, pp. 58–60.

amount of work per week: in 1837, for example, William Thom, then working in Dundee, was limited to weaving only one piece of cloth at 5s. per week.[1]

On the whole, manufacturers seem to have preferred to keep on all their hands, but if necessary at a limited amount of work and lower piece-rates. But in the worst recessions of the wartime, and again in 1826, 1829, 1837, and 1841–2, many weavers received no work at all, and there was heavy unemployment, sometimes for weeks on end. In June 1816, 60 per cent of the looms in the Stockport district were idle.[2] With the onset of a recession in May 1825, there were 5,000 weavers unemployed in and around Glasgow,[3] and at the end of the following year there were still 10,682 unemployed out of a total population of 73,000 in the Blackburn district (from Accrington to Walton-le-dale).[4] At the height of this recession, in the spring of 1826, the vicar of Great Harwood found that 148 of the 177 looms in the village of Lowertown were standing empty.[5] Fortunately, unemployment on this scale was usually shortlived, although it recurred with painful regularity; and, save for the bad years, even after the great slump of 1826, it was low wages, rather than a lack of work, of which the remaining weavers complained. John Fielden's survey of the state of the poor in thirty-three Lancashire and Yorkshire weaving townships in 1833, whilst suggesting terribly low earnings, found only 2,287 employable persons out of a total population of 50,000 who were not actually at work.[6]

Just as there were factors liable to reduce gross earnings calculated from the simple piece-rate, so there was one important means by which earnings could be increased. A domestic system of manufacture gives many opportunities for the workers to indulge in embezzlement; the employer needs to be generous in giving out the materials to be worked up, to allow for normal wastage and breakages. By a variety of stratagems, a handloom

---

[1] Thom, *op. cit.* p. 12.
[2] P. M. Giles, *The social and economic development of Stockport, 1815–36* (Manchester M.A. thesis, unpublished, 1950), p. 164.
[3] *Manchester Mercury*, 31 May 1825. [4] *PP. 1826/7 (237)* v, pp. 211–12.
[5] *Great Harwood parish papers*, Lancashire Record Office, PR. 163/6. See above, p. 62.
[6] *PP. 1833 (690)* VI, pp. 668–71. See below, p. 126.

weaver might economize on the use of materials and dispose of what he had saved to some manufacturer for money. The savings might be made in several ways. The Stockport manufacturers in 1799 spoke harshly of those weavers who

defraud the manufacturers of their property by purloining or embezzling the weft, or exchanging it for others of an inferior quality, or destroying it in a wasteful and careless manner; altering, removing or destroying the marks on their warps and stretching them to an unusual and extraordinary length to obtain large fents; taking part of the breadth of their warps and putting them in coarser reeds; and such like practices.[1]

Traffic in the pilfered materials was carried on by small manufacturers who were able to obtain warp and weft more cheaply in this way than they could from spinners.[2] David Whitehead, who was for a time a chapman and hawker in his youth, found that country shopkeepers in north-east Lancashire would exchange their groceries for weft with the local weavers, and claimed that one of the shopkeepers actually tried to dispose of some of this weft in exchange for Whitehead's shop goods.[3] Samuel Bamford declined the opportunity to set up as a manufacturer following his release from prison after Peterloo, on the grounds that he would only have been able to compete with better-established men by using a proportion of embezzled goods.[4] Sometimes these dishonest small manufacturers were discovered and brought to trial: as late as 1839, two Blackburn manufacturers were fined £20 and costs, and were made to forfeit fifty pieces of cloth, for working with embezzled materials. Seventy-nine of the 117 pieces in their warehouse appeared to have been made from warp and weft illicitly obtained.[5]

It is obviously impossible to estimate the extent to which these practices were carried on in cotton weaving, but they were sufficiently widespread for some contemporaries to advocate the use of the powerloom largely as a means of reducing the manu-

---

[1] *Manchester Mercury*, 2 April 1799.
[2] The agents of these manufacturers were alleged to go through the streets of Manchester offering apples and similar bribes to the weavers' children in return for 'waste' cotton (*Manchester Guardian*, 27 Jan. 1827).
[3] Whitehead, *op. cit.* p. 17.
[4] S. Bamford, *Homely rhymes, poems, and reminiscences* (London, 1864), p. 7.
[5] *Manchester Guardian*, 1 June 1839.

facturers' losses by embezzlement.[1] In many towns, the manufacturers formed associations to prosecute embezzlers: Stockport
had one as early as 1781, Bolton in 1799 kept names of offending
weavers in a black book, and at Burnley the association seems to
have been particularly active in 1809.[2] The local press contains
many accounts of the prosecution of weavers for embezzlement;
of their punishment by fining, whipping, and imprisonment; of
stocks of embezzled materials recovered by the constables; and of
public apologies by repentant offenders. It is difficult to say whether
there was an increase or a decrease in embezzlement as the period
went on.[3] As the price of cotton yarn fell, there was obviously less
financial advantage to be gained from petty pilfering, unless, that
is, it could be carried on on a larger scale; yet greater knowledge
among manufacturers of the amounts a weaver needed should
have made it relatively difficult to increase the scale of activity.
Although common-sense seems to suggest that a decrease in embezzling took place, contemporaries went on complaining of it in
bitter terms; and in 1838, assistant commissioner Muggeridge concluded that it was still extensive in north-east Lancashire.[4] As
piece-rates fell, it became both less easy and more necessary for a
handloom weaver to think about increasing his earnings in this
fashion.

III

Only if all these important limitations are remembered can the piece-
rate be used as a tentative basis for calculating handloom weavers'
earnings. Fortunately a limited amount of information about actual
earnings at particular dates does exist, and can be used to supplement or modify the general picture which piece-rate calculations
can offer. But even this information raises its own problems.

The chief difficulty is that, with the major exception of the
Oldknow papers,[5] no substantial sets of manufacturers' wage-

---

[1] See above, p. 72.
[2] *Manchester Mercury*, 7 Aug. 1781, 26 Feb. 1799, and 24 Jan. 1809.
[3] At the time of the 1834 s.c., knowledgeable contemporaries differed as to whether
embezzlement had increased (*PP. 1834 (556)* x, QQ. 1875 and 5030).
[4] *PP. 1840 (220)* XXIV, p. 627.
[5] In the John Rylands Library, Manchester. They formed the basis of G. Unwin, *Samuel
Oldknow and the Arkwrights* (Manchester, 1924).

books exist for the cotton handloom weaving industry; much of the limited material on actual earnings comes, therefore, from printed sources, particularly from parliamentary papers. A process of selection was obviously involved in deciding what figures were actually put into print, and it is therefore very important to examine the motives of those who brought each particular set of facts forward.

What look like unassailable figures may often have been gathered by prejudiced parties, or compiled in a slipshod fashion. A survey of the poor in thirty-three Lancashire and Yorkshire townships was presented as evidence to the 1833 select committee on manufactures, commerce, and shipping.[1] It was drawn up under the direction of John Fielden, M.P., and however simple-minded Fielden's opinions, no-one would deny his honesty or his good intentions;[2] the information from each township was certified by the local overseers or similar reputable persons. The survey involved only the poorest inhabitants—50,000 people out of a total population of 200,000, half of whom were at work, chiefly as handloom weavers. The average weekly earnings per worker were 3s. 8⅜d. and the average income per head of population, before any working expenses were deducted, was 1s. 9⅝d.

Despite its reputable origins, the reliability of the survey was widely questioned. The choice of townships was unrepresentative; with the exception of Blackburn, the larger towns were omitted in favour of the country villages. Secondly, the organizers had a declared interest in emphasizing poverty, and they dealt with only the very poorest 25 per cent of the population; as one critic said, 'if it be given out...that an inquiry is to be set on foot for the purpose of proving that the people are in a wretched condition, any man who will go from house to house in furtherance of that inquiry will, even in the very best of times, hear of as much distress as he chooses to inquire for'.[3] Finally, the full details of

---

[1] PP. 1833 (690) VI, pp. 668–71.

[2] A correspondent, replying to the *Manchester Guardian's* criticisms of the survey, wrote: 'I would as soon believe that the sun had fallen from its socket into St Stephens to make a report as I can believe that Mr Fielden would wilfully make a false statement in that House' (*Manchester Guardian*, 30 March 1833).

[3] *Manchester Guardian*, 16 March 1833.

the survey—actual names, numbers of families, and so on—were never published, and their accuracy could not be checked.

The most unreliable of all sources of wage information, however, were the weavers themselves. A manufacturer kept a week-by-week record of his actual wage payments in his books; but there is no evidence that any group of weavers did the same for their earnings. There was a perfect illustration of the resultant tendency for weavers to understate their earnings in an effort to win popular sympathy and support in Manchester in 1830. On 16 January, the *Manchester Courier* printed the result of a private inquiry into the circumstances of forty-one families of handloom weavers in the New Town district; to give authority to the statement, full details of names and of the size of the families were given. It appeared that the total weekly earnings of these families were £14. 10s. 10d., and that the average income per head, when working expenses had been deducted, was 1s. 2d. To find out whether people really were living on twopence a day, the church wardens sent the overseer to check the survey, and his report was published in the *Manchester Guardian* a fortnight later. This second statement revealed that the total income of the families was, in fact, more than £30, and that if no deductions were made for the questionable item of working costs the average income per head was 2s. 11d., or fivepence a day.[1]

Problems such as these are sufficient to raise doubts as to the value of some of the printed evidence for earnings. And it was precisely because there still existed considerable disagreement of what 'the facts' of the weavers' situation really were in the 1830s that the select committee of 1834-5, dominated by committed humanitarians like Fielden and Maxwell, had to be followed by the more sober and impartial royal commission of 1837-41, consisting of Nassau Senior and his fellow economists. The first inquiry was unsatisfactory because it chose its facts to fit a case; the second merely sought to establish what had really happened.[2] Whatever his inclinations, the historian must take Senior, not Fielden, as his model.

What, then, can safely be concluded about the earnings and the

---

[1] *Manchester Guardian*, 30 Jan. 1830.   [2] See below, pp. 160-7.

standard of living of the cotton handloom weavers over the relatively brief period in which they played their part in English economic history? Obviously, during a serious industrial recession —1807–8, 1811–12, 1816–17, 1826–7, 1829, 1837, 1841–2—there was unemployment, low piece-rates, and, as a result, low wages and widespread poverty of the most distressing and demoralizing kind. But if these abnormal spells are set aside—after all, other classes of industrial workers apart from handloom weavers also suffered acutely on these occasions—how did the normal earnings and living standards of the remaining handloom weavers in the 1830s compare with those of the 1790s? There can be no doubt that, with the piece-rate falling so much more sharply than any cost of living index, no matter how unreliable, handloom weavers were less well-off in the latter period than in the former. Contemporaries were unanimous in agreeing that the weavers were worse-off than any other group of workers and persistently excepted them from any statements about the general prosperity of the working classes.[1]

How much worse-off it is difficult to say, but it seems clear that they were not enjoying what was then regarded as the basic comfortable standing of living. John Doherty, the Lancashire spinners' leader, once lamented that the workers did not in general seem 'to know what ought to be a sufficient renumeration for their labour', and proceeded to supply his own rather curious definition as 'what would give to the operative and his family four comfortable meals a day with flesh meat at each, and a pint of beer for himself and another for his wife and family at dinner, and the same at supper; a good suit of clothes for everyday wear, and a better one for Sundays; a good bed to lie on, and sufficient means to give a good education to his children'.[2] Few workers in the 1830s can have achieved this standard, and the general definition of comfort might have been more modest. James Orr, a Paisley weaver, estimated in 1834 that a family needed an income of 3s. 6d. per head per week 'to subsist with anything like comfort', which he seemed to consider as involving, apart from the rent of a house and the

---

[1] PP. 1833 (690) VI, QQ. 3819, 5203, and 5519.
[2] *Manchester Guardian*, 21 May 1831.

basic diet of bread, oatmeal and potatoes, 'three-quarters of a lb of meat to each individual in the family by the week, and tea and sugar, and shoes for the children'.[1]

Given the drastic decline in piece-rates, many weavers' families are unlikely to have enjoyed an income of 3s. 6d. per head in the 1830s, and consequently they did not enjoy the modest comforts described by James Orr. In 1829, nearly one-third of the inhabitants of Colne were said to be subsisting on 1s. 2¼d. a week, or twopence a day, and another quarter on 1s. 9¾d. a week or threepence a day; and in the following year, nearly 2,300 Blackburn families, consisting of over 11,000 persons, were alleged to have a weekly income per head of only 1s. 7d.[2] The statements of individual weavers show what such low incomes meant when translated into a standard of living. Richard Needham, an old Bolton weaver, recounted a conversation with a fellow weaver who had a wife and five children to support: 'When I asked him how he lived, he said "I buy a pound of meal and make it into porridge, and I buy two quarts of buttermilk, and those amount to threepence, and from that threepence the whole family breakfasts". "What do you get for your dinner?" I said. "We get", he says, "two quarts of buttermilk again, and as many potatoes as three-halfpence will buy. If potatoes are cheap, we make a tolerable putting-on for dinner, but if they are dear we are likely to do with less than is sufficient." I said, "What do you get the remainder of the day?" "Sometimes nothing, and sometimes we muster two quarts of buttermilk again, and one pound of meal".'[3] James Brennan, a Manchester weaver with two children and a wife who did unskilled factory work, also provided details of his daily life for the 1834 select committee: he had never been able to buy furniture, but had fortunately inherited some from his parents; he could not afford to join a friendly society, but seemed to regard a penny a week to a burial club as a wiser investment; and his only indulgence was 'two or three gills of ale' of a Saturday night.[4]

There can be little doubt that, for the cotton handloom weavers, the real permanent dividing line between relative (although not

[1] PP. 1834 (556) x, QQ. 1264-5.
[2] Manchester Guardian, 2 May 1829 and 30 Jan. 1830.
[3] PP. 1833 (690) VI, Q. 11747.   [4] PP. 1834 (556) x, QQ. 6462-6474.

unbroken) comfort and a standard of living normally below that of other workers came with the slump of 1826, when the piece-rate really tumbled and never subsequently recovered to any appreciable degree.[1] As the rector of Wilmslow said in 1827, before the recent slump, 'a family could well maintain themselves on two looms'; but now, 'no family was considered to be capable of maintaining themselves with fewer than three looms'.[2] The account-book of William Varley, the Higham calico weaver, furnishes the strongest evidence that even in the early 1820s it was possible for a country weaver to live comfortably. It is true that this family's diet was monotonous—chiefly oatmeal, milk, and butter, with some potatoes, onions, and cheese; but sugar, treacle, and small amounts of coffee and tea were regularly purchased, together with hops and malt for home-brewing every autumn; and in addition Varley had cabbages and fruit-trees in his garden, and kept a pig and some poultry. More significant, however, are the large sums spent on items other than food: a family which could afford 10s. for a new hat for father, 5s. for a silk handkerchief, 2s. for a bound 'Life of Napoleon', and a total of more than £5 on clothing between February and October 1821 was a good way above the subsistence line.[3] The contrast with the anguish and suffering displayed in Varley's diary in the later 1820s is very marked; it was then that the days of oatcake and porridge really arrived.

IV

Certain factors help to modify this general picture of decline and warn us against over-exaggerating its severity. First, it is important to avoid too rosy a picture of conditions in the 'golden age' of handloom weaving at the end of the eighteenth century. As Miss Collier pointed out more than forty years ago, 'although all sections of the weavers suffered a diminution of income, many of them were earning but a modest sum to commence with. The weavers in all branches of the manufacture did not experience a

---

[1] See above, table 3, p. 105. [2] PP. 1826/7 (237) v, Q. 464.
[3] The Varley household is discussed in W. Bennett, History of Burnley (Burnley, 1948), III, 234–6 and 271–4. Mr Bennett's transcript of the account-book is in Burnley Reference Library.

descent from great prosperity to adversity.'[1] It is unlikely that William Radcliffe was speaking of anything like a majority of the handloom weavers when he claimed that 'every family was bringing home weekly 40, 60, 80, 100, or even 120 shillings'.[2] In the 1780s fustian weavers do not appear to have earned more than 8s. or 9s. a week;[3] and the weavers of Samuel Oldknow averaged from 17s. 7d. a week for fancy muslins down to 12s. for plain calico and 9s. for coarse linen in 1787.[4] Nor did weavers escape the consequences of trade recessions in the early years; William Rowbottom, the Oldham annalist, confided to his diary on 1 August 1793 that 'the relentless cruelty exercised by the fustian masters upon the poor weavers is such that it is unexampled in the annals of cruelty, tyranny, and oppression, for it is nearly an impossibility for weavers to earn the common necessaries of life, so that a great deal of families are in a most wretched and pitiable situation'.[5]

At first sight, it is difficult to reconcile low actual earnings with the high piece-rates which certainly prevailed in the early days— for instance, in 1784-5, Samuel Oldknow was paying 18s. a piece for ordinary calico, or 33s. where the weaver was also responsible for his own spinning.[6] The conclusion is inescapable: whether from disinclination or incapacity, Oldknow's weavers did not work very hard—indeed, many of them produced less than one piece of calico per week, although it was usually agreed in later years that a hardworking man could produce four such pieces in a week's work.[7] This suggests that the average industrial worker in the eighteenth century did as little work as was consistent with maintaining a certain fairly low, but conventionally acceptable, standard of living; once he had earned enough to pay the rent, keep himself in clothes, and buy food and beer, he probably felt

[1] F. Collier, *The family economy of the workers in the cotton industry, 1784–1833* (Manchester, 1964), p. 6.
[2] W. Radcliffe, *The origin of the new system of manufacture called powerloom weaving* (Stockport, 1828), p. 62.
[3] *Manchester Mercury*, 21 June 1785; *PP. 1834 (556)* x, Q. 5366.
[4] Unwin, *op. cit.* p.114.
[5] 'Annals of Oldham' (*Oldham Standard*, 26 March 1887).
[6] *Oldknow Papers*, John Rylands Library, English MSS 755.
[7] See above, p. 115.

9-2

little obligation, unless he was socially ambitious, to do any more work. Arthur Young and other eighteenth-century economists were, therefore, not too far wrong when they lamented the bad effects of low prices and high wages on working men's behaviour. After his visit to the north in 1770, Young complained that the Manchester workmen 'never worked six days in a week; numbers not five, nor even four; the idle time spent at alehouses, or at receptacles of low diversion; the remainder of their time of little value; for it is a known fact that a man who sticks to his loom regularly will perform his work better'. He added that 'the master manufacturers of Manchester wish that prices might always be high enough to enforce a general industry and to keep the hands employed six days for a week's work'.[1]

This is not to say that some weavers in the late eighteenth century did not earn the sort of wages which William Radcliffe alleged; James Ramsbotham, a Whitefield manufacturer, paid a woman nankeen weaver 50s. in December 1802 for five days' work.[2] With the heavy demand for fancy cottons in the early 1790s, which led to increases of up to 25 per cent in Oldknow's weaving prices between 1787 and 1791,[3] the weavers of these goods must have done very well. Nor was it merely exceptional demand which contributed to the prosperity of some of the weavers at this time; the belated introduction of the fly-shuttle in Scotland about 1788 'increased the wages of a man beyond all proportion to any other trade'.[4] Under such circumstances, industrious weavers could earn good money, and ambitious ones might even succeed in raising their social status.[5] But these were freak conditions applying only to particular branches of the trade under exceptional circumstances; within a few years, weavers were to confess that, in the 1790s, 'the wages were too high'.[6]

---

[1] A. Young, *Six months tour of northern England* (2nd edn, London, 1771), III, 193.

[2] The woman had been weaving 18 hours a day (*PP. 1803 (114)* III, part 4, p. 44). It should be remembered that E. Gilboy found evidence for a marked general rise in Lancashire wages in the late eighteenth century (E. Gilboy, *Wages in eighteenth-century England* (Harvard, 1934), pp. 194–5).

[3] *Oldknow Papers*, John Rylands Library, English MSS 797.

[4] *PP. 1834 (556)* X, Q. 166.

[5] John Kingan, a Glasgow weaver, claimed (*ibid. loc. cit.*) that 'two late Lord Provosts of Glasgow (Monteith and Dalgleish) were handloom weavers in my remembrance'.

[6] *PP. 1808 (177)* II, p. 100.

A second qualifying factor is immediately apparent throughout the period—the great contrast between the high earnings of a few good and industrious weavers, and the low average performance of the labour force as a whole. As Kirkman Finlay, a leading Scottish manufacturer and M.P., put it: 'I was myself engaged in business, and employing 2,000 handloom weavers, and at the best work; and when some men were getting 30s. a week, I never found the average above 10s.'[1] A Scottish weaver, James Orr, concurred: 'I find,' he said, 'that as you increase the number of weavers or extend the time of employment, the average always decreases.'[2] In 1790 the best of a group of twenty of Samuel Oldknow's weavers averaged 33s. a week; but the average of the whole group was only 12s. 7d., a staggering difference.[3] Likewise, in 1838, the average gross earnings of ten of the best weavers of J. R. and J. Ferguson, Carlisle, were 10s. a week, whilst the average of eleven inferior weavers was only 5s. 10d.[4]

The reasons for this contrast are not difficult to find. A large part of the labour force consisted of inferior labour—young children, women, and old people—who, even if they had the incentive or the inclination, did not have the physical strength to equal the output of the best male weavers. But physical factors were a minor part of the explanation; to these junior members of the family, weaving was a by-occupation to keep them out of mischief, or, more particularly, to enable them to support themselves at least in part. It was not intended to interfere with the more basic duties, the playtimes, or the quiet rests, of the women, children, and old people respectively. Given such an essentially casual attitude to work, low average earnings were inevitable. Yet, as commissioner Hickson rightly argued, 'the case of the old and the infirm, and the victims of intemperance, have no direct relation to the main inquiry'.[5] To find out what 'steady and industrious handloom weavers with youth and strength in their

---

[1] *PP. 1833 (690)* VI, Q. 1202.   [2] *PP. 1834 (556)* X, Q. 890.
[3] Unwin, *op. cit.* p. 113. The wage books of two small Colne manufacturers (kindly loaned by W. Spencer, Esq., of Colne) for the late 1840s and early 1850s show that the difference between the well-paid few and the badly-paid majority was just as marked in the last years of handloom weaving as it had been in Oldknow's time.
[4] *PP. 1840 (220)* XXIV, p. 607.   [5] *PP. 1840 (639)* XXIV, p. 648.

favour' could earn, Hickson went to the handloom factories, where weavers worked full-time. He realized that one could not fairly compare the earnings of women and children weaving casually at home with the wages of women and children working under supervision twelve and more hours a day in a factory, where they were bound to constant attendance on the unceasing motion of the steam-engine.[1]

In the 1830s, indeed, the wages of the factory handloom weavers, as Hickson soon discovered, did not compare too badly with those of other groups of workers. The outdoor weavers of John Spencer of Patricroft, Manchester, averaged only 8s. 1d. a week in 1838, and from this they had to deduct working expenses; on the other hand, Spencer's indoor weavers averaged 9s. 8d. with all expenses covered.[2] In the early 1830s, the outdoor weavers of Jonathan Hitchen at Bolton averaged only about 6s. per week, gross earnings;[3] in the late 1830s, however, Hickson found that many of the weavers at Bailey's handloom shed, Preston, were earning over 10s. a week, and he concluded that in general indoor weavers would earn on an average at least 2s. a week more than cottage weavers.[4] Calico weavers in dandyloom shops would also do much better than calico weavers in the country: their looms were more efficient, the method of payment gave bonuses for higher output, and the weaver did not have to bear working expenses.[5] Thus, in the early 1830s, the dandy weavers at Preston averaged 10s. or 11s. a week clear earnings,[6] whereas the many women and children weaving in the cottages of north-east Lancashire would be lucky if they made more than 4s. in many cases.[7]

If these shop weavers' wages are compared with those of factory

---

[1] The contrast in output, and therefore in earnings, between handloom weavers in cottages and those in sheds was also noted in north America. One New England firm, Almy and Brown, claimed in 1809 that 'a hundred looms in families will not weave so much cloth as ten at least constantly employed under the immediate inspection of a workman'. Quoted C. F. Ware, *Early New England cotton industry* (New York, 1931), p. 51.

[2] *PP. 1840 (220)* XXIV, p. 605.

[3] *PP. 1833 (690)* VI, p. 706; *PP. 1834 (556)* X, p. 441.

[4] *PP. 1840 (639)* XXIV, pp. 646–9.

[5] *PP. 1834 (556)* X, QQ. 5044 and 5882.

[6] *PP. 1835 (341)* XIII, Q. 1762.

[7] James Grimshaw, a manufacturer at Barrowford, near Colne, had a total weekly wages bill for his 400 weavers of 'about £80 to £90' (*PP. 1833 (690)* VI, Q. 10188).

workers, they do not come off badly. It is erroneous to think that most factory workers—many of whom, again, were women and children—received high wages in the early nineteenth century. Leonard Horner reported in 1842 that 'with the exception of the mule-spinners, dressers, overlookers, mechanics, and a few others, all of whom constitute but a small proportion of the whole, the majority of workers in a cotton mill receive very moderate wages'.[1] Powerloom workers, with whom the most direct comparison can be made, were said to be earning the following wages in Manchester in the late 1820s:

Winding (women 18–25 years)	8s. to 10s. a week
Winding (women 12–16 years)	5s. to 7s. a week
Warping (women 18–25 years)	10s. to 12s. a week
Two-loom weaving (male or female, 14–22 years)	7s. 6d. to 10s. 6d. a week[2]

Many of the inferior workers in other departments of cotton mills were likewise poorly paid. The average of all the workers in Joshua Milne's Oldham mill was 9s. 3d. a week in 1833; but the card-room hands earned only from 5s. 6d. to 8s. 6d., the throstle-piecers from 7s. to 9s., and the doffers from 4s. to 7s.[3]

In some of the old-fashioned throstle-spinning mills in the 1830s, wages were even lower. At Greg's Styal mill in 1831, spinners earned 6s. 6d., creel-tenters from 2s. 3d. to 3s. 6d., doffers 2s. to 3s., and winders 2s. to 4s.—wages even lower than those for plain calico weaving.[4] Since the basic situation in this old water-powered mill—low-grade labour and obsolete machines—in some ways resembled that of the domestic weavers, the comparison is particularly revealing. The most glaring difference between hand-loom weavers' and factory workers' wages was in the case of adult men, for here the comparison must be with well-paid mule-spinners and powerloom overlookers, whose earnings often exceeded 20s. a week. It was these adult men who were the real sufferers, for their earnings compared badly with those of agri-

---

[1] PP. 1842 (31) XXII, p. 365.   [2] PP. 1826/7 (237) V, Q. 361.
[3] PP. 1833 (690) VI, QQ. 10948-9.
[4] Collier, op. cit. p. 42. W. R. Greg himself admitted that wages at Styal were particularly low (PP. 1833 (690) VI, Q. 11346).

cultural workers and outdoor labourers,[1] and even with hand weavers in silk and wool.[2]

The final qualifying factor as regards the standard of living is, of course, the question of total family earnings. Factory inspector Horner noted that, in general, 'where several persons in one family are employed, as is very often the case, their aggregate wages afford the means of living in comfort; but single persons earn a scanty subsistence, and when there is a wife and a family of young children not employed there must be great privations'.[3] Horner was thinking of factory workers, but his observation applies equally to handloom weavers. It is important to realize that in many weavers' families, especially in the towns, it would not be a case of complete dependence on one wage-earner or even on one kind of employment; and even where weaving was the only job available, there would often be more than one loom in the house.

The earnings of the whole family had long been a vital element in economic life in the north of England.[4] Even in the prosperous early days, a weaver with a large but young family would not find life easy; in 1791, for example, the *Manchester Mercury* solicited subscriptions from its readers for a poor weaver's family which consisted of thirteen children (including two sets of twins) all under 15.[5] Conversely, even at the end of the period, when piece-rates were low, a small family with most of its members working would be fairly comfortable; the prosperity of William Varley in the early 1820s may have been enhanced by the fact that he had two looms in a family of only four people.

Individual case-histories show that weavers' families in which there were several workers did not compare too unfavourably in total earnings with their factory-working neighbours. Indeed, a survey of 243 families in a poor district of Preston in 1834 showed that the average weekly income per head was 2s. 2½d. for the whole number, whilst the average of the handloom weavers'

---

[1] During the 1826 slump, weavers who accepted road-work could earn from 10s. to 12s. a week; but as soon as weaving became available at 6s. to 7s. they went back to it because 'the labour was too severe for their habits' (PP. 1833 (690) VI, Q. 3899).

[2] Hickson concluded that the cotton weavers were worse off than all the others (PP. 1840 (639) XXIV, p. 645).

[3] PP. 1842 (31) XXII, p. 366.   [4] Gilboy, *op. cit.* pp. 196 and 221.

[5] *Manchester Mercury*, 26 Nov. 1791.

families (who numbered more than half of the whole) was 2s. 3½d. per head—although this latter figure took no account of working expenses.[1] To cite specific families, Joseph Sherwin, a prominent Stockport weaver in the post-war period, had a total income of 22s. 6d. a week in 1824 for a family of six, earned as follows:[2]

	s. d.
Sherwin, weaving	6 6
His wife, winding	3 0
Son, aged 15, in factory	7 0
Son, aged 10, in factory	6 0
	22 6

William Pilling of Bolton had an income of 25s. 9d. in 1833 for a family of eight:[3]

	s. d.
Pilling, weaving	9 0
Two daughters, weaving	8 3
Son, aged 14, in factory	5 6
Son, aged 10, drawboy	3 0
	25 9

These earnings are no lower than those of similar families at Styal in 1831. According to Miss Collier, the average of two families of five workers was 24s. 6d., and of two families of four workers, 30s. 9d.[4] Everything, in short, suggests that, except in the years of severe unemployment, many handloom weavers' families were only in a very relative sense living in more impoverished circumstances than many of the families of other workmen around them.

V

The overall change in the handloom weavers' way of life in the industrial revolution was once summed up as a move to 'long hours and short wages'.[5] Before the coming of the weaving

[1] PP. 1834 (44) XXVIII, pp. 909–10.   [2] PP. 1824 (51) V, p. 419.
[3] PP. 1833 (690) VI, Q. 11968.   [4] Collier, op. cit. p. 54.
[5] The phrase was used by the Bradford woollen weavers in 1834 (G. P. Scrope, *Political economy versus the handloom weavers* (Bradford, 1835), p. 8).

factories, the handloom weaver often found that a very modest amount of toil would earn him enough money to live at a conventionally comfortable standard of living. But as piece-rates fell, this conventional standard could no longer be enjoyed with the old desultory habits of work. Once the textile industries had been transformed by the use of power-driven machines, the hand worker was not merely technologically at a disadvantage, but was also anachronistic in his attitude to work. The great changes of the first half of the nineteenth century made cotton operatives work, if not harder, at least for longer hours and in a more regular fashion. But whereas for factory workers this was accompanied in the long run by an improved standard of living, for the handloom weavers it meant at best remaining stationary, and, at worst, actual deterioration.

CHAPTER 7

PUBLIC OPINION AND THE HANDLOOM WEAVERS

THE DEBATE ON 'MACHINERY'

DETAILED analysis of the economic problems which the cotton handloom weavers came ultimately to face has, on the whole, enabled a less horrifying picture of their sufferings to be painted. Yet even with the emotional varnish removed, and the exaggeration curbed, their fate remains a sad one. If their economic well-being did not suffer an unbroken decline from the beginning of the nineteenth century; if the casual nature of much of the employment and the weavers' increasingly archaic attitude to work make direct comparison with the new factory operatives difficult; if they had suffered horribly at times even before the powerloom came to affect their position; and if the location of industry as much as its technical development tended to aggravate their problems, the suffering entailed in the elimination of the handloom weavers as an element in economic organization is still the most disquieting aspect of the English industrial revolution. Theirs was, if not the first, certainly the largest case of redundancy or technological unemployment in our recent economic history;[1] the contraction of the cotton industry in our time, particularly in the 1920s and 1930s, affords an interesting parallel.

The extensive distress which certainly existed among the handloom weavers even before the 1820s has indicated that their problems did not arise simply from the coming of new machines; indeed, it could be maintained that their long-term prospects were distinctly uninviting so long as weaving remained a domestic trade bedevilled by all the problems of underemployment and

---

[1] The supersession of hand spinning by the water-frame and mule factories at the end of the eighteenth century was an earlier instance. Little is known about it, but it appears to have been much quicker and less painful. Many of the displaced spinners easily found new domestic employment in handloom weaving (see above, p. 42).

exploitation inherent in such occupations. Nevertheless, because of its immediate short-term consequences, the actual coming of the powerloom in the cotton industry gave Britain her first bitter taste of the problems which result from the application of science to manufacturing industry, and as such it rightly forms the central strand in the present story. No collective solution to these problems was found at the time, although they affected a large number of people; in the last resort, each individual weaver and each individual manufacturer had to decide for himself what action he would take. Thus the ultimate disappearance of the handloom weavers seems all the more tragic because of the complete failure of the means suggested for stopping or softening the process of displacement. The adoption of the powerloom moved on relentlessly, its brief delays serving only to worsen the weavers' position rather than to improve it, by protracting the death-scene. 'The history of the hand workers', wrote Engels in 1845, 'has been one of continued retreat in face of the advance of the machine.'[1]

Yet we should not assume that their disappearance was inevitable, nor forget the many attempts which they made to bolster up their position. Not the least of their efforts was the persistent way in which they brought their problems to the notice of the country's rulers. Although in the event parliament probably could not, and certainly would not, do anything to help them in their struggle against the developments in technology and industrial organization which were proving so fatal to them, the ruling class did not coldly acquiesce in the destruction of the weavers through ignorance, or without subjecting the matter to debate and controversy. So acute were the weavers' problems on occasions, and so widespread their sufferings, that parliament was several times obliged to inquire officially into their situation, and to give serious consideration to various possible remedies and improvements.

More than this, the ultimate fate of the handloom weavers sparked off within the ruling element in society a much wider debate on the desirability or otherwise of Britain's becoming a nation chiefly dependent for her prosperity on manufacturing

[1] F. Engels, *The condition of the working class in England* (1845) (English edn by W. H. Chaloner and W. O. Henderson, Oxford, 1958), p. 14.

industry. In the 1830s and 1840s there was a spasmodic but by no means minor controversy within the ranks of educated opinion as to whether the replacement of men by machines and of cottages by factories was really beneficial. The supporters of the 'machine', usually men of fairly radical political opinions, included professional economists such as Charles Babbage, Travers Twiss, Andrew Ure, and G. P. Scrope, as well as serious journalists like William Cooke Taylor, and Edward Baines. Those who were to some degree hostile to machinery on the whole carried less intellectual or political authority, and were generally Tory in their sympathies; they numbered among them such figures as Richard Oastler, Joseph Rayner Stephens, Feargus O'Connor, and W. B. Ferrand. The spirit of their various arguments calls for a brief discussion before the narrative of the handloom weavers' attempts at different times to win the active assistance of parliament is told.

Neither contemporaries nor later historians quite presented the argument in purely black and white terms. Few people would have maintained that the large-scale adoption of the powerloom was not accompanied by serious problems, and equally few would have taken the view that all technical progress is inherently and absolutely evil in its consequences. No one argued that all had been perfect before the powerloom came along, and no one claimed that its coming had seen the immediate dawning of a happier age.[1] But for all that, the protagonists of the pro- and anti-machinery factions held their views with great tenacity, and advanced them with vigour.

Unfortunately, the debate tended to be confused by various red herrings. Ignorance, or at any rate the lack of sufficient factual material upon which to build an empirical case either for or against 'machinery', was one. As a result, both parties advanced their opinions on the most slender evidence, particularly when they were trying to illustrate the condition of industrial workers before the coming of 'the machine'. Under these conditions, reminiscence and a colourful imagination were more relied upon than hard fact, and 'the good old days' came to be described

---

[1] The two figures who probably came nearest to expressing the most extreme views for and against machinery were respectively Ure and Ferrand.

in exaggerated language; the very real sufferings to which all domestic outworkers were liable and which the handloom weavers had experienced often enough before 1820 were conveniently forgotten. Yet, as the Hammonds remind us, 'scarcely any evil associated with the factory system was entirely a new evil in kind. In many domestic industries the hours were long, the pay was poor, children worked from a tender age, ...and both home and workshop were rendered less desirable from the combination of the two under a single roof'.[1]

The biggest confusion arose, however, because the protagonists usually failed to separate with sufficient rigour two different, though by no means disconnected, types of argument. The purely economic effects of machine-production—the altered use of the labour force, the effect on wages, the increase or decrease in cyclical or seasonal unemployment, the new workshop conditions, the changed relationship between employer and workman, and the physical problems which resulted from people being crowded together to live as well as to labour, became indiscriminately confused with the 'moral' consequences, in particular with the splitting-up of the family unit, the alleged decline of religion, morality, and patriotism, and the destruction of small-scale community and village life. Some attempt must be made to sort out the tangle.[2]

On purely materialistic grounds, those who doubted the advantages of adopting new machinery could fairly easily be confounded. 'The coming of machinery', said Cooke Taylor, 'has provided additional employment and increased wages',[3] and this argument was not easily refuted. Furthermore, it was commercially suicidal not to make practical use of new inventions, since if England did not use them, her competitors certainly would. As Joseph Brotherton, M.P. for Salford, argued in 1843, 'if they stopped the machines and went back to handloom weaving and spinning and allowed the manufacturers on the continent to use

---

[1] J. L. and B. Hammond, *The town labourer* (London, 1917), p. 18.
[2] For a discussion of this confusion among both contemporaries of the industrial revolution and its later historians, see R. M. Hartwell, 'Interpretations of the industrial revolution in England', *Journal of Economic History*, XIX (1959), 229–49.
[3] W. Cooke Taylor, *Handbook of silk, cotton, and woollen manufactures* (London, 1843), p. 82.

all the newly-invented machinery which British ingenuity and skill had discovered and applied to the production of its manufactures',[1] the country would be rapidly impoverished.

Thus the argument of O'Connorite Chartists was not that new machinery should not be used, but that in some undefined way it should not be *abused*:

Our machinery [ran a *Northern Star* editorial] has always hitherto been applied ...to the raising and gathering together of large heaps of wealth for the 'great' owners of it and to driving from the workshop the man who had to 'earn his bread by the sweat of his brow' and dragging into his place (where a sentient being was still needed) the woman and the child, inflicting upon them LONGER HOURS of toil than the man had to endure before his supersession; and involving all in a race of commercial strife which continually takes from the wages of the work-woman and the work-child and inflicts suffering and poverty upon all who have to live by daily toil. Tell us not that these things must continue...A better and more just distribution of the fruits of toil must be made...That which is of itself one of the greatest of blessings must not continue to be made into the greatest of scrourges and curses. IT MUST BE REGULATED! It must be used within due limits; and its benefits must be diffused amongst and secured to all concerned.[2]

Even those who questioned the replacement of the handloom by the powerloom, like Peter Gaskell, did not claim that the change-over had prevented factory workers from earning 'what is amply sufficient to supply all their wants',[3] Only the most prejudiced paternalist Tory, like W. B. Ferrand, could seriously attribute the plight of industrial workers during a depression to the fact that manufacturing was now done in factories with the aid of steam-power and not in cottages on handlooms.[4]

Where the opponents of machinery tried to demonstrate its adverse economic effects, they were usually on shaky ground. They might claim that the housing conditions of factory workers were worse than those of the old handloom weavers—an arguable case, perhaps, when applied to weavers in some of the country villages, but very dubious as regards those who worked in damp urban cellars and who contributed as much as the early factory

---

[1] *3rd Series Hansard*, vol. 66, col. 790.   [2] *Northern Star*, 5 Feb. 1842.
[3] P. Gaskell, *The manufacturing population of England* (London, 1833), p. 7.
[4] See, for example, Ferrand's speeches in the Commons in February 1843, in *3rd Series Hansard*, vol. 66, cols. 306 and 523.

hands to swelling the rapidly-growing manufacturing towns. They might argue, as the Hammonds did, that the most unbearable aspect of the transfer to the factory was that it subjected the worker to 'the discipline of a power driven by a competition that seemed as inhuman as the machines that thundered in factory and shed'.[1] The deterioration of physique under the stricter factory regimen might also provide an argument against the machine.[2] But none of these propositions was really capable of proof, if only because there was no detailed evidence in the 1830s (apart, that is, from unreliable memories and vague impressions) of what things had really been like thirty or forty years earlier.

In any case, the confusion was further increased because the discussion was not very clear about what comparison was being made. Was it between the condition of the domestic worker of long ago and the factory worker of the present who was his heir, or was it between the pauperized handloom weaver of the 1830s and his contemporary in the mill? The fact that a direct comparison could be made, that the change from hand to power did not take place immediately, and that the two forms of industry co-existed for twenty years after the disastrous slump of 1826—made the case for machinery more difficult to sustain than it would have been had the powerloom taken over suddenly and speedily.

Faced with the unpleasant fact that the domestic weaver had not been magically transformed overnight into the mill hand, political economists could offer little immediate encouragement as they extolled the long-term advantages of harnessing new discoveries to manufacturing processes. The best that Charles Babbage could offer was to urge that workers liable to be made technologically redundant 'should be aware of the effects [of a new machine], and that they should be able to foresee them at an early period in order to diminish as much as possible their injurious results'.[3] Travers Twiss could only submit that the victims of economic change had suffered even worse in the past:

Pitiable...as may be the condition of the workman who suddenly finds the demand for his labour to cease, and most deserving as he is of the sympathy and

---

[1] Hammonds, *op. cit.* p. 19.   [2] Gaskell, *op. cit.* pp. 158–9.
[3] C. Babbage, *On the economy of machinery and manufactures* (London, 1832), p. 229.

succour of the community to whose general welfare his interests are sacrificed for a time [he wrote], yet his lot is far less wretched than that of the individual members of those hapless bands of emigrants whom famine drove forth in olden times from their homes, and whose track across Europe was marked out for the next comers by the bleached bones of those who had perished on the way.[1]

This was probably true as far as it went, but, even when uttered with all the authority of the professor of political economy of Oxford University, it could have given little comfort to a weaving family in Bolton or Colne which had lived through the miseries of 1826, 1829, 1832, 1837 and 1842.

The opponents of machinery perhaps failed to make enough, not of the evils of machinery *per se*, but of the special problems which resulted from the particular way in which the powerloom was introduced into the cotton industry. They tended to argue in vague generalities, instead of citing concrete examples. The fact that in the first part of the nineteenth century cotton hand weaving provided in terms of numbers the largest manufacturing employment in the country, that the technical perfection of the powerloom was only slowly achieved, and that the weaving factories, when they came, were often set up in the wrong place at the wrong time (from the weavers' point of view)—none of these received very much emphasis. Yet such factors, rightly stressed, would have done something to strengthen the argument that the wholly unregulated introduction of machinery on so large a scale and with such striking consequences for the workers was bad, and that remedying its evil consequences should be a matter of public concern. Even then, it is likely that any parliament, reformed or unreformed, in the early nineteenth century would have lacked the means, even if it had the will, to undertake the kind of regulation which the problem demanded. But the argument would at least have looked more convincing.

Those who criticized the effects of machinery usually showed more confidence when they relied on the 'moral' arguments. Their case was most ably put by Peter Gaskell in his two books *The manufacturing population of England* (1833) and *Artisans and*

---

[1] T. Twiss, *Two lectures on machinery* (Oxford, 1844), pp. 54–5.

machinery (1836).[1] The consequences of which he complained were not greater poverty, more fatiguing work, or even greater ignorance. He was more concerned with the demoralization of the factory worker as compared with the old handloom weaver, which, he claimed,

has arisen from the separation of families, the breaking-up of households, the disruption of all those ties which link man's heart to the better portion of his nature—viz. his instincts and social affections, and which alone can render him a respectable and praiseworthy member of society both in his domestic relations and in his capacity of a citizen, and which have finally led him to the abandonment of the pure joys of home, and to seek his pleasures and his excitements in pursuits fatal alike to health and to moral propriety.[2]

Stated in these terms, the argument that evil consequences followed the adoption of steam machinery seems more plausible. For such factors as the separation of children and parents in the mills were evidently causes of great concern and resentment to workers.[3] J. R. Stephens, leader of the Lancashire anti-Poor Law movement in the late 1830s and a popular speaker at the early Chartist mass meetings, attributed the 'high moral character' of the handloom weavers 'to the fact of their having their children more immediately under their own eye. Father, mother, and off-spring still make up one household. The natural affections and social sympathies, and the relative duties of man to his neighbour and to his God are implanted and cherished in this native school.'[4] He went on to lament that the government had 'allowed this nursery of religion, morals, and loyalty to have been almost destroyed', while it had done nothing to prevent the growth of 'that system of manufactures which impairs the health, injures the morals, and destroys the social character of our home population'.

The break-up of the family, the desertion of the closely-knit village community with its traditions and social obligations for the impersonality of the big town where men's mutual relation-

---

[1] The latter is merely a second edition of the first, revised in view of the evidence collected in 1833–4 by the royal commissions on the Poor Law and the factories, and by the select committee on the handloom weavers.

[2] Gaskell, *op. cit.* pp. 7–8.

[3] See N. J. Smelser, *Social change in the industrial revolution* (London, 1959), pp. 279–87.

[4] Stephens's evidence to assistant commissioner Muggeridge is printed in *Northern Star*, 23 June 1838

ships and duties were ill-defined, and the replacement of a blissfully ignorant but healthy people by a discontented, half-educated, and wholly-demoralized proletariat—all these arguments could be, and were, used to interpret the passing of domestic industry (of which the largest and best-known example was handloom weaving) as a case of the corruption of innocence and the strangulation of virtue.

But by their very nature, such interpretations must remain hypotheses, because they concern matters incapable of factual verification, and because there are enough indications to make a completely opposite view tenable. The old handloom weavers were not always noted for independent-mindedness, self-improvement, and self-respect. Depending entirely on personal temperament and inclination, the 'freedom' to work as one pleased, and the relatively easy wages of the early days, were just as likely to lead to idleness, drunkenness, and general demoralization.[1]

Furthermore, it can be argued that the coming of the factory system and its concomitants first provided opportunities for the development of educational and social institutions—savings banks, mechanics institutes, trade unions, and the like—without which working men would still be in a very low state of education, economic well-being and self-development. For instance, no cases are known of educational facilities having been provided by the employers of handloom weavers, whereas the offspring of factory workers often enjoyed some schooling, however primitive, which had been arranged by the manufacturer.[2] And again, it could be maintained that the emancipation of working women could not have begun until they had become independent wage-earners in factories, and had ceased to be subordinate casual employees within the household.[3]

All in all, the intellectual case for preserving domestic industry, particularly in the form of handloom weaving, was not very well argued. The efforts of the opponents of machinery were even less convincing when they tried to offer any practical solution to the

[1] PP. 1816 (397) III, p. 290.
[2] This point was made as early as the s.c. on children in manufactories, 1816 (PP. 1816 (397) III, p. 509).
[3] I. Pinchbeck, *Women workers in the industrial revolution* (London, 1930), p. 313.

weavers' problems. Gaskell, for example, had no sympathy for local wages boards, taxes on powerlooms, or state-aided emigration. By rejecting all these ideas, he and the 'Young England' Tories and the O'Connorite Chartists of the 1840s who thought on the same lines were left with only one suggestion—'back to the land'.[1] The cultivation of the supposed 'waste lands' of the United Kingdom was seen as the only way of keeping the working population virtuous and happy, of employing those who were made redundant by technical developments, and of enabling England to remain economically self-contained and self-sufficient. Pleasantly idealist as it sounds, it was far less practical and realistic than anything the weavers themselves hoped to achieve. Their own efforts to persuade parliament to protect them must now be examined.

PARLIAMENT AND THE HANDLOOM WEAVERS

The debate on 'machinery' belongs to the latter years of the handloom weavers' history. Long before the powerloom came into effective operation, the weavers had found that periodically their economic well-being was seriously threatened, and had been obliged to take steps to improve their position.[2] It was in 1799 that the cotton weavers first approached parliament with a statement of their sufferings and a remedy of their own devising for which they required legislative support. Their grievances were obvious. The uncertainties of the trade, which was disrupted by war, together with the bad harvests and the recent suspension of cash payments, had meant a sharp drop in piece-rates at a time when prices in general were rising rapidly.

In face of this, a committee of thirty weavers, representing the towns of Bolton, Manchester, Stockport, Oldham, Wigan,

---

[1] P. Gaskell, *Artisans and machinery* (London, 1836), pp. 45–55. The 'back to the land' movement of the 1840s can be seen in action in the Chartist land scheme (see the essay by J. MacAskill in *Chartist Studies*, ed. A. Briggs (London, 1958)), and in the report of the Young England-inspired s.c. on the labouring poor (allotments of land) in *PP. 1843* (*402*) VII.

[2] The most detailed and comprehensive account of the different movements among the handloom weavers between 1800 and 1826 will be found in J. L. and B. Hammond, *The skilled labourer* (London, 1919), to which the reader is referred for a fuller narrative.

Warrington, Blackburn, Chorley, Newton, Bury, Whitefield, Chowbent, and New Chapel near Leigh, met at Bolton in May 1799. Styling themselves 'The Association of Weavers', they issued on 13 May an 'Address to the Public', signed by John Seddon their President and James Holcroft their Secretary. In it, they took great pains to stress their law-abiding intentions and their loyalty: 'We shall neither interfere with Church nor State but strictly confine ourselves to a private grievance which we wish to lay before government', they promised, and went on to argue that the government could easily pass legislation to allow the fixing of statutory minimum wages for cotton weaving, as was already done in the Spitalfields silk-weaving industry.[1]

It is vain [their proclamation went on] to talk of bad trade, for if goods are actually not wanted they cannot be sold at any price; if wanted, twopence or threepence per yard will not stop the buyer; and whether does it appear more reasonable that twopence or threepence per yard should be laid on the consumer or taken from the labourer? A single twopence per yard would increase wages from eleven to twenty-one shillings...consider how little it would affect the one, and how important to the other. How impressed with gratitude must that man be with five or six small children when informed that Government has devised certain measures, that where he now received only eleven shillings he might receive about twenty shillings for his work.[2]

The authorities' reaction to the weavers' attempts at organization was dictated in the first instance by fear of sinister Jacobinical plots against the government. Local magistrates were panic-stricken, and parliament was prevailed upon, partly as a result of the weavers' activities, to pass the most comprehensive and famous Act against Combinations of Workmen in July 1799.[3] Undeterred, however, the weavers continued to petition for some form of defence against the continued wage-reductions which their capricious and cruel masters allegedly forced upon them, and the government was prepared to make some soothing gestures. Pitt would not go so far as to pass a wage-fixing statute, although it

---

[1] For the Spitalfields legislation, see J. H. Clapham, 'The Spitalfields Acts, 1773–1824', *Economic Journal*, XXVI (1916).

[2] Address of 'The Association of Weavers', Bolton, 13 May 1799. Enclosed in J. Singleton (Wigan) to Home Office, 27 May 1799 (*HO. 42. 47*).

[3] See A. Aspinall, *The early English trade unions* (London, 1949), pp. xi–xiii.

would appear from an unsigned, undated, and almost illegible memorandum in the Home Office papers that he at least considered the possibility;[1] and in the end he produced the so-called Cotton Arbitration Act of 1800.[2]

This provided that when a dispute arose between an individual employer and an individual weaver about piece-rates, bad materials, or fines and abatements for faulty workmanship, each party could name an arbitrator to adjudicate. The arbitrators' decision, if unanimous, was binding; but if they failed to agree, the case was referred to a magistrate.

The working of this Act soon caused general dissatisfaction, and in 1802 there was further petitioning for it to be amended. The result was a committee of the House of Commons to examine the petitions and consider the effects of the Act. It was set up in February 1803, at the instigation of the government, the motion for its appointment being introduced by Addington, the prime minister.[3] The evidence heard by this committee and the resolutions it reached in March 1804 marked the first time that parliament inquired directly into the problems of the handloom weavers.[4] Its method of proceeding was rather different from that of the later select committees on the same subject. The weavers and the manufacturers each presented witnesses, prominent among the weavers being Richard Needham, Thomas Thorpe, and James Holcroft, who had been secretary of the weavers' association of 1799. Each side was also represented by a solicitor or agent, Mr Mundell appearing for the workers and Mr Richardson for the masters. Contrary to later practice, whereby the questions were

[1] HO. 42. 55. The relevant document runs: 'On looking into Barnes' *Justice*, Title *Servants*, head *Rating of Wages*, Mr Pitt will see the authority given to Magistrates to settle the wages of all artificers and labourers by the day, week, or month. If anything can be done as suggested by Mr Bayley [the Manchester Magistrate] it appears to Mr King [the author of the Memorandum?] that it must be grounded on the Acts there mentioned...' Bayley does not in fact seem to have advocated a Minimum Wage Act, for on 8 May 1800 he wrote to J. King that 'the measure they solicit is altogether so absurd and impracticable that many of their number see their interest is in its overthrow, which I hope for the peace of the country will be *very speedy* and by a *great majority in a full House*, and this I beg may be intimated to Mr Pitt' (HO. 42. 50).
[2] 39 and 40 George III, cap. 90.
[3] *1st Series Hansard*, vol. 1, cols. 1080–2.
[4] The evidence is printed in PP. *1803 (114)* III, part 4; the resolutions in PP. *1804 (41)* IV, part 1

put to witnesses entirely by the M.P.s who made up the committee, most of the examining and cross-examining was undertaken by these two agents. Because of this, the whole inquiry had very much the atmosphere of a case in a law court.

Much of the evidence taken by the 1803 committee was of a fairly trivial nature and concerned individual cases and experiences. But the investigation showed that two factors were chiefly responsible for the failure of parliament's only attempt to placate the cotton weavers by legislation. One was the strong opposition of the employers to any form of government interference. As early as February 1802, the Manchester manufacturers had denounced the 1800 Act as 'productive of much inconvenience, expense, and litigation, as well from its principle as its particular provisions'.[1] They were opposed to any attempt to extend the Act, hoping rather for its repeal, and formed a committee to secure these objectives. By the beginning of 1804, they had spent over £2,000 in sending witnesses to London and putting their case to the select committee.[2] Apart from trying to annul the Arbitration Act in this way, the manufacturers were also accused of trying to evade it in practice by appointing arbitrators who lived at a great distance. As the Act had made no provision to compel the arbitrators to meet, a case where an absent arbitrator was involved would simply never be settled.[3]

The manufacturers' attitude becomes more understandable, however, when the second factor in the Act's failure is taken into account. For it is clear that the weavers had tried to make the Arbitration Act much more than a quick and cheap mechanism for settling occasional individual disputes. The leading weavers in the Manchester and Bolton areas had become in effect full-time professional arbitrators; James Holcroft alone had been called to adjudicate in three hundred disputes.[4] The manufacturers feared the creation of permanent legal machinery which would by-pass the J.P.s who had settled such disputes in the past, give the power of summary justice to unqualified men, and encourage 'a spirit of

[1] *Manchester Mercury*, 2 March 1802. [2] *Ibid.* 14 Feb. 1804.
[3] This point was used by Addington to justify his motion for the 1803 committee.
[4] *PP. 1803 (114)* III, part 4, p. 33.

insubordination among some of the lower orders of society'.[1] Most important of all, however, some weavers hoped to manipulate the Act in order to regulate wages. Although the 1800 law was not intended to deal with collective disputes, the weavers of Whitefield, near Manchester, hit on the idea of reversing a recent wage reduction by simultaneous individual arbitrations against all their employers. Such organized and unanimous action was in effect a general refusal to work for the wages offered, and an attempt to throw the burden of fixing a different rate on the arbitrators, or, in the last resort, on the local justices.[2]

Had the Whitefield attempt been successful, a form of wage-fixing would have been established in cotton weaving via the back door, contrary to the intention of the Arbitration Act. Accordingly, the select committee stressed that the original object had not been to fix wages. To prevent a repetition of the Whitefield case it urged that the power of naming arbitrators be removed from the contending parties. All future disputes should be settled either by the local justices or, if the disputants preferred, by two arbitrators, selected one by each side from a shortlist nominated by the magistrates.[3] This would cut out the 'professional' arbitrator, and place the responsibility for settling industrial disputes with the J.P.s, to whom it had formerly belonged. It was hoped that the weavers would be appeased because their employers could no longer nullify the law by appointing distant arbitrators, and because manufacturers were now required to give out weaving-tickets, setting down in full the terms on which any piece of work was put out. Against the continued opposition of the manufacturers, who had the assistance of the Lancashire M.P.s, a bill embodying the committee's recommendations became law on 20 July 1804.[4]

---

[1] The view of James Ramsbotham, a Whitefield manufacturer, *ibid.* pp. 40–7.
[2] James Holcroft was named as arbitrator in no less than nine hundred of the actions at Whitefield. He claimed, however, that the interpretation of the Act as a wage-fixing measure was peculiar to Whitefield (*ibid.* p. 34).
[3] 44 George III, cap. 87. (It was repealed by 5 George IV, cap. 96.)
[4] The resolutions are in *1st Series Hansard*, vol. 1, cols. 1172–3.

II

These amendments made the machinery for settling disputes so similar to what it had been before 1800 that the new Act seems to have been largely inoperative; for it could no longer be converted to a wage-fixing measure as the weavers had hoped. Although it was invoked occasionally to settle individual disputes,[1] and although even in the 1840s magistrates might still be applied to successfully by weavers with grievances,[2] the amended Act did not make the rate of wages any less dependent on the arbitrary whim of the individual manufacturer. On the other hand, to have retained the Act at all in view of the manufacturers' opposition says a great deal for the strength of the weavers' organization and the skill of Holcroft and his associates. The heavy financial costs which their organization must have entailed also indicate their prosperity and high social status in these early years, and provide a marked contrast with the poverty and demoralization to which they were to sink.

Nonetheless, the tameness of the second Arbitration Act necessitated further applications to parliament whenever wage-regulation seemed the only remedy for their economic decline. Nor was it long before the cotton weavers were again clamouring for some measure to halt the disastrous drop in earnings after the renewal of the French war in 1803. The piece-rate index for muslins fell from 100 in 1805 to 56 in 1808, and another large-scale organization to secure a 'minimum wage' bill was built up, again centred on Bolton, with leaders such as Richard Needham prominent once more. In February 1807, a petition reached parliament allegedly containing 130,000 signatures. It prayed for a bill to set up machinery which would lay down a minimum wage for weaving, below which no manufacturer could go. The petitioning, which was kept up into the following year, was supported by many merchants and employers, although it is uncertain whether their

---

[1] Assistant commissioner Muggeridge was told of its being used in Preston in 1838 (*Preston Observer*, 2 June 1838).

[2] For example, two Carlisle weavers secured compensation in 1841 for time lost through the failure of their employer to provide weft for their particular warps, and through his refusal to give them alternative work (*Northern Star*, 4 Sept. 1841).

sympathies were sincere, or merely judicious.[1] On behalf of the new Portland administration, G. H. Rose, of the Board of Trade, agreed to a select committee to examine the petitions and advise on legislation. It is quite obvious, however, as far as the government was concerned, that the committee was merely a piece of window-dressing to humour the workers. It met six times, and heard only nine witnesses—three merchants, two manufacturers, and four weavers.[2] The final report of 1809 maintained that 'fixing a minimum for the price of labour in the cotton manufacture is wholly inadmissable in principle, incapable of being reduced to practice by any means which can possibly be devised, and, if practicable, would be productive of the most fatal consequences'.[3] Even before this report was published, it was obvious what the committee's attitude would be; for on 19 May 1808 Rose had half-heartedly brought in a minimum wage bill with the admitted intention of simply appeasing the weavers by a show of sympathy. All the speakers in the ensuing debate had opposed it strongly, and it was quickly dropped.[4] Disappointed by the government's refusal to help, the cotton weavers turned to industrial action in the strike of 1808.[5]

They were soon petitioning again for wage regulation, as the brief prosperity of 1810 receded. On 30 May 1811, Blackburne and Stanley, the Lancashire M.P.s, presented petitions from Manchester and Bolton signed respectively by 40,000 and 7,000 workers. Their prayer was not specifically for a minimum wage, but merely that 'parliament will enact such salutary laws as will give employ and suitable wages to the industrious inhabitants'.[6] The government, whilst admitting in Spencer Percival's words that 'it was impossible to hold out to them any expectation of a favourable nature without exposing them to the certainty of disappointment',[7] agreed to another select committee to satisfy the

---

[1] Among the sympathizers—as on later occasions—was Colonel Ralph Fletcher, the Bolton magistrate. See Fletcher to Lord Hawkesbury, Feb. 1808 (*HO. 42. 95*) and *idem* to J. Beckett, 11 April 1812 (*HO. 40. 1/1*).

[2] The evidence is in *PP. 1808 (177)* II; the final report in *PP. 1809 (111)* III.

[3] *PP. 1809 (111)* III, p. 311.

[4] The debate is in *1st Series Hansard*, vol. 11, cols. 425–8.

[5] See below, pp. 189–91.   [6] *1st Series Hansard*, vol. 20, col. 343.

[7] *Ibid.* col. 431.

weavers 'that every attention had been paid to their claims in that House'.[1]

The perfunctory nature of this new inquiry is indicated by the extremely small number of witnesses, one of whom was in any case Joseph Hanson of Manchester, who had already made himself *persona non grata* with the authorities for his part in the strike of 1808.[2] Furthermore, the committee met on only four occasions and its report was a model of *laissez-faire* thinking. A limitation of the number of apprentices, a ban on mechanical improvements, or a direct grant of financial relief from the Treasury—all these were rejected on the grounds that

no interference of the legislature with the freedom of trade or with the perfect liberty of every individual to dispose of his time and of his labour in the way and on the terms which he may judge most conducive to his own interest can take place, without violating general principles of the first importance to the prosperity and happiness of the community; without establishing the most pernicious precedent; or even without aggravating after a very short time the general distress.[3]

It was the inevitable conclusion.[4]

III

The refusal of the unreformed parliament to take any step in 1808 or 1811 to help the handloom weavers, even when their proposals had the ostensible sympathy of the local magistrates and manufacturers, seems to have left them with little hope of legislative action for many years. Several parliamentary committees of the next two decades—those on the Orders in Council in 1812, the employment of children in factories in 1816, and the laws relating to artisans and machinery in 1824—turned up evidence about the weavers, but it was purely incidental to other matters. Realizing

[1] *Ibid.* col. 437.
[2] See below, pp. 191–3.   [3] *PP. 1810/11 (232)* II, p. 389.
[4] Within another two years the government had confirmed its adherence to the new principles of political economy by repealing much of the old mercantilist wage-fixing legislation. For an account of the breakdown of the workers' former legal defences at this period, see E. P. Thompson, *The making of the English working class* (London, 1963), esp. pp. 543–5, and T. K. Derry, 'The repeal of the apprenticeship clauses of the statute of apprentices', *Economic History Review*, III (1931–2).

that little could be expected from parliament, most weavers turned in their next bouts of industrial depression either to radical politics, as in 1816–17 and 1819, or particularly to industrial action, as in the strike of 1818 and the efforts of 1819 and 1826 to get their employers to agree to a negotiated wage-fixing scheme.[1]

They did not entirely desert the old parliamentary methods, however. In 1816–17, William Radcliffe was again active, and together with 'loyal' weavers such as Thomas Thorpe and Richard Needham organized renewed petitions for a ban on yarn exports, which had increased from under 10 million lb to over 16 million lb between 1815 and 1816.[2] Manufacturers and merchants joined with weavers to memorialize the Prince Regent. The cotton manufacturers of the West Riding, for example, complained that 'by the present unrestricted traffic, the foreign manufacturer is enabled to buy yarns on the same terms as Your Memorialists; and owing to the high price of provisions, the heavy pressure of taxes, and the unceasing increase of the poor rate...the foreign manufacturer is enabled to manufacture his goods at a lower rate than Your Memorialists', and they begged the Regent to adopt 'the policy of taking off the duty now existing on imported cotton wool, and imposing the same on exported yarns'.[3]

Sympathetic magistrates might also still urge the government to act. The Rev. W. Prescott of Stockport, for example, wondered whether the government might not itself buy materials and give out work in order to prevent further unemployment.[4] This novel and obviously unacceptable scheme was recommended on the grounds that the government would 'export to distant markets, as they would have the conveyance at a much lighter expense, and they could afford to lay out of their money much better than individuals'. Perhaps the best indication of the weavers' attitude to the possibilities of parliamentary help in these years, however, is shown by the behaviour of their most prominent Stockport leaders, Joseph Sherwin and Simon Lilly. In May 1816 they were

[1] See below, pp. 171–2, pp. 194–6, and pp. 211–13.
[2] Hammonds, *op. cit.* pp. 90–1; *PP. 1817 (141)* XIV, p. 269. For the movement to prevent yarn exports about 1800, see above, pp. 68–70.
[3] *PP. 1817 (482)* XIV, p. 357.
[4] P. M. Giles, *The social and economic development of Stockport, 1815–1836* (Manchester M.A. thesis, unpublished, 1950), p. 171.

petitioning parliament and memorializing the Prince Regent for the prohibition of yarn exports and for a minimum wage bill. By October of the same year they were calling for parliamentary reform.[1] It hadn't taken long to realize that they could expect little from parliament as then constituted.

There was one final inquiry by an unreformed House of Commons directed specifically at solving the problems of the handloom weavers. This was the select committee on emigration, which sat after the slump and the widespread unemployment of 1826. For the cotton industry as a whole this was the most serious depression it had yet known in peace-time; for the handloom weavers in particular, it was a demonstration that their problems were now of a different order, since the powerloom had first been adopted on an appreciable scale during the few preceding years. Under these circumstances, it seemed a reasonable conclusion in 1826 that there must be a vast population of hand workers in the manufacturing districts who would in future be redundant. Direct grants of public money,[2] an early proposal, were obviously only a short-term method of reducing distress. A few serious-minded politicians led by R. J. Wilmot Horton, M.P. for Newcastle-under-Lyme and a junior member of Lord Liverpool's administration, turned to the possibilities of a government-sponsored scheme of emigration for this 'surplus' population.

In March 1826, Horton secured a select committee to examine the idea; it was renewed in the following year, and published four reports.[3] One of them was concerned specifically with the Lancashire cotton weavers, whose problems were regarded as 'a special case...so serious and so urgent as to induce [the committee] to devote to it their principal attention'.[4] After hearing a good many witnesses with first-hand experience of the distress, among them Bishop Blomfield of Chester and W. H. Hyett, the secretary of the London manufacturers' relief committee, their report provided a very perceptive analysis of the particular sufferings of the country weavers, whose location made them less likely to obtain

[1] *Ibid.* pp. 141, 163 and 168.
[2] See debates in both Houses of Parliament, 1 and 2 May 1826, in *New Series Hansard*, vol. 15.   [3] *PP. 1826 (404)* IV, and *PP. 1826/7 (88)*, *(237)*, and *(550)* v.
[4] *PP. 1826/7 (237)* V, p. 4.

alternative work, but whose small-farming habits made them potentially suitable as emigrants to the colonies. The committee recommended that the government should operate an emigration scheme to help them, but as usual parliament had neither the inclination nor the means to carry out such a major proposal. This does not necessarily diminish the significance of the emigration committee, however. For it was the first time that M.P.s had voluntarily and spontaneously considered the possibilities of large-scale government action to solve the problems which the coming of the powerloom had now made pressingly urgent. True, emigration was not a proposal which necessarily commended itself very strongly to most of the weavers.[1] But at least it showed that the old unreformed parliament was by no means so out-of-touch with the 'problems of a new industrial society' nor so ill-disposed to consider doing something about them, as is often implied.

IV

After the reform of parliament in 1832, the handloom weavers could again entertain serious hopes that the legislature would intervene to bolster up their position. Among the new M.P.s were John Fielden and John Maxwell, who had a long-standing interest in the weavers' problems. Their very strenuous efforts to make the recent Reform Act bring direct benefits to working men, particularly to the weavers, have never been recorded in any detail. Yet it was largely thanks to them that the voluminous evidence of the select committees of 1834–5 and of the royal commission of 1837–41, which still remains the primary source of information on the subject, ever came to be amassed.

Fielden's career has been particularly neglected, partly because he sometimes attached himself to unpopular and unwise causes— for example, he shared the eccentric opinions of his fellow M.P. for Oldham, William Cobbett, on currency. But even where the objectives for which he fought were achieved, as was the case with the Ten-hours Act for factory workers in 1847, Fielden's part in the campaign was usually overshadowed by more forceful per-

[1] See below, p. 174, n. 2.

sonalities such as Lord Ashley. Fielden's unimpressive parliamentary manner, and the impossibility of giving him a party label—he was usually know as a radical, yet he had more in common with such Tories as Oastler, Stephens, and Ferrand than with Joseph Hume and William Molesworth—combined to weaken his influence in the Commons. Yet there was probably no-one in parliament at that time who took a more active interest in such a wide variety of causes affecting the welfare of the working classes, or whose personal experience of their problems was so extensive. John Fielden was as prominent in opposing the new Poor Law and the restoration of the gold standard of 1819 as he was zealous in advocating a statutory minimum wage for handloom weavers, shorter working hours in factories, the extension of the franchise, and a reduction of the burden of indirect taxation. It is particularly unfortunate that the lack of personal papers has never permitted the biography of this eccentric but interesting figure to be written.

It is perhaps unusual that a self-made man like Fielden should have continued to side with the mass of working people, when it would have been so easy for him to have followed the example of industrialists such as the first Sir Robert Peel in being accepted into the ruling class simply by adopting its outlook and habits. In the case of the domestic weavers, a cynic might easily see the pangs of conscience at work in a man whose Todmorden business once employed three thousand handlooms, but who in 1835 was the biggest operator of powerlooms in the West Riding.[1] Yet no-one among his contemporaries seems seriously to have questioned the genuine humanity of his motives, or the warmth and sympathy of his disposition. Even before the first reformed parliament had met in 1833, Fielden was gathering information on the state of the poor in Oldham 'which he intends to make use of. . . in his parliamentary capacity',[2] and as soon as the Commons assembled he was calling for action. He supported Hudson and Attwood in their unsuccessful attempt of 7 March to reduce all public salaries in the same proportion as rents, capital and wages

[1] J. Holden, *History of Todmorden* (Manchester, 1912), p. 162, and *PP. 1836* (24) XLV, pp. 150-1.
[2] *Manchester Guardian*, 19 Jan. 1833.

were said to have fallen as a result of deflation since 1819.[1] A fortnight later, with the bold statement that 'if he were of opinion
that the relief of public distress could not be affected by the
legislature, he would take his hat and walk away, and not come
within the walls of St Stephens again',[2] he urged the need for a
committee to examine the causes and the extent of the distress.

By the beginning of May, the representations of Fielden and
his allies seemed to be taking effect. A select committee was set
up 'to inquire into the present state of manufactures, commerce
and shipping in the United Kingdom'. Among its thirty-nine
members were Althorp, Goulburn, Henry Parnell, and Poulett
Thomson, as well as Fielden, Thomas Attwood, Joseph Brotherton, and other radicals. There was nothing perfunctory and formal
about this committee's proceedings. It sat on thirty-three days and
heard evidence relating to most branches of trade and industry
from seventy witnesses, a quarter of whom dealt wholly or partly
with the problems of the handloom weavers.[3] When the parliamentary session ended in August 1833, however, the committee
had done nothing beyond publishing the evidence it had taken,
nor was it subsequently reappointed.

The weavers' supporters were not easily disappointed, and
renewed their efforts in the following year. On 5 March 1834, the
economist Robert Torrens presented three petitions from his
Bolton constituents—one from the weavers, one from the magistrates and clergy, and the third from forty-five manufacturers.
All prayed for a specific inquiry into the weavers' problems, and
advised the establishment of local 'boards of trade' to fix a
minimum wage by agreement between a majority of the employers and their workmen.[4] Two months later, John Maxwell
moved that a select committee be appointed, and on 11 June the
Commons agreed by 70 votes to 42. The lateness of the session
prevented the committee from making any specific recommendations, but it had managed to hold nearly thirty sittings and hear
over forty witnesses before it broke up at the beginning of August.
Its evidence, which occupied more than 600 pages,[5] was mainly

[1] 3rd Series Hansard, vol. 16, cols. 353–69.   [2] Ibid. col. 953.
[3] The report is in PP. 1833 (690) VI.   [4] 3rd Series Hansard, vol. 21, col. 1144.
[5] The report is in PP. 1834 (556) X.

directed towards proving the feasibility of the 'boards of trade', and manufacturers and weavers were produced in almost equal numbers to press the claims of this new panacea.

As the select committee had left its work unfinished, it was not difficult for Maxwell to secure its reappointment in 1835, ostensibly to hear any opinions against the proposed boards.[1] The new committee produced a further 300 pages of printed evidence, and its final report of 1 July 1835 actually recommended the adoption of the 'boards of trade'.[2] The entire report bore very clearly the fingerprints of those who had all along been the weavers' most zealous friends. It attributed their sufferings to the powerloom, to high taxation, to the deflation which had followed the return to a gold currency after the Napoleonic war, and to the free export of yarn. It concluded: 'to the sentiment that Parliament cannot and ought not to interfere in cases of this nature Your Committee is decidedly opposed... Your Committee therefore recommend that a Bill of the nature of the one proposed by Mr Fielden should be immediately introduced into Parliament.'[3]

This suggestion that the government should sanction a scheme for regulating wages was, in an age when *laissez-faire* was popularly regarded as the eleventh commandment, quite outlandish, and it is not surprising that no notice was taken of it. Nor did the government's neglect create a great public outcry. For the select committees on the handloom weavers, like Sadler's committee on factory conditions of 1831 or the 1840 committee on import duties, were quite obviously biased and partial bodies.[4] Both were completely dominated by the two M.P.s—Fielden and Maxwell—who were most willing to overturn the accepted ideas of political economy to help the handloom weavers.

Most politicians seem to have been completely apathetic about

---

[1] *The agricultural and industrial magazine* (vol. II, 1835), p. 2.
[2] The report is in *PP. 1835 (341)* XIII.
[3] *Ibid.* p. 15. Fielden's draft bill was to create local boards of trade to fix a minimum wage which would be based on the average piece-rate paid by the leading manufacturers during a given period. Once it was worked out, manufacturers would be forbidden by law to pay less than the minimum.
[4] On Sadler's committee, see W. H. Hutt, 'The factory system in the early 19th century', *Economica*, VI (1926), 78–93. For the s.c. on import duties, see L. Brown, *The Board of Trade and the free-trade movement, 1830–42* (Oxford, 1958).

the whole affair, so convinced were they that parliament could do nothing in such cases. Whenever the weavers' problems were debated in the Commons the attendance was very sparse;[1] this situation also obtained at committee sittings, with the result that Maxwell and Fielden and a handful of sympathizers could easily push through their pet schemes. It was only by one vote, for example, that the 1834 committee allegedly rejected their proposal for 'a grant of one million sterling of public money for the relief of the weavers'. As the Whig *Manchester Guardian* commented, 'it is surprising that at this time of day, in the improved state of political science...such a proposition as this could receive the support even of a single individual legislator'. It dismissed the whole committee as 'a burlesque on parliamentary investigations'.[2]

More strange facts about the committee's behaviour were revealed by John Bowring during the debate in which Maxwell sought leave to bring in the bill which the 1835 committee had advocated. Bowring, who had himself been a member, claimed that the report had been the work of a small minority. Of the sixty-seven nominal members 'a very large majority never attended at all'. Only twenty-five were present at the crucial final session when the report was drawn up, and only fifteen of them— less than a quarter of the whole committee—actually voted in favour of its adoption.[3]

The inquiries of 1834-5 display very well the weaknesses of the select committee system, and go far towards explaining why, in the interests of greater accuracy and impartiality, they were followed by a royal commission on the same subject a few years later.[4] Their influence on the government or on informed public opinion was bound to be limited by the suspicion that their work had been unduly hurried—which was certainly true of the first committee. Secondly, their membership had been far too large for efficiency, with the result that the less enthusiastic members

---

[1] At a debate on popular distress, 2 April 1833, there were only twenty present (*3rd Series Hansard*, vol. 17, col. 28), and only fifty when Maxwell first proposed a select committee on 15 May 1834 (*ibid.* vol. 23, col. 1097).

[2] *Manchester Guardian*, 6 Sept. 1834.

[3] *3rd Series Hansard*, vol. 29, col. 1164.

[4] For criticisms of the select committee system, see H. M. Clokie and J. W. Robinson, *Royal commissions of inquiry* (Stanford, 1937), pp. 64-5.

had stayed away and left the zealots to do as they pleased. Thirdly, the selection of witnesses had been noticeably onesided, as was usually the case with select committees, because they were confined to Westminster, and depended for verbal evidence entirely on people summoned specially to the capital. Fielden and Maxwell took good care to call up personally those whose testimony was most likely to give weight to the wage-fixing idea.[1] They did not try to exclude potential opponents, but they took less pains to obtain them. Thus in 1835 they sent down a request for 'a Manchester manufacturer' to attend, but a manufacturers' meeting found 'considerable difficulty in appointing any gentleman, because if he were adverse to the proposed measure he would probably become exceedingly obnoxious to the operatives'.[2] As a result, little was said to either committee against the proposal for fixing wages. There is no need for us to go as far as the *Manchester Guardian* in assuming that 'some members of the committee' had wanted merely to acquire a 'cheap reputation for humanity and spurious and worthless popularity',[3] or in being 'disgusted to see time spent and public money thrown away in such enquiries so conducted as that in which the handloom weavers' committee have been engaged'.[4] But one must conclude that the select committee, instead of deciding whether or not wage fixing was feasible, tried to prove from the very beginning that it was.

In view of the patent bias behind the 1834 report and its unorthodox economic thinking, it is not surprising that, when Maxwell applied for leave to bring in a bill to establish 'boards of trade' on 28 July 1835, he was defeated by 129 votes to 41.[5] The Commons rallied to Poulett Thomson's call to 'resist this first proposition which had been made for a series of years to interfere with the rate of wages, and, by at once expressing a decided

---

[1] William Longson, a Stockport weaver, told a Manchester meeting that 'he had recently received a letter from John Fielden Esq....requesting him to hold himself in readiness to proceed to London' (*Manchester Guardian*, 28 June 1834). Another witness in 1834, John Ashworth of Newchurch-in-Rossendale, who belonged like Fielden to the Methodist Unitarian sect (a small group peculiar to the weaving villages of north-east Lancashire) was summoned to London 'probably at Fielden's suggestion' (H. McLachlan, *The Methodist Unitarian Movement* (Manchester, 1919), p. 132).
[2] *Manchester Guardian*, 4 April 1835.   [3] *Ibid.* 20 June 1835.
[4] *Ibid.* 11 July 1835.   [5] The debate is in *3rd Series Hansard*, vol. 29.

opinion against it, to put an end to all such attempts in future'.[1] Among the 41 who thought that in this case accepted economic doctrines could be brushed aside, obscure Tories bulked large. Such Whigs as followed Maxwell were chiefly representatives of manufacturing towns where handloom weavers constituted a problem. An attempt to introduce the bill a second time on 12 July 1836 suffered a similar defeat.

V

The efforts of Fielden and Maxwell and their few supporters to use the committee system to help the weavers had failed. The only remaining hope of parliamentary action lay, therefore, in a second inquiry whose findings and recommendations would carry greater weight by being less obviously biased. In other words it meant admitting what the *Manchester Guardian* in 1834 had called 'the desirability of confiding the business rather to a [royal] commission than to a committee of the House of Commons'[2]. Accordingly, on 4 July 1837, John Maxwell moved that 'an humble address be presented to her Majesty praying her to issue a commission of inquiry into the condition of the unemployed handloom weavers, with instructions to report whether any and what measures could be devised for their relief'. Whereas in 1834 the weavers' case had been somewhat weakened by their relative prosperity, in 1837 they were experiencing large-scale unemployment; and it was perhaps for this reason that a thinly-attended House agreed to Maxwell's motion on a fairly close division of 53 to 45.[3]

The royal commission set about its work far more thoroughly, and with a more obvious detachment, than the select committees of the early 1830s had done. The four commissioners were respected men of proven impartiality and unquestioned economic orthodoxy: Nassau Senior, the country's leading economist; Samuel Jones Loyd, a prominent banker; William Edward Hickson, philanthropist and enthusiast for popular education; and John Leslie. Unlike the select committees, they were under no obligation to rush their work, and it was not until February 1841 that

---

[1] *3rd Series Hansard,* vol. 29, col. 1160.
[2] *Manchester Guardian,* 6 Sept. 1834.
[3] The debate is in *3rd Series Hansard,* vol. 38.

their final report was published.[1] Nor was their evidence restricted by the need to rely on a small number of selected witnesses summoned to London. The material which they examined and published, and on which they based their final recommendations, had been carefully gathered over the three intervening years by assistant commissioners who had spent a considerable time in each of the major weaving districts.

The instructions from the central board upon which these assistants acted were very thorough indeed.[2] They were told to distinguish between weavers on different fabrics and qualities of cloth. In gathering material on wages they were to be sure that it referred to full-time weavers, that careful deductions had been made for working expenses, and that the information covered a period of at least two years, 'that being the shortest time that will afford average results'. The weavers' moral and intellectual condition was to be treated as a separate issue. The causes of distress were to be divided into those over which the weavers had no control and those which might have resulted from their sins of omission or commission. Finally, the assistants were to examine all the stock remedies, such as wage fixing, and to look critically at any new proposals.

It is small wonder that with such a precise plan of action the royal commission produced several volumes of detailed but carefully arranged evidence, and a very judicious final report. The material on the Lancashire cotton weavers was collected by Richard Muggeridge in the spring and early summer of 1838. His method of proceeding was to give advance notice that he was about to visit some particular town, and to invite weavers, manufacturers, and other interested parties to prepare written or oral evidence to be submitted to him. The actual visit took the form of a public meeting, with spectators and reporters present; anyone might come forward and submit his testimony. The hearings were usually conducted in an atmosphere of informality and good humour,[3] and J. R. Stephen's fears that the weavers would be

---

[1] PP. 1841 (296) x.

[2] They are printed in full in *Manchester Guardian*, 28 Feb. 1838.

[3] See, for example, the reports in *Preston Observer*, 2 June 1838, and *Carlisle Journal*, 23 June 1838.

reluctant to tell the whole sad truth about their position to a prying commissioner[1] do not seem to have been justified. There was none of the boycotting which had accompanied the 1833 factory commission.[2]

On the other hand, there was a marked difference between Muggeridge's reception in the country areas, where handloom weavers were still numerous and their problems pressing, and in the factory towns, where they were few, unimportant, and largely apathetic. In the former, the commissioner's visit was an event which might affect for good or ill the future of an entire community. The public sessions in the small villages around Burnley attracted very large audiences—over three hundred at Padiham, and almost as many at the hamlet of Haggate.[3] By contrast, at Preston Muggeridge's audience was only a hundred and eighty;[4] at Manchester the few remaining weavers were upbraided by Samuel Bamford for having prepared no evidence for the commissioner's visit;[5] whilst at Blackburn 'there was great apathy among the weavers', and 'they appeared to take no interest in the business'.[6] It is significant that the greatest interest in the commission's work was to be found in those very villages where Chartism was currently attracting most support among weavers.[7] By the late 1830s, the zeal and energy of the countrymen was in marked contrast to the general apathy of the urban weavers.

It was, of course, very much a foregone conclusion that a royal commission with such orthodox members as Nassau Senior and Jones Loyd would feel unable to recommend any of the weavers' favourite remedies. The Whig *Preston Chronicle* had remarked just before Muggeridge's visit that 'there seems no prospect whatever of any important practical good resulting from the commission'.[8] Yet its report was one of the most intelligent analyses of the problems which the industrial revolution had raised, and of the very limited weapons with which parliament could meet them, given the prevailing climate of economic thinking and the

---

[1] *Northern Star*, 23 June 1838.
[2] C. Driver, *Tory radical: the life of Richard Oastler* (Oxford, 1946), pp. 222–36.
[3] *Blackburn Standard*, 11 April 1838.   [4] *Preston Observer*, 2 June 1838.
[5] *Manchester Guardian*, 7 April 1838.   [6] *Blackburn Standard*, 1 Aug. 1838.
[7] See below, pp. 225–8.   [8] *Preston Chronicle*, 14 April 1838.

inadequacy of the administrative machinery to hand. It recognized that the principal cause of the weavers' long-term decline was that the supply of labour was not geared to the fluctuating demands of the textile industries.[1] The only way to improve the situation was to steady the demand and reduce the supply.

In the short run, there was little the government could do to achieve either of these ends. In order to put British overseas trade on a firmer basis and to reduce the cost of living at home, the commission strongly recommended the repeal of the Corn Laws and other radical alterations in the tariff—such as a reduction in the duties on imported raw materials used in the building trade and on the semi-luxury articles in general consumption.[2] But in the long run, the commission's only answer lay in pleading the cause of popular education, on the same grounds as J. R. McCulloch, who had argued in the 1820s that 'the poor ought to be taught that they are in a great measure the architects of their future...We ought to endeavour to make them acquainted with the principles that must determine their condition in life.'[3] A public system of education would enable groups like the handloom weavers to realize for themselves in good time when their livelihood was being threatened. 'We cannot close our labours', their report concluded, 'without expressing our regret that in the matter of education the government of this country owes a duty to its people which it has not performed.'[4] When one considers the sectarian squabbles and the attitude of many prominent Tories towards popular education at this time, the neglect of successive governments is not surprising: Lord Londonderry, after all, extolled 'the superior advantages of a practical education in collieries to a reading education';[5] Lord Lowther maintained that 'over-education produces the greatest mass of floating discontent that pervades this country and France';[6] and even Lord Shaftesbury, fearful that national education would not be sufficiently moral and

---

[1] *PP. 1841 (296)* x, p. 326.   [2] *Ibid.* pp. 346–7 and 354.

[3] J. R. McCulloch, 'The rise, progress, present state and prospects of the British cotton manufacture', *Edinburgh Review*, XLVI (1827), 38.

[4] *PP. 1841 (296)* x, p. 399.

[5] J. L. and B. Hammond, *Lord Shaftesbury* (4th edn, London, 1936), p. 78.

[6] A. Aspinall, *Politics and the press* (London, 1949), p. 12.

evangelical, once expressed the view that 'idleness is ten times more dangerous than ignorance'.[1] Yet the commissioners were clearly right. In a society ruled by *laissez-faire* principles, man can only be the judge of his own best interests if he has sufficient knowledge on which to base his decisions. A national system of education to train the people to live wisely in a free society was not the least valuable of the suggestions of the royal commission on the handloom weavers.[2]

By the time the final report appeared in 1841, the cotton weavers' problems were of rapidly diminishing importance. In the last few years before its publication, John Fielden made a final vain attempt to secure some relief for the weavers by advocating a change of emphasis in fiscal policy from indirect taxation which fell on the working man to a direct tax on property—a move which Peel made when he reintroduced income tax in 1842.[3] After the royal commission, however, the cotton weavers' problems ceased to be raised in parliament because, with the prosperity and the expansion of factory employment in 1843-5, their numbers dwindled.[4] Like the Midland framework knitters, the handloom weavers lost their place in society without the legislature having done anything to help them keep it. It remains to consider whether any of the remedies for which they had sought support would have been either practicable or effective.

THE REMEDIES PROPOSED

The most frequently canvassed scheme for relieving their misery, and the one most persistently favoured by the cotton handloom weavers themselves, was wage regulation. They hoped that parliament would legislate to prevent unscrupulous manufacturers from paying lower rates than the more generous employers were able to offer. The weavers regarded this 'cut-throat competition' among their many masters as the main cause of continued wage

[1] Hammonds, *op. cit.* p. 236.
[2] It is interesting to note how many of the commission's ideas Peel attempted, whether consciously or not, to implement during his ministry of 1841-6.
[3] *3rd Series Hansard*, vol. 39, col. 1406; vol. 49, cols. 236 and 1256.
[4] See above, p. 90 and below, pp. 267-8.

reductions, and it has already been shown that piece-rates did, in fact, vary between manufacturers within the same town, as well as between different weaving districts.[1] It is clear, too, that there were times when contracting markets led to intense competition, in which the poorer masters with large stocks on hand could avoid bankruptcy only by undercutting their rivals, lowering their prices, and paying their weavers less—moves which the other manufacturers usually had to follow.

Furthermore, as the weavers were a numerous, widely scattered, and heterogeneous body, they found large-scale industrial bargaining with their employers extremely difficult.[2] They needed the help of parliament to compensate for their own weaknesses. A statutory minimum wage below which no manufacturer might go would 'take the power of fixing the rate of wages out of the hands of those who were disposed to grind down the labourer to the last extreme and place it in the hands of respectable and opulent manufacturers'.[3] The intention was never that parliament itself should lay down a list of piece-rates, or even that this duty should fall on the local justices; the weavers' object was simply to create machinery by which a wage-list could be negotiated between masters and men according to the state of the trade. Once such a list had been agreed, a manufacturer would be legally forbidden to pay, or a weaver to accept, a lower rate.

Is it true, as Mr E. P. Thompson has recently claimed,[4] that it was no more outlandish or impracticable to ask parliament to sanction a scheme on these lines than it was to seek a legal restriction of factory hours? Would any of the proposals for a 'minimum wage' actually have worked? The earliest project of 1808 was justified by those manufacturers who supported it on the grounds, first, that it would prevent the weavers from starving, and second, that if they were adequately paid, there would be no need for them to overwork, and no danger of their overproducing.[5]

Just how these two desirable ends were to be achieved was not

---

[1] See above, pp. 97–8.   [2] See below, pp. 177–8.

[3] Speech of Mr Gillon in the debate on Maxwell's motion to relieve the weavers, 28 July 1835 (3rd Series Hansard, vol. 29, col. 1161).

[4] E. P. Thompson, The making of the English working class (London, 1963), pp. 299–300.

[5] PP. 1808 (177) II, p. 106. Evidence of T. Ainsworth, a Bolton manufacturer.

made very clear in 1808, and the vagueness and indecision help perhaps to explain why parliament had so little trouble in rejecting the proposal. The weavers seem to have wanted a uniform wage list for all England, to be negotiated by masters and men, and enforced by law. In order not to prejudice their case, they were at pains to point out that the minimum must be a 'moderate' one— in other words not so high as to encourage complacency and sloth among weavers, nor, as one perceptive witness put it, to 'encourage the trade being carried on by machineries [*sic*] in factories'.[1] But the witnesses were uncertain as to whether the scheme's success depended on the minimum being enforced in Scotland and Ireland too—John Honeyford claiming that it was unnecessary to apply it outside England, whilst Jeremiah Bury regarded this as very desirable.[2]

Confusion of this kind gave the scheme's opponents—prominent among them being the same Manchester manufacturers who had objected so strongly to the Arbitration Act of 1800[3]— ammunition with which to attack it. When G. H. Rose, for the government, made his half-hearted gesture of bringing in a minimum wage bill in May 1808, he framed it to apply only in those towns which had specifically petitioned for it.[4] This was far from what the weavers themselves expected, and its weakness could easily be demonstrated by alleging that, as in the case of the Spitalfields Acts in the silk industry, the only effect would be for the industry to remove itself to areas where the regulations did not apply.[5] Nor was the ineffectiveness of a minimum which operated only partially the sole argument used against the weavers in 1808. Davies Giddy, M.P., argued, very plausibly, that the weavers' troubles arose 'not from the wages being too low, but because at one time they had been too high, a circumstance which induced more people to adopt this trade than there was a demand for, or than it could support'.[6] A minimum wage, he argued,

---

[1] *PP. 1808 (177)* II, p. 100.   [2] *Ibid.* pp. 122 and 98.
[3] See, for example, *Manchester Mercury*, 17 March 1807.
[4] *1st Series Hansard*, vol. 11, col. 425. See above, p. 154.
[5] Sir Robert Peel, senior, justified his opposition on these grounds in an open letter in *Manchester Mercury*, 7 June 1808.
[6] *1st Series Hansard*, vol. 11, col. 426.

would encourage the overstocking of the trade to continue. All these factors could only serve to strengthen the conviction of most M.P.s that there was no case here for departing from the principles of *laissez-faire*.

A statutory minimum wage having been refused, a voluntary one could always be attempted. But it is unlikely that any beneficial effects resulted from various spontaneous efforts on the part of the more generous manufacturers to prevent needless wage reductions. On several occasions between 1815 and the early 1830s, leading employers in different parts of the weaving area agreed on a wage list, and urged weavers who were offered less than the list to leave their employers and seek work from a manufacturer who promised to adhere to the list. A proposal on these lines was made by the leading masters in north-east Lancashire in 1819,[1] a similar one at Preston ten years later,[2] and the existence of some sort of agreed list at Paisley was confirmed by several witnesses at the select committees of the early 1830s.[3]

One particularly interesting scheme was suggested during the slump of 1826.[4] Its prime mover was John Fielden, and the occasion marked probably his first appearance as a public figure and his first effort to help the handloom weavers. The manufacturers, who met at Burnley on 14 April 1826, promised the local overseers of the poor that they would pay a certain minimum wage, provided that the townships would support any weaver unable temporarily to get work at the minimum rate. The scheme never came into effect, because within two weeks of the manufacturers' meeting the weavers had taken their own initiative and destroyed the powerlooms in north-east Lancashire, thereby alienating their employers.[5] The Hammonds doubted very much whether the proposal would have commended itself to the Poor Law authorities, who would have found it impossible to support a large number of men, virtually on strike for higher wages, for very long.[6] As the scheme was devised near the beginning of

[1] J. L. and B. Hammond, *The skilled labourer* (London, 1919), pp. 121-6.
[2] *Blackburn Mail*, 1 July 1829.
[3] *PP. 1833 (690)* VI, Q. 11317; *PP. 1834 (556)* X, QQ. 727 and 929.
[4] Hammonds, *op cit., loc. cit.*   [5] See below, pp. 199-203.
[6] Hammonds, *op. cit.* p. 126.

what proved to be a protracted and severe depression, it seems certain that in the long run it must have broken down for this reason. Initially, however, it probably stood a reasonable chance of being accepted. The authorities of Marsden [modern Nelson], for example, resolved to pay relief only to those weavers who could not get work because they demanded the minimum.[1]

The confusion which had been apparent in 1808 in working out a legal minimum wage was again evident in the early 1830s. The more naïve proposals to the select committees of 1834–5, such as that of Richard Needham, the veteran Bolton weaver, assumed that it was possible to take the average of the piece-rate for any particular type of cloth over the whole country, and make that average the national minimum.[2] John Fielden's own proposals, prepared in the form of a draft Act of parliament, were more subtle, however; they marked the most serious attempt to establish a practicable scheme of wage regulation.[3] Instead of a uniform national average, Fielden wanted a minimum which differed from place to place. Within each parish, the average would be taken of the rates paid by the largest manufacturers, and this average would then become the minimum for the parish.[4]

Although this scheme avoided the obvious pitfalls of a uniform national minimum—a country manufacturer with additional transport costs would hardly be able to pay as much as an urban employer—it was not without its own drawbacks. From a purely administrative viewpoint, its operation would initially be very complex. For both a national and a local average, detailed schedules would have to be sent out to all manufacturers to obtain the necessary statistics, and then collected and worked out. The whole process would be lengthy, and by the time the average had been reached, the state of the trade might have changed considerably from what it was when the figures were given in. There was also the possibility that some manufacturers might make false returns.

But there were more fundamental difficulties. In the first place, even if the administrative problems could be disregarded, a minimum wage scheme at a time when handloom weavers were com-

[1] W. Bennett, *History of Marsden and Nelson* (Nelson, 1957), p. 164.
[2] *PP. 1834 (556)* x, Q. 5439.   [3] See above, p. 161.
[4] *PP. 1834 (556)* x, pp. 630–1.

peting, directly or indirectly, with the powerloom was a very different matter from such a scheme in the old days when the powerloom's role was negligible; and the Fielden scheme took no account of the fact that, even when competition was indirect, the labour costs which a handloom manufacturer could afford to incur would be heavily influenced by the costs of powerloom production. If the latter fell, as they were likely to do with increasing technical efficiency, the handloom manufacturer could not have gone on paying the old minimum.

Secondly, the Fielden plan was unsound because it took no account of the likelihood of an industrial depression. Its basic assumption was that after the first average had been taken, the weavers' wages could never again fall—they could only rise. But as John Bowring pointed out,[1] such a situation could not continue if there was unemployment. During a slump, the alternatives facing a manufacturer would be either to give out work at less than the minimum, or to cease giving out work at all; whereas the weaver would have to decide whether he would accept work at the lower rate, or resort to the Poor Law. Both were likely to take the former rather than the latter course. Furthermore, a system of minima which differed from parish to parish would substitute for the rivalry of individuals 'the competition of district against district'.[2] The Fielden plan, in short, failed to take account either of the supply and demand situation for weavers, or of the very variable markets with which the cotton industry had to deal.

It is difficult to avoid the conclusion that the amount of government interference required to secure effective wage regulation would have been many times greater than that needed to prevent young people and women from working more than ten hours a day in textile factories. And as Clapham said long ago about the Spitalfields Acts which had attempted to fix wages for silk-weaving, 'You could not have one locality, or even one whole industry, controlled in this way, and all others left to free and open competition'.[3] Once the principle of legislative control had been accepted, the regulation of factory conditions in the early

---

[1] *3rd Series Hansard*, vol. 29, col. 1173.   [2] *Ibid.* col. 1172.
[3] J. H. Clapham, 'The Spitalfields Acts, 1773–1824', *Economic Journal*, XXVI (1916), 471.

nineteenth century was a problem of manageable proportions: the appointment of a handful of inspectors with simple and specific duties was the answer. But to ensure that handloom weavers received an adequate remuneration would have necessitated government activity on a scale which contemporaries understandably regarded as not only undesirable, but unworkable: for the productive capacity of the industry would have to be regulated both by restricting entry to the trade and by controlling the introduction of new machinery, whilst its markets—many of them overseas—would have to be static and unchanging. Both these tasks would have overwhelmed the feeble administrative resources currently available, and in any case, by this late stage, the effort would hardly have been worthwhile.

Ineffective as the wage-fixing schemes were likely to have been, they were at least positive proposals to help the handloom weavers maintain their position. Most of the rival projects, on the other hand, were largely negative. The most obviously negative was the suggestion that the problem could be swept aside if the state were to help the 'surplus' weaving population to emigrate.[1] Except on special occasions and in particular places, this scheme was unlikely to be very acceptable, first, because the weavers themselves usually took the Oastlerite view that 'every man born in England has a right to live well in England',[2] and, secondly, because a government believing in *laissez-faire* would neither force people to do what they didn't want to, nor help them to do what they had voluntarily decided to do for themselves. Apart from this basic disinclination on both sides, the huge cost and vast organization required to move the number of weavers who seemed 'surplus' in the 1826 slump told against it. It was in any case

[1] See above, p. 157. In the 1830s, the possibilities of emigration were again canvassed by the economist G. P. Scrope, M.P., in *Political economy versus the handloom weavers* (Bradford, 1835), pp. 5–6.

[2] This was, for example, the attitude of the Bradford woollen weavers, as they showed in their public debate (in which Oastler assisted them) with Scrope (*ibid.* pp. 15–16). In the depression of 1819, whereas the Carlisle weavers voted 'to petition the Regent to send them all to America' (*Manchester Mercury*, 18 May 1819), the Glasgow weavers a few weeks later rejected emigration and instead demanded annual parliaments and universal suffrage (*ibid.* 29 June 1819). The surviving handloom weavers in Manchester around 1840 again turned to the possibility of assisted emigration (*Manchester Guardian*, 23 Sept. 1840 and 14 Aug. 1841).

misleading to think of the cotton weavers after 1826 as 'surplus' in the sense of being permanently unemployed. They were merely unfortunate in that they lived in an age which had little experience of cyclical industrial unemployment, and even less of rapid technological progress.

Other proposals involving parliamentary intervention were never taken seriously. A tax on powerlooms was occasionally suggested by the cotton weavers—for example in 1811 and 1823[1] —and again in the early 1830s by the Yorkshire woollen weavers.[2] By this stage, however, the latter saw that their best chance of limiting the use of machinery lay rather in giving support to the Ten-hours movement among the factory workers.[3] The cotton weavers, however, do not appear to have been associated with the short-time movement in the 1830s, nor did they seriously suggest taxing powerlooms again. Perhaps they realized that the powerloom was an aggravation, not a prime cause, of their condition, and that a tax on machinery alone would do little to steady the disproportionate relationship between the inflexible supply of weavers and the all-too-flexible demand for their labour.

The only real answer to this basic dilemma was clear enough, and it was not one which any government of the early nineteenth century—or, indeed, of many years later—could give. Supply and demand could be made to agree only if there was an absolute limitation on the numbers of workers, whether hand or power, in the industry, and if the markets for cotton goods could be guaranteed and unvarying. In the circumstances of the early nineteenth century, these problems could be solved only by the cumulative effect of countless individual decisions by weavers and entrepreneurs, each judging where his own best interests lay. As the 1841 royal commission suggested, the most that could reasonably be done at the time was for the people to be educated so as to judge their interests wisely, and for the government to do its utmost, by its fiscal and commercial policy, not to lose markets, even though it could not actually create and guarantee them.

---

[1] PP. 1810/11 (232) II, p. 395; *Manchester Mercury*, 3 June 1823.   [2] Scrope, *op. cit.* p. 9.
[3] *Ibid.* p. 17, and J. T. Ward, *The factory movement* (London, 1962), p. 125. Peter Gaskell also thought that factory regulation would help the handloom weavers (*Artisans and Machinery* (London, 1836), p. 45).

CHAPTER 8

ORGANIZED INDUSTRIAL ACTION AMONG THE COTTON HANDLOOM WEAVERS

IN common with other workers in industries organized on a capitalist, private-enterprize basis, the cotton handloom weavers' most immediate and direct method of putting pressure on their employers lay in some form of 'industrial' action.[1] A combination of workmen, using the ultimate sanction of a strike, is the 'normal' retaliation against any threatened deterioration in the conditions of work or fall in wages, regardless of whether or not the employers seem directly responsible for it. At a time when parliament was slow to act, and when political reform offered only a vague panacea, the most obvious response to some sudden challenge was prompt local action against those masters whose decision to lower wages had thrown down the challenge in the first instance.

As the handloom weavers suffered many wage reductions, one might expect them to have turned frequently to industrial action in their efforts to halt the decline. Yet it was a matter of general comment among contemporaries that they seldom did so. The docility of the cotton weavers was often contrasted with the violence of the factory spinners, who in the 1820s and 1830s were usually regarded as the most ardent of trade unionists. Thus the Tory *Blackburn Standard* could claim in 1838 that 'for many years a strike or combination amongst the handloom weavers has been

---

[1] The story of trade unionism among the cotton handloom weavers has been well told by a number of eminent historians, in particular by J. L. and B. Hammond in *The skilled labourer* (London, 1919), and by H. A. Turner in *Trade union growth, structure, and policy* (London, 1962). The main source of information in detail is the Home Office Papers in the Public Record Office, and it is fortunate that the most important documents from this quarter were published in A. Aspinall, *The early English trade unions* (London, 1949). For further details of the narrative of events, the curious reader is referred to these authorities.

totally unknown. Those pernicious and dangerous conspiracies are chiefly promoted by the most designing and disreputable of that large body of persons who work in factories—who are better paid and have less reason to violate the law and injure their employers. The handloom weavers', it concluded 'cannot in justice be charged with leaguing against capital...'[1] Far from there being a permanent division of interest or lack of contact between worker and employer, as was allegedly the case in the cotton factories, industrial relations in handloom weaving were often cordial. In that same year, 1838, for example, a Bolton firm, R. and J. Magnall, celebrated Queen Victoria's coronation by providing a feast for their weavers.[2] The fact that the weavers had never had an effective union against their masters was indeed cited by many contemporaries as the direct cause of their long sufferings.

A brief reflection will show why the handloom weavers should have played an insignificant part in the development of modern trade unionism. Like every other trade before 1824, they were hampered by the Combination Laws. And after the 1826 slump, they were largely unable to take advantage of the recent, if still limited, legality of unions because of their habitual poverty, and because their problems were different in kind from what they had been before 1820 once the powerloom had come into widespread use. After they had become only a marginal element in the productive process and were liable to be often unemployed or underemployed, they could do little to inconvenience their masters by witholding their labour, and their earnings were too low to support a large union fund or to allow them to indulge in the luxury of a voluntary cessation of labour.

Even before the coming of the powerloom, however, there had been factors inherent in the structure of the industry which had acted as a strong bar to effective unionism. Indeed, it is highly surprising that strikes on the scale of 1808 and 1818 took place at all. One factor was that the old handloom manufacturer could not easily be subjected to industrial pressure: unlike a factory owner who had capital sunk in buildings and machinery, he suffered no

---

[1] *Blackburn Standard*, 28 Feb. 1838.   [2] *Bolton Free Press*, 7 June 1838.

loss when these buildings and machines stood idle.[1] The second was the great size, wide distribution, and varied composition of the labour force in cotton weaving: as a Scottish weaver put it in 1834, 'we being scattered over the whole face of the country cannot communicate with each other, and we are easily routed by our masters'.[2] Under such conditions, a unanimous, spontaneous, and simultaneous strike was almost unobtainable.

The weakness of the handloom weavers in effective industrial action is revealed in the attitude of other groups of workers to the weavers and their problems. The other trades, seeing the weavers' misery, regarded a combination amongst themselves as the only means of avoiding the handloom weavers' fate. The woollen weavers of Rochdale, for example, observed during the slump of 1826 that 'if we cannot maintain this [weaving] price [by a combination], we can clearly foresee that our wages will be brought down in the same way that the calico weavers' have been, and it will be found that the employed will be in no better condition than the unemployed'.[3] In 1834, a Stockport witness also told the select committee that 'the awful example' of the handloom weavers had stimulated the formation of unions among other workers.[4]

Unions in other trades were also accused of maintaining a 'closed shop' at the expense of the handloom weavers, whom they prevented from finding alternative employment. Archibald Alison, sheriff of Lanarkshire, told the 1838 select committee on combinations of workmen that 'the distress of the handloom weavers is mainly and almost entirely to be ascribed to the exclusive monopoly established by the forcible conduct of the trades in all other lines, which prevent their [the weavers'] sons getting into any other line'.[5] This may well have been true at Glasgow in the 1830s, where the cotton spinners' union was particularly active

---

[1] PP. *1834* (*556*) x, Q. 2645. It is significant that the biggest handloom weavers' strikes after 1826 were among those who worked in sheds on looms provided by their employers, and whose position was thus very similar to that of factory workers (see below, p. 184).

[2] PP. *1834* (*556*) x, Q. 991. The chronology of the strikes of 1808 and 1818, which began in Manchester and then spread slowly over the weaving area, illustrates the difficulties of achieving concerted action.

[3] Printed enclosure, dated 29 May 1826, in *HO. 40. 19*.

[4] PP. *1834* (*556*) x, Q. 7260   [5] PP. *1837/8* (*488*) VIII, Q. 2116.

and violent. But it is important to remember the other side of the story. The other trades, especially the factory workers, were ill-disposed towards the handloom weavers because the latter were on several occasions used as strike-breakers by factory owners who saw them as a valuable reserve of blackleg labour.

During the great spinners' strike at Ashton in 1829, numbers of handloom weavers from the Burnley and Colne district came into south Lancashire to take the jobs of those on strike;[1] and in 1831, the weavers of the same area, faced with a turn-out of calico block-printers, whose idleness might lead to stagnation throughout the cotton industry, 'volunteered to assist the masters in keeping the peace and protecting all such of the blockprinters as may be disposed to free themselves from the controul of the Club and return to their employment'.[2] Clearly, after 1826, the cotton weavers, unable to manage an effective union of their own, had little notion of 'working-class solidarity', or of the necessity for a general 'union of trades'. Thus it is not surprising that even a personal visit from John Doherty, the great spinners' leader, could not persuade the handloom weavers of Bolton to join his 'general union' in 1829–30.[3]

The public sympathy which the weavers often won during their attempts at industrial action further demonstrates their basic weakness. Whereas the spinners' strikes were usually regarded as aggressive and selfish acts by men already enjoying relative prosperity, it was generally recognized that the handloom weavers were stirred into action only when their conditions had deteriorated very markedly. Local magistrates frequently complimented the weavers on their decent and orderly conduct in times of adversity: Mr Marriott of Prestwich told the Home Office in August 1818 that he could 'with truth say that I found them extremely well behaved, and always thankful for a very moderate pittance of parochial relief'.[4] Thus when the weavers did turn out, their case was usually regarded as a legitimate one, which the employers ought to do their best to satisfy. James Norris of Manchester

---

[1] *Manchester Guardian*, 18 April 1829.   [2] *Manchester Guardian*, 27 Aug. 1831.
[3] *Ibid.* 4 Dec. 1829 and 2 Jan. 1830.
[4] W. Marriott to H. Hobhouse, 17 Aug. 1818 (*HO. 42. 179*).

claimed in 1818 that 'the public feeling is certainly in favour of the men—they are the most suffering class',[1] and the Rev. W. R. Hay mentioned 'a general acknowledgement that their masters might raise their wages considerably with their own profits'.[2] Similarly, during the Scottish strike of 1812, it was reported that 'the landed interest take their [the weavers'] part, and have given them employment in agriculture, to which they resort with pleasure and activity'.[3] In view of this widespread sympathy, it is small wonder that in 1818 the weavers of Manchester felt able to request public subscriptions to their funds,[4] or that in 1825 a correspondent of the *Manchester Mercury* could seriously suggest that wealthy individuals and employers should actually subsidize the weavers' union, so as to enable them to organize strikes against the low-paying masters.[5]

Another indication of the basic weakness of combinations among the handloom weavers is the fact that, when not seeking legislative assistance or toying with political radicalism, they were often obliged to adopt extraordinary and strictly 'non-industrial' methods of voicing their dissatisfaction in an immediate local context. These outlets, frequently characterized by pointless physical violence, were a throwback to the disorganized activities of a pre-industrial age, and not a forerunner of modern collective bargaining.

Of these 'old-fashioned' modes of action, the smashing of powerlooms was undoubtedly the most spectacular.[6] But there were others. The deliberate withholding of rent was practised by some Bolton weavers in 1826.[7] Riots or 'strikes' were also directed against shopkeepers who were alleged to be offending against the old notion of a 'just price'. In the depression of 1829, weavers at Bolton, Wigan, and Preston organized 'food strikes' and agreed not to buy milk and butter until their price fell. At Bolton,

---

[1] J. Norris to Lord Sidmouth, 2 Aug. 1818 (*HO. 42. 179*).
[2] W. R. Hay to H. Hobhouse, 9 Aug. 1818 (*ibid.*)
[3] A. Aspinall, *The early English trade unions* (London, 1949), p. 147.
[4] See below, p. 196, n. 1.
[5] *Manchester Mercury*, 14 June 1825. Sympathy was, of course, also shown by those generous manufacturers who made various voluntary attempts to fix wage rates for the benefit of their weavers (see above, pp. 171–2).
[6] See below, pp. 197–204.   [7] *PP. 1834 (556)* x, QQ. 4987 and 4989.

unrepentant shopkeepers had their windows broken, and in the butter market 'all who made purchases were assailed with hooting and hisses'.[1] At Manchester in 1837 and Wigan in 1842, handloom weavers unemployed during the depression went round the streets in large parties calling on, and allegedly intimidating, house-holders with demands for charity.[2] Such pathetic demonstrations were the admission of weakness by men in the last extremes of demoralization and incapable of pursuing a course of industrial bargaining with their employers. This aimless, despairing, desul-tory violence of the last years of handloom weaving was epito-mized in such events as the riot at Colne in June 1837, when a crowd of unemployed weavers attacked a few of their fellows who had had the good fortune to obtain a little work. As the *Manchester Guardian* said, 'it seems as if the jealousy of the unemployed, sharpened by hunger, could not bear that there should be anything but a "fellowship of grief", and no exception'.[3]

II

Nonetheless, in spite of the huge natural obstacles to trade unions in handloom weaving, they did exist, and they did act, throughout the period of the industrial revolution, especially in the years before the powerloom had fatally weakened the weavers' position as an element in economic organization and their capacity to bargain with their employers. What form did these unions take, how many workers did they include, and was their existence con-tinuous or intermittent? These are the problems which need to be considered before a narrative of the great weavers' strikes can be given.

The 'natural' character of the associations among handloom weavers has recently been well described by Professor Turner, who claims that they 'probably had their roots, quite simply, in the regular social meetings of men working at the same trade in the same place'.[4] For, although the hand weaving process was

[1] *Manchester Guardian*, 13 June 1829. The 'food strike' went on into July.
[2] *Ibid.* 19 April and 15 July 1837; 23 April 1842.
[3] *Manchester Guardian*, 28 June 1837. See also *pp. 1840* (220) XXIV, pp. 627–8.
[4] H. A. Turner, *Trade union growth, structure, and policy* (London, 1962), p. 79.

carried on in some degree of isolation, the opportunities for the weavers meeting together—on 'bearing-home day' or in the village inn of an evening—were frequent. From the convivial meeting it was but a short step to the development of the 'friendly society', a form of organization particularly widespread at the end of the eighteenth century, after the legislation of 1793–5.[1] By 1801 there were more than 800 of them in Lancashire, and handloom weavers were prominent among their members.[2]

Friendly societies were not nominally organizations through which workmen in a particular trade could negotiate with their masters—such organizations were in any case illegal before 1824. Nevertheless they did not always restrict themselves to providing sick and funeral benefits for their members. In 1800, for example, the societies of Manchester formed a union with objectives similar to those of a more modern co-operative society—buying in the wholesale market and retailing at lower-than-usual prices to the members of the society.[3] Of more particular interest to the cotton weavers were the friendly societies' funds, on which they drew for strike pay both in 1808 and in 1818.[4] The part played by the societies in aiding the handloom weavers was regarded with grave suspicion by local magistrates, and in 1813 the leading Manchester justice, the Rev. W. R. Hay, submitted to the Home Office the draft of a bill whose object was 'to prevent the friendly societies from being perverted to purposes of public mischief'.[5]

The local friendly society and its 'box' provided one strand in the development of weavers' unions. The second stimulus came from the long existence of 'shop unions' among the weavers on specialized products who usually worked together in small workshops. The unions among the Manchester small-ware and check weavers of the mid-eighteenth century, with their twofold tradition of maintaining restrictions on the numbers in the trade, and of providing for the 'tramping journeyman', have been excellently described by A. P. Wadsworth.[6]

---

[1] Turner, *op. cit.* p. 80.   [2] Aspinall, *op. cit.* p. 214.
[3] *Manchester Mercury*, 30 Sept. and 14 Dec. 1800.
[4] Aspinall, *op. cit.* pp. 102 and 300.   [5] *Ibid.* pp. 156–8.
[6] A. P. Wadsworth and J. de L. Mann, *The cotton trade and industrial Lancashire* (Manchester, 1931), pp. 340 *et seq.*

Professor Turner suggests that the 'shop union' tradition among the skilled workers provided the same stimulus for town weavers to unite as did the friendly societies in the country villages.[1] And although this is perhaps an oversimplification, it remains true that the strength of these two basic influences is reflected in the history of the handloom weavers' unions throughout the industrial revolution. For these unions appear to have been of three kinds: the small, specialized unions of skilled weavers on finer fabrics, who often worked in large workshops; combinations which attempted to embrace all weavers within a limited locality; and finally, general unions aiming at concerted action throughout the whole weaving area. Unions in 'skilled lines', which were based on the old 'workshop' tradition, and in particular towns, which probably owed more to the friendly society influence, were much the more important; and they proved both more effective in action, and more persistent in attempting a continuous existence, than did the general combinations.

Skilled workers in specialized trades are traditionally the first people to form unions to protect their interests against the employers. Their very skill both limits their numbers and makes them indispensable to their masters—two factors which render industrial action both simple and effective. Not surprisingly, therefore, small unions of skilled weavers were in existence from the very beginning of the modern cotton industry in the mid-eighteenth century. The small-ware weavers of Manchester were prominent among the groups which organized well and early, and references to their union's activities can be found from the 1750s until at least the 1830s.[2] Their objectives were those of a traditional skilled trade, seeking to limit their own numbers; their rules of 1815 provided that no widow of a weaver should marry out of the trade, and severely restricted the number of apprentices to be allowed to masters who had not themselves served a formal apprenticeship.[3] To achieve these ends, the small-ware weavers of Manchester organized strikes in 1781[4] and 1817[5], and they were still an

[1] Turner, op. cit. p. 80.
[2] For their early history, see Wadsworth, op. cit. loc. cit.
[3] Manchester Mercury, 11 March 1817.
[4] Ibid. 7 Aug. and 18 Sept. 1781.   [5] Ibid. 11 March 1817.

apparently flourishing association in 1834, when they were represented at a great meeting of the Manchester unions which
discussed the fate of the Dorsetshire labourers.[1]

Another well-organized group in Manchester were the gingham
and shirting weavers, largely Irish, who worked in handloom
sheds. They were particularly active around 1830, when several
violent strikes took place. Weavers would march to a shed where
the employer was alleged to have lowered his wages, and would
force the weavers there to turn out.[2] Perhaps the most serious
outbreak, which also spread to Ashton, was in the early months
of 1832,[3] and coincided with the ferment which accompanied the
passing of the great Reform Act; the magistrates do not, however,
seem to have connected it with the political movements. The
trouble arose because one gingham manufacturer, James Orrell,
had not only lowered his piece-rates by 10 per cent, but 'had even
given out work without naming the price at which it was to be
paid, and reserving to himself the right of fixing the price when
the work was brought in', a form of behaviour which lost him
the sympathy of J. F. Foster, the leading local magistrate.[4] On this
occasion, the gingham weavers seem to have succeeded in making
Orrell revert to the prices which other manufacturers were
paying.[5]

The skilled weavers at Bolton also maintained effective unions
for many years. In 1829, the bed-quilt weavers ran a successful
strike against a manufacturer who made a unilateral reduction.
But their numbers were small, they were still well-paid, and as a
result their combination was a wealthy one. It drew £60 in subscriptions in one quarter-year, and those members who in the
depression of 1829 were 'stinted' to only ten shillings worth of
work per week (a sum very much greater than a calico weaver,
however industrious, could earn) were allowed to pay a lower
subscription.[6] The Bolton counterpane weavers too, had an active

[1] *Manchester Guardian*, 10 May 1834.
[2] *Ibid.* 5 Sept. 1829; 17 April and 11 Dec. 1830; and 2 April 1831.
[3] *Ibid.* 21 Jan. and 25 Feb. 1832.
[4] Foster to Home Secretary, 26 Feb. 1832 (*HO. 52. 18*).
[5] *Manchester Guardian*, 5 March 1832.
[6] *Ibid.* 21 Feb. and 6 June 1829.

union in the 1840s, and their last survivors forty years later still kept up some kind of association.[1]

Although in these specialized lines the existence of trade unions can be observed throughout the period, it does not necessarily follow that they enjoyed a continuous history. Yet, as Professor Turner reminds us, 'the formal disbanding of a society, even the seizure of its committee, funds, and records could of itself make only a temporary impact on its members' organizational capacity'.[2] The smaller the trade, the easier it was to keep an informal organization in being. With the larger unions in individual towns, these problems were magnified, but still not insuperable; so that the town unions were able to maintain a fairly continuous, if sometimes shadowy, existence, especially before 1820. The vast petitioning of 1799–1802, 1807–8, 1811 and 1816–19 could not have been achieved without the existence of at least an informal weavers' committee in such centres as Manchester, Bolton, Stockport, Carlisle, Glasgow and Paisley. Nor could the big strikes of 1808, 1812, and 1818, to say nothing of isolated ones such as those of 1816 at Preston[3] and 1820 at Glasgow,[4] have been organized and sustained without the presence of acknowledged leaders in the principal weaving towns.

After 1820, however, the local unions became increasingly ineffective. An attempt at Manchester to form a union after the repeal of the Combination Acts in 1824 was not a success, and following the slump of 1826 the weavers tried to re-establish it.[5] Their efforts were evidently fruitless yet again, as there was a further attempt to re-form it in 1831. It is an indication both of the falling numbers of Manchester weavers and of the apathy of those who remained in the trade that 'not more than 150 to 200 persons' attended the public meeting on this last occasion,[6] and it is not surprising that J. F. Foster in 1838 'did not know that there had been any permanent or long established union amongst them'.[7]

Some of the smaller towns, where the handloom weavers

---

[1] Turner, op. cit. p. 51. [2] Ibid. p. 85.
[3] Manchester Mercury, 27 Aug. 1816. [4] Ibid. 11 April 1820.
[5] Wheeler's Manchester Chronicle, 15 Sept. 1827.
[6] Manchester Guardian, 5 Nov. 1831. [7] PP. 1837/8 (488) VIII, Q. 3343.

remained an important element in the population longer than they did in Manchester, probably kept their local unions longer. At Bolton there must have been an active weavers' committee in 1833-5, since Bolton men were particularly prominent in pressing for wage fixing by 'boards of trade'. Moreover, during the prosperity of 1836 they actually took the offensive, resolving that 'with the present excessive demand for their labour the low-paying masters might be brought up to the prices given by the respectable manufacturers, or otherwise lose their workmen',[1] and they appear to have re-formed their union with a similar objective during the 'revival of trade' in 1843.[2] The comparable periodic revival of a union at Paisley over the same years was likewise regarded as 'a proof of returning prosperity'.[3] There is, however, one major gap in the history of the local handloom weavers' unions. Neither in the years of prosperity nor in the years of decline can their existence be traced in the calico-weaving region of north-east Lancashire—except, that is, in the town of Blackburn.[4] Here, the weavers' larger numbers, wide geographical dispersion, more casual composition, and lower pay all served to prevent the operation of an effective combination. Brief bursts of physical violence—as in the strike of 1818, the great loom-breaking of 1826, and the Colne riot of 1837—were the characteristics of industrial action in this area.[5]

III

General unions of all cotton weavers had a much more tenuous existence. Professor Turner has suggested that they 'were only proposed when sectional conditions deteriorated'—in other words they were the unanimous response to a worsening situation, not an aggressive attempt to force concessions from their employers in good years.[6] Whilst this seems indeed the basic *raison d'etre* of the attempts at general union, it is, however, difficult to accept his

[1] *Manchester Guardian*, 6 Feb. 1836.   [2] *Northern Star*, 4 Nov. 1843.
[3] S.c. on distress in Paisley, 1843 (*PP. 1843 (115)* VII, Q. 1089).
[4] There was, for example, a weavers' committee in Blackburn in 1810 (Aspinall, *op. cit.* pp. 114-15).
[5] See below, pp. 196 and 199, and above, p. 181.
[6] Turner, *op. cit.* p. 51.

assumption that, since 'the record of weavers' activities...is almost
continuous from 1799 to 1819', then 'some form of general combination existed over the whole period',[1] even when the qualifications he adds to that statement are borne in mind.[2] Except perhaps
for the years 1807-12, the continuous existence of a general cotton
weavers' union cannot be demonstrated. For it is here, and not in
the specialized or local unions, that the 'difficulties of communication' which Professor Turner tends to discount,[3] really were an
obstacle. It is true that within the compact semi-circle of towns
around Manchester—from Bolton through Bury and Ashton to
Stockport—concerted action was possible, and the weavers of one
place were able 'to march in procession to "turn out" the neighbouring centres', as they did in 1818.[4] But in the great calico-
weaving belt of north Lancashire, from Preston to Skipton, there
does not appear to have been even a shortlived general union; nor
was communication between this region and the Manchester area
very easy, as a result of the physical barrier imposed by the
Rossendale hills. In 1810, the weavers of Bolton and Blackburn,
towns separated by ten miles of moorland, do not appear to have
had much contact; for in June the Bolton weavers sent out hand-
bills announcing their future meetings, and merely 'hoped that
our brethren (the poor and oppressed weavers of Blackburn and
its neighbourhood) will join them'—hardly a sign of regular co-
ordination between the two districts.[5] Similarly, in 1818, the more
remote calico weavers both came out and stayed out later than
did those nearer Manchester[6]—a time-lag which is accounted for
only by the difficulties of communication and the lack of habitual
contact.

On certain exceptional occasions, contact of a purely *ad hoc* and
temporary kind was achieved between the weavers in different
trades and localities. Such a 'general union' consisted, at its most
sophisticated level, in meetings of delegates from the various

[1] *Ibid.* p. 53.
[2] These are: (i) the unlikelihood that the unions 'connected even a majority in formal
membership' (*Ibid.* p. 87), and (ii) the fact that they existed 'primarily to compile and
forward pleas for legislative regulation' (p. 82).
[3] *Ibid.* p. 81.   [4] See below, p. 195.
[5] Enclosure in H. Feilden to Lord Hawkesbury, 6 June 1808 (*HO.* 42. 95).
[6] See below, pp. 195-6.

districts, or, more crudely, in visits from delegates representing one town to the weavers' committee in another. Bolton or Bury was usually the most convenient centre for a general delegate meeting: in 1799, the agitation for the Arbitration Act was managed by a delegates' committee in Bolton;[1] at the time of the great strike of 1818, there was a committee of delegates in existence to negotiate with the employers from late July,[2] although the strike did not begin until the end of August, whilst on 5 September, an even larger meeting of fifty-two delegates assembled at Bury to consider 'whether the whole weaving body of this country, together with that of the manufacturing districts of Cheshire and Derbyshire, should turn out or return forthwith to their employment';[3] and again in 1825, after the repeal of the Combination Acts, delegate meetings were held at Bolton, Stockport, and Manchester to consider the establishment—unsuccessful in the event—of a general weavers' union.[4] Regular delegate meetings do not, however, appear to have taken place over the period as a whole; and the only successful general combination which effectively drew together several localities seems to have been that which managed the Scottish strike of 1812.[5] The more casual contacts, where delegates from one town consulted with the weavers' leaders in another, were more frequently recorded; for example, during their 'militant' phase in the boom of 1836 the Bolton union was visited by delegates from the weavers of Preston

---

[1] See above, p. 149.

[2] Printed handbill in HO. 42. *178* headed 'To the Cotton Manufacturers of Lancashire, Yorkshire, Cheshire, Derbyshire, etc.', dated 'Bury, 27 July 1818', and signed 'John Hibbert, President, and Robert Ellison, Secretary'. It concluded, 'the Weavers...for the purpose of framing this address, have delegated a number of their own trade from Manchester, Bolton, Bury, Blackburn, Burnley, Padiham, Higher Darwen, Lower Darwen, Heywood, Haslingden, Todmorden, Walshawlane and Tottington, Cockey Moor, Prestwich, Pilkington, Stockport, Ashton-under-Lyne, Chadderton, Middleton, etc.'. In addition, a letter from R. Fletcher to H. Hobhouse of 26 July 1818 (HO. 42. *178*) mentions 'a meeting of weavers' delegates' which had taken place at Prestwich during the previous week. The handbill and the relevant section of Fletcher's letter are not printed by Aspinall, although the former appears in full in Hammonds, *op. cit.* pp. 111–12.

[3] W. Chippindale to Lord Sidmouth, 6 Sept. 1818 (HO. 42. *180*).

[4] *Wheeler's Manchester Chronicle*, 15 Jan. 1825.

[5] See below, p. 197. The high degree of organization behind the Scottish strike was frequently commented on at the time, and a proclamation of the Lanarkshire magistrates in December 1812 specifically described it as 'a general combination among the operative cotton weavers in Scotland' (Aspinall, *op. cit.* p. 141).

and Carlisle.[1] But there is nothing to suggest that these occasional and informal communications led to concerted action between the areas concerned.

IV

The existence of handloom weavers' unions—initially reasonably effective and, even in the last years, fairly persistent in particular trades and localities, but weak and temporary when it came to a general combination—is thus established beyond doubt. On only three occasions, however, did the cotton weavers as a whole attempt to defend their economic position by a full-scale strike; in 1808 and 1818 in England, and in 1812 in Scotland. Each deserves a brief examination to show how far, if at all, the hand-loom weavers were able to overcome the tremendous natural obstacles which stood in the way of effective industrial action on their part.

The strike of the Lancashire cotton weavers in May and June 1808 had an obvious immediate cause. The government's half-hearted minimum wage bill, for which the weavers had been petitioning over the previous year, was rejected in the Commons on 19 May 1808, and hope of halting the recent drastic decline in wages by legislative intervention had to be abandoned.[2] The response to this disappointment came surprisingly quickly. On the morning of 24 May, many Manchester weavers struck work, and assembled near St George's Church. They created no disturbance, but the local magistrates took fright; and when the weavers re-assembled in still greater numbers on the following day, the Riot Act was read, and the crowd was dispersed by the dragoons and the local volunteer corps. During the course of this operation, one man was killed, several wounded, and a number arrested.[3]

The weavers now changed their policy. Big meetings were abandoned, and the more active weavers concentrated on ensuring that the cessation of labour would be complete and continuous until their demand for a 33⅓ per cent increase had been met by the

---

[1] *Manchester Guardian*, 19 Oct. 1836   [2] See above, p. 154.

[3] The soldiers and their officers salved their consciences for the bloodshed by giving up a day's pay to support the family of the dead man (*Manchester Mercury*, 31 May 1808).

employers. This they did by touring the town in small parties collecting shuttles from the houses of their less keen brethren (often, it was alleged, using violence, or at least threatening it), so as to prevent their carrying on weaving. In some cases, the strikers even went so far as to take the actual piece out of the loom. The magistrates tried to encourage those still willing to work by stationing military patrols 'at the different avenues of the town, in order to protect and secure the well-disposed weavers in receiving and returning their work'.[1]

Despite the magistrates' efforts, however, the 1808 strike was lengthy, extensive, well-organized and apparently effective. By 1 June, Mr Farrington, J.P., of Manchester was reporting to the Home Office that 'the discontents...extend to every part of the manufacturing districts in the county of Lancaster'.[2] The towns grouped closely around Manchester—from Bolton to Stockport —joined in very quickly, and in some cases experienced more violence than did Manchester itself: the Rochdale gaol was burnt down and several imprisoned weavers released; a Heywood manufacturer, Mr Ashton, was dragged from his bed and made to sign a wage agreement; and at Oldham many house-windows were broken.[3] The more distant weaving centres were also involved: at Wigan (where at this period 'the principal employment of the people is in the cotton manufactures') there was a very smoothly-managed shuttle-gathering operation on 30 May;[4] there were 'disturbances' at Blackburn; around Clitheroe and Burnley there were food riots, and a large meeting of weavers was broken up by the Craven volunteer cavalry.[5]

The organization of the strike in Manchester was particularly effective, and the leaders escaped detection for many days. Even on 4 June, with the strike well into its second week, Farrington had to report to the Home Office that 'a committee sit who direct operations...but no discovery has been made so as to enable us

---

[1] *Manchester Mercury*, 7 June 1808. [2] *HO. 42. 95.*
[3] *Manchester Mercury*, 7 June 1808. At Oldham, the weavers' leaders seem to have lost control of the crowd, for they published an apology to the manufacturers whose property had been attacked.
[4] Mayor of Wigan to Lord Hawkesbury, 15 June 1808 (*HO. 42. 95*).
[5] *Manchester Mercury*, 14 June 1808; Rev. Dr Collins (Gisburn) to Home Office, 9 June 1808 (*HO. 42. 95*).

to seize them'.[1] The whole affair lasted at least a month, and not until 5 July could the *Manchester Mercury* report that 'all the late differences appear to be adjusted'. As early as the 31st of May, a Manchester correspondent reported to the Home Office that 'the manufacturers have agreed to give to the weavers an advance of 20 per cent upon their wages, and as soon as this can be generally known it is expected to produce general satisfaction in every town and place in this vicinity where the public mind is now disturbed.'[2] This partial advance did not win general and immediate acceptance, but within a short time a division of opinion as to whether or not to stand out for the whole rise naturally weakened the strike's impetus. Those who stayed out in Manchester became increasingly violent, damaging work in looms, attacking weavers on their way to the warehouse, and burning in effigy unpopular manufacturers.[3] By the end of June, however, peace had been restored, and some advance in wages had been generally secured.

It is doubtful whether in the long-run the strike would have had much effect on the handloom weavers' wages, had it not been reinforced by the recovery of trade in 1809–10. But a short-term gain was undoubtedly made. The weavers benefited to some degree from the widespread public sympathy for their case. The mayor of Wigan told the Home Office that 'the present distresses of the weavers and their families are such as were never before experienced',[4] and the *Manchester Mercury* hoped that 'their employers will candidly consider their case and contribute to their future comfort by granting them equitable wages'.[5] The weavers who were tried for acts of violence or intimidation were leniently treated—a sure reflection of the goodwill which local notables felt towards them.[6]

The treatment of Joseph Hanson, Gentleman, of Strangeways Hall, Manchester, was much harsher. For he had publicly sympathized with the weavers' cause and addressed their second mass

[1] *HO. 42. 95.* The arrest of thirty 'delegates of the weavers' was reported in *Manchester Mercury*, 7 June.
[2] Ralph Wright to Spencer Perceval, 31 May 1808 (*HO. 42. 95*). This letter is not printed by Aspinall.
[3] *Manchester Mercury*, 28 June 1808.
[4] Mayor of Wigan to Lord Hawkesbury, 15 June 1808 (*HO. 42. 95*).
[5] *Manchester Mercury*, 7 June 1808.   [6] Hammonds, *op. cit.* pp. 80–1.

meeting in Manchester on 25 May. To some extent the authorities' reaction may have been dictated by fear of one of their own kind putting himself at the head of the revolutionary mob, for Hanson, whose father had made money as a manufacturer, was clearly a traitor to his class. But it is more likely that whatever words of encouragement Hanson may or may not have addressed to the weavers on this occasion were used merely as an excuse to punish him for many previous transgressions beyond the pale of upper-class solidarity. For even before 1808, Hanson had already marked himself out as an extremely unconventional and controversial character. In 1804, when he founded his own regiment of rifle volunteers on the renewal of the war, he became involved in a trivial but unpleasantly personal wrangle over seniority with a brother officer—a dispute which was ultimately dragged into the open.[1] The following year saw the publication by Hanson of a controversial pamphlet on 'The Present Volunteer Establishment', which brought him further unpopularity.

But it was in 1807 that Hanson really became *persona non grata* to the authorities. First of all he stood as radical candidate at Preston in the general election of that year, and denounced the prevailing political influence of the Stanleys and Horrockses. He also pledged himself to support the weavers' minimum wage bill if elected.[2] Then secondly, at the end of the year, he became a public advocate of 'an honourable peace', denounced the war for increasing distress at home, and resigned his commission in the volunteers.[3] His behaviour in the 1808 strike, added to his past record, was merely the last straw, and gave a first-rate opportunity of making a public example of one who had long been a general nuisance. Hanson was tried in May 1809, fined £100, and imprisoned for six months; he died, unmarried and still quite a young man, two years later. The handloom weavers recognized his sympathy by organizing a subscription on his behalf, to which nearly 40,000 were said to

---

[1] *Manchester Mercury*, 17, 24 and 31 July 1804.
[2] *Manchester Mercury*, 26 May 1807 and 31 May 1808. It is an indication of the limited value of a wide franchise, such as Preston enjoyed under the unreformed parliament, that the families of the leading local landowner and the chief manufacturer could easily defeat a radical like Hanson, despite the fact that the latter supported a policy likely to appeal to many poorer voters.
[3] *Ibid.* 15 Dec. 1807.

have contributed; the fund was used to purchase for him an inscribed gold cup.[1]

When industrial depression returned in 1811–12, the Lancashire weavers did not organize another general turn-out: after petitioning unsuccessfully for a minimum wage once more, their 'industrial' action was of the disorganized, desultory kind—attacks on powerlooms, and food riots. Four years later, in December 1816, there was again an alarm that a general weavers' strike would break out, and a number of Manchester weavers did turn out briefly. But the whole thing was over in a couple of days, much to the magistrates' relief; for as William Chippindale of Oldham wrote to Colonel Fletcher on 5 December, 'it was a most fortunate circumstance for the peace of this neighbourhood that the weavers in Manchester had returned to work before the news of the Spa Fields Riots in London arrived. The Lord knows what would have been the consequence had they been out upon the occasion'.[2]

The Lancashire strike of 1818 was the last occasion on which the cotton weavers, not as yet threatened by the powerloom, tried to secure a wage increase by organized and unanimous industrial action. In the two preceding years, the handloom weavers had pursued different, disorganized lines of action—parliamentary petitioning, political radicalism, even brief local strikes, as at Manchester and Preston in 1816. Once again, in 1818, it was a specific event which united the weavers behind the strike, in this case the example of the factory workers, both spinners and the few weavers, who came out for a wage increase in July. Other trades in and around Manchester—the builders and joiners, the dyers, and later the miners—were also on strike in the summer of 1818 (which was said, incidentally, to have been the hottest since 1779),[3] and it is hardly surprising that the handloom weavers were moved by this prevailing 'general strike' atmosphere[4] to test the advantages of industrial action. But it is a sign of their weakness

---

[1] A. Prentice, *Historical sketches of Manchester* (Manchester, 1851), p. 33.

[2] Enclosure in R. Fletcher to J. H. Addington, 7 Dec. 1816. (*HO. 40. 3/1*). This enclosure is not printed by Aspinall.

[3] *Manchester Mercury*, 4 Aug. 1818.

[4] Plans for a 'general philanthropic society' involving a union of all the trades of Manchester were in fact formulated in August 1818 (Aspinall, *op. cit.* pp. 272–4).

as compared with other trades that it needed such a widespread example to start them moving, and that they only came out when the other strikes were under way.

Slow though the weavers were to come out, the possibility that they would ultimately do so was widely recognized from July 1818 by local magistrates, who lamented that the manufacturers were doing little to placate them.[1] Weavers' meetings in the individual towns took place within a few days of the factory workers' turn-out: as early as 20 July, the Stockport weavers requested that the magistrates should call a public meeting 'to take into consideration any means to secure to the workman a competence for his labour',[2] and on the 27th a meeting of weavers' delegates from all parts of Lancashire met at Bury, where they formulated their demand for an all-round increase in wage-rates of seven shillings in the pound.[3] Negotiations seem then to have begun in pursuit of this claim between the weavers and their employers in the individual towns, and these dragged on for the greater part of August. In most towns the magistrates refused to call public meetings, and the number of manufacturers prepared to sit down and talk with the weavers about their claim seems to have been small.[4] Unable to get a generally favourable response from their employers, a further delegate meeting at Bury on 22 August played its final card: the weavers would strike work on 1 September if the requested increase was not granted.[5] On the last day in August, numerous small parties of weavers came into Manchester to ask their respective employers whether they were willing to pay the increase; since the replies they received were still not unanimous, the strike began on the following day.[6] In Manchester, the normal shuttle-gathering tactics seem to have

---

[1] See Aspinall, *op. cit.* pp. 252, 255, and 258.

[2] J. Lloyd to H. Hobhouse, 23 July 1818 (*HO. 42. 178*).

[3] See above, p. 188, n. 2.

[4] A meeting at the 'Bull's Head' tavern, Manchester, on 11 August was attended by 'fifteen delegates of the weavers and three or four masters' (J. Lloyd to H. Hobhouse, 12 Aug. 1818 (*HO. 42. 179*).

[5] Enclosure in *idem* to *idem*, 25 Aug. 1818 (*HO. 42. 179*).

[6] J. Norris to R. H. Clive, 31 Aug. 1818 (*HO. 42. 179*). From the extract from this letter in Aspinall (*op. cit.* p. 281) it might appear that 31 August was the first day of the actual strike. The letter as a whole, however, makes it clear that the manoeuvres on this day were a final attempt at negotiation.

taken a subordinate place, and the main features of the strike were monster processions through the streets to impress or even over-awe their masters and the authorities with a display of solidarity. There was very little violence. On Tuesday, 1 September, the first day of the strike and also Manchester's market day, three columns marched from different directions through the town centre and past the Exchange and the Post Office, 'as if threatening defiance'.[1] On the following Thursday, the Manchester weavers marched to Stockport to bring out their fellows there, and the next day they set out with a similar objective to Ashton. By these means, the weavers' strike very quickly embraced the towns nearest Manchester, nor was it long in spreading to the more distant parts of north Lancashire. On 5 September, a big delegate meeting was held at the 'Spread Eagle', Bury, to promote concerted action throughout the weaving area. The delegates agreed, after a long and heated discussion, in which Robert Pilkington—a prominent radical in 1817—deprecated anything less than the full increase, that they were prepared to accept an increase in two instalments of 4 shillings immediately and 3 shillings on 1 October, and ordered weavers not to take work from manufacturers who would not agree to make the increase.[2]

The Bury delegate meeting, although showing a certain degree of skill in organizing united action, also sowed the seeds of the strike's rapid collapse. The partial increase of the first instalment, to which many manufacturers had already agreed,[3] left most of the weavers inclined to begin work at once, whilst the action of the leaders in ordering that people 'should not take out work unless at certain rates' was used by the authorities as an excuse to arrest them on a charge of 'combining, conspiring, and confederating'.[4] Ellison, Kay, and Pilkington were arrested for having signed and published the Bury resolutions, and subsequently imprisoned. With their objective partly gained, and their leaders put away before 1 October, when the strike was to have been renewed

---

[1] *Manchester Exchange Herald*, 8 Sept. 1818.
[2] See the account of the meeting by Robert Ellison, Bolton, who took the chair, to s.c. artisans and machinery, 1824 (*PP. 1824 (51)* v, pp. 394–6).
[3] Aspinall, *op. cit.* pp. 286 and 288.
[4] J. Norris to Lord Sidmouth, 16 Sept. 1818 (*HO. 42. 180*).

if the second increase had not been made, it is small wonder that the handloom weavers rapidly drifted back to work, especially as they, unlike the factory workers, lacked a union fund from which to sustain a long strike.[1] By 11 September, most of them were back at work in the Manchester region, but in north Lancashire they remained out over a week longer.[2] Here the strikers used the more violent methods which the Manchester weavers had tried to avoid. 'The hundred of Blackburn', reported the Rev. Dr Whitaker, J.P., on 17 September, 'is in a state approaching to that of a general insurrection...The houses of the weavers who are willing to work are visited, their looms and work marked, and themselves inhibited from proceeding.'[3] At Burnley there was a riot of sufficient magnitude to cause the building of a permanent military barracks the following year, and at nearby Padiham a troop of soldiers leading prisoners to Preston was stoned by the populace.[4] By the 22nd however, peace had generally been restored, and even the remote districts were back at work. On the face of things the strike was a success in that it resulted in some immediate advance in wages; but this was quickly nullified as industrial depression returned in 1819, the year of Peterloo.

The strike of the Scottish cotton weavers in 1812, although taking place outside the main cotton area, affords some interesting contrasts with the Lancashire strikes, and deserves a brief mention. This strike was said to have made 50,000 to 60,000 looms idle,[5] and as in Lancashire in 1808, it had a specific immediate cause.[6] The Glasgow weavers, who had, like their fellows in Lancashire, been anxious for a minimum wage, tried after the failure of the select committee of 1811 to use old statutes which empowered magistrates to fix wages. After strenuous lobbying by weavers, the Lanarkshire justices had laid down a list of weaving prices

---

[1] Agents had been sent out to collect funds from distant parts of the country (Aspinall, *op. cit.* pp. 282 and 295), and public notices appeared in the streets of Manchester soliciting donations from wealthy sympathizers (*Manchester Mercury*, 16 Sept. 1818).
[2] J. Norris to Lord Sidmouth, 11 Sept. 1818 (*HO. 42. 180*).
[3] Whitaker to Lord Sidmouth, 17 Sept. 1818 (*HO. 42. 180*).
[4] *Manchester Mercury*, 22 Sept. 1818.   [5] *PP. 1824 (51)* v, p. 481.
[6] See B. and S. Webb, *History of Trade Unionism* (1920 edn), pp. 58–9 and 81–2, and the documents in Aspinall, *op. cit.* pp. 137–51, 153–6, and 159–61, for further details of the Scottish strike.

which the Edinburgh court of sessions upheld on 10 November 1812. The manufacturers denied the magistrates' competence to act in this way, and since no order was ever made to enforce the new list, the weavers immediately began a strike to oblige their masters to accept the new rates. The weavers naturally regarded their case as a particularly strong one, since it had been established at great expense through the normal channels of litigation, and since it enjoyed widespread public sympathy. The leaders of the combination were at great pains to avoid the use of force in obtaining their just rights; 'they consider themselves legally justified in their proceedings', a Glasgow correspondent told Lord Sidmouth, 'and seem particularly cautious to avoid Luddism'.[1] Inevitably, however, some violence crept in in the attempt to make the stoppage complete as it dragged on into the new year, and cases of intimidation and damage to property provided the authorities with a charge of 'illegal combination' to level against the organizing committee of five weavers; they were tried and sentenced in March 1813 to terms of from four to eighteen months imprisonment.

The capture of their leaders marked the end of this well-organized strike by the Scottish handloom weavers. No increase in wages seems to have been obtained as an immediate result, and the obsolete statutes which the weavers had tried to use were hastily repealed by the government. Fortunately, as the Napoleonic war drew to its close in 1813, prosperity returned and secured for the handloom weavers the better wages which they had been unable to achieve by industrial action in the previous year.

v

1818 was the last general strike by the cotton handloom weavers. Their remaining phase of industrial action—which was neither constructive in design nor well-organized in practice—was the great loom-breaking in north Lancashire in 1826. The earlier history of the weavers' tactics has already shown that the calico weavers of this area never sustained an effective combination; even

---

[1] Aspinall, *op. cit.* p. 147.

in 1818, the brief and desultory violence in Burnley had been in marked contrast with the well-organized but peaceable processions in Manchester. It is not surprising that these 'country weavers'—poorer, less sophisticated, and more widely scattered than their fellow workmen in Manchester and its neighbouring towns—should have been guilty of this major act of blind vandalism.

The 1826 episode, although the biggest, was not the first occasion on which handloom weavers had broken up the new and threatening machines. Messrs Grimshaw's factory—the first in Manchester to operate Cartwright's powerloom—was attacked and burnt down by irate handloom weavers on 13 March 1792.[1] Cartwright had patented his first loom only a few years before, and this particular factory had been operating only two years. Its destruction was held by William Radcliffe to have inhibited entrepreneurs from developing the powerloom for many years.[2] Loombreaking was also a feature (and a minor one, in view of the small part played as yet in the manufacturing process by the powerloom) of the disturbances in Lancashire during the critical year 1812.[3] In March, irate handloom weavers at Stockport attempted to fire William Radcliffe's factory and warehouse; their activities were explained to the Home Secretary by John Lloyd, the clerk to the local magistrates, on the grounds that 'Mr Radcliffe was the original projector of the obnoxious looms that the weavers have thought proper to complain of as the cause of their present distress, and is the proprietor of a patent of a machine for dressing cotton warps to be made use of in such looms, and it is thought that the weavers have considered him as the most proper object for the first act of their resentment'.[4] Some weeks later, on Monday 20 April, a mob which the *Manchester Mercury* compared with 'the very Goths and Vandals of antiquity' attacked Daniel Burton's factory at Middleton and attempted to destroy the looms.[5] The

[1] *Manchester Mercury*, 20 and 27 March 1792.   [2] See above, p. 76.
[3] For an account of the mixture of political radicalism, food-rioting, and machine-breaking of 1812, see Hammonds, *op. cit.* chapter x; E. P. Thompson, *The making of the English working class* (London, 1963), pp. 565–9; and below, pp. 208–10.
[4] J. Lloyd to Home Office, 21 March 1812 (*HO. 40. 1/1*).
[5] *Manchester Mercury*, 28 April 1812. Local colliers from Oldham and Hollinwood were said to have been particularly active in the work of destruction (W. Chippindale to R. Fletcher, 23 April 1812 (*HO. 40. 1/1*)).

armed defenders of the mill fired on the crowd, and dispersed it before any damage had been done. Three men were killed and twenty-seven wounded; and on the following day, Burton's house was attacked and damage done to the estimated value of £2,000. Four days later, there was a successful attack on Wroe and Duncuft's weaving factory at Westhoughton, near Bolton.[1]

The vandalism of 1826 was on a much grander scale than any of these previous attacks. The years 1821–5 had seen the first large-scale adoption of the powerloom in cotton, whilst 1826 had brought the most severe peace-time depression the industry had yet known. Not unnaturally, the handloom weavers saw the second factor as the direct consequence of the first, and their Luddism of 1826 was a blind display of hatred against an improved machine which must be destroyed before it took away the old weavers' livelihood. This differed from the sporadic and small-scale frame-breaking of 1811–12 and the immediate post-war years in the Midland hosiery industry: in the Midlands, the chief object of Luddite attack was the hated system of frame-renting and its evil concomitants, not the development of a new kind of machine which was robbing men of their jobs. A less sophisticated object lay in the minds of the poor, ignorant, disorganized country weavers when they broke the powerlooms in north Lancashire in 1826.[2]

At the end of December 1825, the boroughreeve of Manchester sanguinely informed the Home Office that 'there appears to be no reason to apprehend the difficulties in the commercial world will lead to any disturbances of the peace in this vicinity'.[3] Unemployment continued to rise and wages to fall in the new year, but even in February the editor of the *Blackburn Mail* upbraided the *Manchester Guardian* for suggesting that 'serious apprehensions are felt for the preservation of tranquillity', and commended that 'truly admirable spirit of resignation and patience which indeed has for a long time been the characteristic of the weavers and operative spinners of this town and neighbourhood, between whom and

[1] *Ibid.* 5 May 1812.
[2] There are accounts of the events of 1826 in Hammonds, *op. cit.* pp. 126–8, and in T. Newbigging, *History of the forest of Rossendale* (London, 1868), pp. 240 *et seq.*
[3] W. Lomas to Home Secretary, 22 Dec. 1825 (*HO. 52. 4*).

their masters there exists the most kindly and sympathizing feeling'.[1] Another month with no improvement in the trade, however, had pretty well exhausted this patience and kindly feeling; by the end of March, the coaches bringing the manufacturers back to Blackburn from Manchester market were being stoned as they came into town.[2]

With such an obvious deterioration in morale, the actual attacks were not perhaps so 'unexpected' as the Hammonds suggest. A week before the actual riots of 24–26 April, the windows of Sykes's mill, Accrington, had been broken by an angry crowd;[3] and on 20 April Colonel Fletcher, the Bolton magistrate who frequently sent spies to workers' meetings, reported that the weavers were planning to destroy all the powerlooms and all the yarn which was awaiting export to be woven abroad.[4] Peel, the Home Secretary, subsequently upbraided local magistrates for their slowness in passing on knowledge or suspicions of the weavers' schemes. Henry Hobhouse, his under-secretary, told the bailiffs of Clitheroe a few days after the riots of the government's regret that Peel

should not have been earlier apprized of the two acts mentioned... [in a letter from Clitheroe of 26 April]... which he has now heard for the first time, viz.: that emissaries have been travelling about the country urging the people to rise and destroy the powerlooms before any military could arrive, and that for several weeks past numbers of pikes have been preparing in the neighbourhood of Blackburn and Burnley.[5]

The actual outrages were not wholly disorganized, for the ability which the rioters showed in evading the military on three successive days demonstrates considerable tactical skill on the part of the leaders. The great loom-breaking began at Accrington on Monday, 24 April;[6] Sykes's factory, which had had its windows broken in the previous week, was the first to be visited. As soon as the news reached Blackburn, the soldiers stationed there were dispatched to break up the riot; the mob, however, evaded the soldiers, and marched on the now-unprotected Blackburn, where

---

[1] *Blackburn Mail*, 22 Feb. 1826.
[2] *Wheeler's Manchester Chronicle*, 25 March 1826.   [3] *Ibid.* 22 April 1826.
[4] R. Fletcher to H. Hobhouse, 20 April 1826 (*HO. 40. 19*).   [5] *HO. 41. 7.*
[6] This account of the first two days of the riots is based on the report in *Blackburn Mail*, 26 April 1826.

they smashed the looms at Eccles's mill in Darwen street. They were at work on Haughton's mill at Grimshaw Park when the soldiers returned and drove them off. The following day, Tuesday 25th, the loom-breakers again avoided the troops, who were sent to Clitheroe to investigate the reported impending attack on the large, isolated weaving mill at Low Moor. In fact, Low Moor was never attacked, but the absence of the soldiers provided an opportunity for the looms of two small mills at Darwen to be broken.

By Wednesday 26th, Major Eckersley, the military commander in Manchester, had been able to make some preparations against future raids: on Tuesday he had sent more troops to Blackburn and Haslingden, and also to Bury, where 'the High Constable and a number of the principal manufacturers' seem, understandably, to have been getting nervous.[1] Yet the third day of the loom-breaking was much the most spectacular, and even these precautions were inadequate to prevent widespread destruction. On that Wednesday, a number of mobs seem to have been active throughout the Irwell valley from Bacup down to Bury; and among the manufacturers who suffered losses at their hands was David Whitehead at Rawtenstall. In two instances, at Aikin's mill, Chadderton, and Turner's at Helmshore, near Haslingden, the loom-breakers clashed with the soldiers, with some loss of life. Major Eckersley himself reported that 'the obstinacy and determination of the rioters was most extraordinary, and such as I could not have credited had I not witnessed it myself'.[2] There was a last echo of the great loom-breaking in the country on Thursday 27th, when a small mill at Gargrave, near Skipton, was attacked and its twenty looms damaged.[3]

The events of April 1826 were a significant contrast with the strikes of 1808 and 1818 because the country, and not Manchester, had taken the initiative. In respectable circles there was the immediate fear that the 'baneful influence' of the events a few miles away would lead to disturbances in Manchester itself. And in the event, on Thursday evening 27 April, a large mob assembled

---

[1] Eckersley to H. Hobhouse, 25 April 1826 (*HO. 40. 19*).
[2] *Idem* to *idem*, 26 April 1826 (*HO. 40. 19*).
[3] M. Wilson to Home Secretary, 26 May 1826 (*HO. 40. 19*).

there, broke the windows of several mills containing powerlooms, and attempted to fire Beaver's mill in Jersey Street.[1] By the following morning, however, order had been restored, and there was no further disturbance.

Throughout the terrible summer of 1826, the fear of further attacks on the factories was strong, and the Home Office papers contain many letters from nervous magistrates and highly-coloured reports from the rather dubious spies they employed. On 3 July, Whiteheads of Rawtenstall, who had replaced their broken looms very quickly, received 'an anonymous letter threatening to destroy by fire or otherwise their factory if they did not within three days decline weaving by power'.[2] On the 9th, General Byng reported that the Low Moor mill was again the object of a threatened attack,[3] whilst later in July, Colonel Fletcher's spy 'Alpha', whose information Hobhouse regarded as 'of little or no value', was reporting 'plans for stopping all the bleachers' waggons that contained powerloom cloth', proposals to raid the provision shops, and a certainly fictitious scheme for attacking the spinning factories which provided yarn for the powerlooms and for 'coupling machinery worked by steam and the machinery of government together and involving all in one common ruin'.[4] None of these fanciful ideas ever reached fruition, however: Peel himself 'had little doubt that the Rev. Mr Whitaker [of Blackburn] has taken too vehement alarm, and that his views have affected the visual organs of the magistrates'.[5]

Yet the magistrates were right to be alarmed, for the violence of 1826 was unprecedented, and contrasted sharply with the docility which the handloom weavers normally displayed. The rioters were not, in fact, severely punished: the millowners who had suffered loss brought actions against the county, and secured damages to the value of over £16,000, this sum being raised by a special rate on the inhabitants of those Hundreds in which the damage had occurred; of the rioters, only 66 were tried, 10 sen-

---

[1] *Manchester Mercury*, 29 April 1826.
[2] Rev. W. Gray (Haslingden), enclosure in Byng to Home Secretary, 6 July 1826 (*HO. 40. 20*).   [3] *Idem to idem*, 9 July 1826 (*HO. 40. 20*).
[4] J. F. Foster to H. Hobhouse, 26 July 1826 (*HO. 40. 20*).
[5] H. Hobhouse to General Byng, 5 July 1826 (*HO. 40. 20*).

tenced to death but transported, and 33 imprisoned for terms of from 3 to 18 months.[1] There can be no doubt, however, that the responsibility was a general not an individual one, and that the mobs who broke the looms included many local handloom weavers. In Rawtenstall, the *Blackburn Mail* reported that 'part of these men were employed by Messrs Whitehead in weaving hand-cloth at the time that they were engaged in destroying the property of those gentlemen'.[2]

Not all the weaving districts were equally implicated: there was no actual destruction in Burnley, and the weavers of Darwen were anxious to prove that the outrages in their village had been perpetrated by outsiders.[3] Nor was there any political content discerned in the riots by contemporaries; the anonymous author of a homiletic pamphlet urging the virtues of patience and courage on the weavers declared himself 'sure that the only motive to those proceedings has been to get work and earn bread'.[4] Francis Place seems to have thought that '*agents provocateurs*' of the government played a part in stirring up the trouble,[5] and certainly, in the later stages, spies of the military and the magistrates may have become overzealous.[6] But it is impossible to see the great loom-breaking of 1826 as anything other than a massive display of resentment on the part of an entire community which appeared doomed to permanent poverty and misery.

The events of 1826 were not repeated. When another slump hit the cotton industry in 1829, fears of renewed violence were voiced; in May, the Blackburn magistrates were warning the Home Office of the handloom weavers' plans for further destruction, but nothing happened.[7] It is true that there were in Manchester attacks on factories by handloom weavers at that time, but

[1] Hammonds, *op. cit.* p. 128.   [2] *Blackburn Mail*, 3 May 1826.
[3] They sent a memorial protesting their innocence to the Home Office on 1 May 1826 (*HO. 40. 19*).
[4] 'William Wish-em-well' (pseud.), *A journey to Blackburn* (Leeds, 1826), p. 9.
[5] G. D'Eichthal, 'Condition de la classe ouvriere en Angleterre en 1828', *Revue Historique*, LXXIX (1902), 82.
[6] A report from General Byng to the Home Office on 22 Aug. 1826 runs: 'There is a man at Bolton, a stout man, but whose name he [Byng's spy, "No. 2"] does not know, who is exciting the people. No. 2 thinks this man is employed to give information by Colonel Fletcher' (*HO. 40. 20*).
[7] *HO. 40. 23.*

'the vengeance of the rioters...has not now, as in 1826, been directed against powerlooms, although some have been destroyed, but against certain establishments for hand weaving'.[1] The owners of these handloom sheds had made themselves unpopular by reducing piece-rates.

A variety of explanations can be offered as to why Luddism was never tried again: the loom breaking of 1826 had done nothing to end the slump—instead it had increased the burden of the county rate; it had not discouraged further investments in powerloom factories by entrepreneurs; and, given the size of the weaving area and the relative efficiency of the forces of law and order, it was impossible that destruction could be complete and simultaneous. But perhaps many of the handloom weavers after 1826 began to see at least some force in Edward Baines's argument that 'these last invented machines are the honour of our age, and their inventors the greatest benefactors of their species; for such machines are the steps we make in the march of civilization, they are the gift of utility made by this country and this age to the whole human race and to all posterity'.[2] Certainly the weavers of Darwen did so, when they resolved in July 1826 that 'it is necessary for some other species of labour besides handloom weaving to be introduced into this district in order to raise the inhabitants from their present state of unexampled distress and misery', and that, to achieve this end, 'nothing presents itself of equal advantage to the powerloom'.[3] After 1826, with organized industrial action impossible and unorganized action ineffective, it was clearly here that the ultimate answer to the handloom weavers' problems lay. The tragedy was that it was a solution which it took another two decades to achieve.

[1] *Manchester Guardian,* 9 May 1829.
[2] E. Baines (Jr.), *Address to the unemployed workmen of Yorkshire and Lancashire* (London, 1826), p. 10.　　　　[3] *Blackburn Mail,* 12 July 1826.

CHAPTER 9

THE WEAVERS AND RADICAL POLITICS

WHEN soliciting parliamentary assistance and applying industrial pressure on their employers had proved ineffective or inappropriate, there was always open to the handloom weavers a third method of halting the decline in their well-being. This was to seek the reconstruction of the institutions of the country—if not, indeed, of the very structure of society—in order to end the evils which had seemed inseparable from the old system of government. The discontented in the early nineteenth century did not lack radical social and political doctrines which they might espouse. In concrete terms, these doctrines usually involved the complete overhaul of the electoral system of Great Britain so as to give free and direct representation in the legislature to all elements in the community, and the end of all legislation which favoured any one class in society at the expense of the rest.

Once the handloom weavers were in full decline after 1826, their connexion with radical politics of this kind became a commonplace both to contemporaries and to many subsequent historians; it was contrasted particularly with their alleged loyalism in past times of prosperity. Old men looking back from the unhappy 1830s were very prone to lament the weakening of loyalty to old institutions. William Radcliffe claimed that 'until the year 1800, the weavers as a body were as faithful, moral, and trustworthy as any corporate body amongst His Majesty's subjects; and before the curse of modern political economists and liberal (meaning retrograde) march of mind were known, they wore their armorial bearings...with as few stains upon their coat armour as any individual or corporate body on whom these marks of Royal favour have ever been bestowed'.[1] When asked by the

---

[1] W. Radcliffe, *The origin of the new system of manufacture called powerloom weaving* (Stockport, 1828), p. 107.

1834 select committee about the weavers' attitude to idle placemen and pensioners who lived on the proceeds of taxation, John Makin replied that 'when wages were high, a man would have been knocked down for mentioning anything of the sort', and claimed to have known 'individuals who were in serious danger for being reformers of the old school'.[1]

Nor does the evidence for the alleged patriotism and political quiescence of the old weavers come solely from reminiscence. The 'public spirit of the youths of Burnley, Colne, and Blackburn' in volunteering for service in the armed forces in 1809 won the admiration of the *Manchester Mercury*,[2] and even in 1812, one of the worst years of wartime depression and disorder, a Stockport manufacturer could still exonerate the 'resident weavers' (as opposed to immigrants from the countryside) from any part in the disturbances.[3]

Even before it had become generally clear that handloom weaving was a doomed trade, however, there had been occasions when some handloom weavers had flirted with radical politics. Invariably, these early departures from the loyalist tradition were the reaction to economic depression. In 1834, Richard Needham, the veteran Bolton weaver, argued that it was 'not the school-master' but 'the steampower' which was 'causing all the revolutions on the continent and in England, and all the reforms',[4]—in other words, it was not the dissemination of ideas which caused discontent, but rather the disastrous effects of industrial development. William Radcliffe made a similar assessment of the economic undertones of weavers' radicalism in a period when the power-loom was still unimportant. Parading his favourite *idée fixe*, he ascribed the disturbances of 1816–20 to the evil consequences for the English cotton industry of the unrestricted sale of yarn to rival foreign manufacturers; and he exhorted the future historian 'never to make use of the words sedition, disaffection to government, or rebellion as he glides over this short period, for I assure him there was not amongst them a single iota of anything of the kind'.[5] As

---

[1] *PP. 1834 (556)* x, Q. 4928.   [2] *Manchester Mercury*, 14 Feb. 1809.
[3] *PP. 1812 (231)* III, p. 269.   [4] *PP. 1834 (556)* x, Q. 5588.
[5] Radcliffe, *op. cit.* p. 196.

a French observer noted, even in 1828, 'dans les temps ordinaires, les Weavers ne s'occupent point, ou presque point, de politique. Quand la dêtresse arrive, ils commencent à s'en occuper, croyant que le gouvernement est la cause de leurs souffrances'.[1]

Most of these sporadic outbreaks of early radicalism among the cotton weavers have been well studied by historians, and their details are readily available in the authorities to which reference will be made. Generally, they have been approached from two different angles: from that of the 'making of the English working class', in E. P. Thompson's phrase, with the gradual development of a consciousness of national politics among all groups of workers; and from that of local history, with its complex interplay of a multitude of sectional interests all combining to give a highly individual flavouring to political stirrings in the different regions. Here the aim will be more modest than either of these, and will be restricted to seeing their occasional sympathies with radical politics as only one element in the handloom weavers' protracted, many-sided, and wholly unsuccessful struggle to maintain their position in a hostile and changing environment.[2]

II

It is difficult to accept that there was much deep-rooted, carefully thought-out, or strenuously supported radicalism among the cotton weavers during the Napoleonic wars, despite the fact that 'sedition' occupied a good deal of the time of the country's rulers at both a national and a local level, as any study based on the Home

---

[1] G. D'Eichthal, 'Condition de la classe ouvriere en Angleterre en 1828', *Revue Historique* LXXIX (1902), 68.

[2] Of the works which examine working-class political movements generally in the period 1800–30, and which devote some attention to radicalism among the cotton handloom weavers, the most useful are: J. L. and B. Hammond, *The skilled labourer, 1760–1832* (London, 1919) and E. P. Thompson, *The making of the English working class* (London, 1963). Of the local approach to Lancashire politics in the early nineteenth century, there is unfortunately nothing to compare with A. Temple Patterson's model work on Leicester. D. Read, *Peterloo: the massacre and its background* (Manchester, 1958), analyses one particular phase of the radical movement, 1816–20, and the same author's 'Chartism in Manchester' (A. Briggs (ed.), *Chartist Studies* (London, 1960), pp. 29–64) gives some insights on the 1830s and 1840s. Careful local histories of individual towns, such as G. E. Miller, *Blackburn: the evolution of a cotton town* (Blackburn, 1951) and W. Bennett, *History of Burnley* (Burnley, 1947–9, 4 vols.) are useful on occasions.

Office papers will testify. So scared was the governing element in society at this time by the outcome of 'revolution' in France, however, that it was inclined to see the hand of Jacobins in every food riot. Of course, the weavers did sometimes express dissatisfaction with the government and with the effects of the war. As early as April 1798, the *Manchester Mercury* published an 'address to the weavers and other artificers', decrying the opinion, which, many weavers apparently held, that a negotiated peace was advisable.[1] It argued that 'an ignominious peace with our inveterate enemies' would destroy English trade and make English workmen 'as wretched as the natives of Holland'.

Rumours of conspiracies against the government were again rife in the weaving districts in the years of high food prices at the turn of the century, when the weavers were in fact actively agitating for an effective Arbitration Act.[2] Nor was the suspicion of political undertones wholly absent at the time of the great weavers' strike in 1808. Perhaps the presence of a traitor to the cause of ruling-class solidarity in the shape of Colonel Joseph Hanson, a radical who openly sympathized with the weavers in Manchester, gave the impression that here was something more than a purely working-class industrial dispute.[3] At any rate, the *Manchester Mercury* 'seriously apprehended that the ...disturbances have been secretly fomented by latent sedition, if not by actual rebellion'.[4]

Fear of revolution in the cotton districts during the war was strongest, however, in 1812, at the depth of the depression which succeeded the brief boom of 1810. Food prices had soared, and the appeal for parliamentary help in 1811 had been unsuccessful. In Lancashire the Luddism of 1812 manifested itself chiefly in food riots and in attacks on some of the few powerloom establishments then in operation.[5] However, some of the outbreaks appeared to have a political significance. On 8 April 1812, the Manchester Royal Exchange was attacked by a large mob whose object was to break up a meeting of the wealthy inhabitants which had been

---

[1] *Manchester Mercury*, 10 April 1798.
[2] Hammonds, *op. cit.* pp. 65–7. For the Arbitration Acts, see above, pp. 149–52.
[3] See above, pp. 191–93.   [4] *Manchester Mercury*, 7 June 1808.
[5] See above, pp. 198–9.

called to draw up a loyal address to the Prince Regent on his acces-
sion to full powers. Having achieved this aim, the crowd then
proceeded to pass certain 'revolutionary' motions unanimously.[1]

Certainly in 1812 there was a general impression that things
could not go on as they were for much longer. At Failsworth, it
was widely held that 'it was almost impossible for the parliament
to carry on', and one local weaver is reputed to have told a neighbour that 'England would be done-up and all destroyed before
his neighbour's chickens were hatched'.[2] The following year,
however, saw, not the outbreak of revolution, but the return of
prosperity and the rapid disappearance from the cotton areas of all
forms of violent disturbance, whether politically motivated or not.

According to the reports of the various spies employed by such
zealous Lancashire magistrates as Colonel Fletcher of Bolton, a
general rising was projected in 1812, and arming and drilling and
secret oath-bound conspiracies accompanied the food riots and the
attacks on looms. The historians, however, are divided as to the
amount of credence which should be attached to these documents
in the Home Office papers: the traditional view of the Hammonds
was that many of the events therein described were purely
imaginary, in that the spies, being paid by results, produced the
kind of evidence which their employers wanted to hear, but
recently Mr Edward Thompson has attempted to show that many
of the reports were well grounded in actual events.[3] Essentially,
the dispute is incapable of final resolution, since it rests entirely on
an assessment of the value of evidence from a source which is not
above suspicion; and in the last resort, those who want to believe
that England came near to revolution at this time will find support
for their belief in these papers, whereas those who do not wish to
believe this will find little difficulty in discounting the records.
Whether or not some of the handloom weavers might have been
preparing to overturn the political system by force in 1812, the
fact remains that no revolutionary outbreak actually occurred,

[1] The editor of the *Manchester Mercury* (14 April 1812) 'refused to sully his pages by their insertion'. The Regent's failure to bring in a Whig ministry seems to have been the chief cause of dissatisfaction (Thompson, *op. cit.* p. 566).

[2] J. Fielding, *Rural historical gleanings of South Lancashire* (Manchester, 1852), p. 222.

[3] See Hammonds, *op. cit.* chapter x, and Thompson, *op. cit.* pp. 565–9 and 591–602.

and under these circumstances no-one can say how near a potential outbreak was; for it is only with hindsight that one can say, if the revolution breaks out today, then the country was on the verge of it yesterday. The considered opinion of General Maitland, who was commander of the military forces in the north at the time, is perhaps the most plausible assessment: 'In regard to their [the radicals'] organization, that they have some understanding and more of method than at any former period is, I apprehend, undoubted...For my part, however, I am a total disbeliever that either such rising [as the magistrates suspect] was seriously intended, or that they were in a state of organization to admit of it.'[1]

What is more certain is that a number of Manchester weavers were interested in the possibility of securing peace and parliamentary reform through the normal constitutional channel of petitioning the Regent and the legislature. For they were prominent among 'the thirty-eight' arrested on 11 June in a Manchester public house after their reform meeting had been betrayed to the constables by a spy. Their trial and subsequent acquittal on a technical point attracted considerable attention, and did much to restore respect for the processes of the law. But it is some indication of the basic lukewarmness of the handloom weavers towards serious reform that only one of the 'thirty-eight'—John Knight, a small manufacturer—acquired any subsequent prominence in radical circles.[2] That some cotton weavers in 1812 hoped to secure reform by peaceful means seems, therefore, well attested. But so far as securing it by force is concerned, the scope for speculation by the historian remains wide open.

III

The most important outbreak of political radicalism in the period of the unreformed parliament in which the cotton handloom weavers certainly played a part came in the post-war depression

[1] Maitland to R. Ryder, 6 May 1812 (*HO. 40. 1/1*).
[2] A. Prentice, *Historical sketches and personal recollections of Manchester* (London, 1851), pp. 76–82.

of 1816–19.[1] Here there were two distinct and quite brief phases of activity—1816–17 and 1819—broken in 1818 when the weavers again resorted to the strike weapon.[2] An anonymous pamphlet of 1817 stated clearly the weavers' grounds for dissatisfaction with the unreformed parliament: in the first place, a truly representative legislature would never have fought the war against revolutionary and Napoleonic France which had had such disastrous effects on the cotton industry; and secondly, such a body would not have raised the money to pay the interest on war loans and other expenses of government by indirect taxation which fell most heavily on the working classes.[3]

In the 1816–17 phase, which began with the establishment of local Hampden clubs designed to seek reform by peaceful and constitutional means, and which culminated in the famous 'march of the Blanketeers' and the alleged 'Ardwick plot' to 'make a Moscow of Manchester', many of the leaders were certainly weavers.[4] Thus, in October 1816, when agents of Sir Francis Burdett and Major Cartwright addressed a Stockport reform meeting, Sherwin and Lilly, the local weavers' leaders, were on the platform, and in the following March the Stockport political union had a weaver, William Ogden, as its secretary.[5] The whole movement must, however, be kept in its proper perspective, for at its height in March 1817, the forty Hampden clubs in the Manchester area had only 8,000 members even at their own estimate—hardly a sign of a massive following for reform ideas.[6]

The evidence in fact suggests that the interest of the bulk of the handloom weavers at this stage was at best lukewarm and certainly short-lived. Contrary to popular belief, it is not even certain that they played the major role in the Blanketeers' march on 10 March

[1] The most accessible and eminently readable first-hand account of Lancashire radicalism in this period is S. Bamford, *Passage in the life of a radical* (ed. H. Dunckley, London, 1893).
[2] See above, pp. 193–6.
[3] 'Operator' (pseud.), *The petitioning weavers defended* (Manchester, 1817).
[4] H. W. C. Davies, 'Lancashire Reformers, 1816–17', *Bulletin John Rylands Library*, x (1926), 291.
[5] P. M. Giles, *The social and economic development of Stockport, 1815–36* (Manchester M.A. thesis, unpublished, 1950), pp. 141 and 168.
[6] D. Read, *Peterloo: the massacre and its background* (Manchester, 1958), p. 97.

1817,[1] the *Manchester Mercury* report being quite emphatic that they did not: 'in justice to a worthy, patient, and most suffering part of the community, as an undoubted fact, it affords us the sincerest pleasure to remark, inasmuch as the weavers are asserted to have formed a prominent part of this body, that several manufacturers who employed many looms in this neighbourhood sent to ascertain how many would be deserted, when it was found that not more than about six looms were idle, although several hundreds were visited. A great proportion of the prisoners, we lament to state, have been cotton spinners, many of whom are known to earn between 30 and 40 shillings per week!—So much for vaunted distress and misery'.[2]

After the failure of the 1818 strike, however, it appears that the handloom weavers' interest in political reform was much stronger in the year of Peterloo, when the industry was again depressed, than it had been in 1816–17. An earlier meeting at St Peter's Field, on 21 June 1819, was called by the weavers to petition either for public relief or for assisted emigration; but it ended in demanding parliamentary reform.[3] Dr Read's recent study of Peterloo shows convincingly that there must have been a substantial shift of opinion among the handloom weavers in Manchester and the surrounding towns and villages during 1819, so that, by the time of the actual 'massacre' on 16 August 1819, they had come to form the backbone of the movement for peaceful reform. Out of 69 of the 300 signatories to the requisition calling the Peterloo meeting whose occupations have been traced, 46 were weavers; and among the 200 sufferers on the books of the Metropolitan relief committee after the massacre were more than 150 weavers.[4]

---

[1] Several local magistrates also regarded the spinners as heavily implicated in the Blanketeers episode. See W. Evans to Lord Sidmouth, 18 March 1817: 'Almost every person holding the position of the lowest shopkeeper decidedly feels an interest on the side of the law. Amongst the operative part of the community there is evidently an opposite spirit, and amongst no class more than the spinners...' (*HO. 40. 5/4*). During the 1818 strike, Colonel Fletcher recalled that it was from the spinners that 'the greater share of pecuniary support to the Blanketeers of 1817 was derived' (Fletcher to Hobhouse, 11 July 1818 (*HO. 42. 178*). Giles, *op. cit.* pp. 117, claims that the Stockport weavers, who lived along the route of the march, held aloof from it.

[2] *Manchester Mercury*, 18 March 1817.

[3] Read, *op. cit.* p. 109.   [4] *Ibid.* pp. 22–4.

The 1819 movement also won extensive support from the weavers outside the Manchester area, although, as in the 1818 strike, they demonstrated their feelings at a later date. At Burnley, where a barracks had been built after the disorders which accompanied the strike, a large reform meeting was held three months after Peterloo. John Knight was the principal speaker, and the crowd, variously estimated at from 4,000 to 10,000, included contingents from nearby weaving villages. Pikes and pistols were carried, 'caps of liberty' worn, and banners with reform slogans displayed. The precise import of the resolutions passed is unclear; Knight contended that they did no more than condemn the government's recent suspension of Habeas Corpus. However, their revolutionary intent was proved to the satisfaction of the authorities, and Knight was imprisoned for two years. Some of his followers received sentences ranging from three to six months.[1]

Although the cause of parliamentary reform seemed to have strong attractions for the cotton weavers in 1819, it quickly evaporated in 1820. The disappearance of mass support, which was as rapid as its accumulation in the previous year, was the result in part of divisions between the various radical leaders and in part of the government's repressive policy.[2] A more important explanation, however, was the return of prosperity. A combination of abundant work and falling food prices made the period 1820–3 the Indian summer of material well-being for the cotton hand-loom weavers,[3] and it is not surprising that, when life again became reasonably comfortable for them, they ceased to call for reform.

That the reform spirit vanished so rapidly, though, is an eloquent testimony to the very shallow impression which serious political ideas had so far made on the minds of most workers. This does not necessarily mean that a vague sympathy towards the reformers' aims wholly disappeared. William Varley recorded in his diary for 1820 the Cato Street conspiracy, the trials of Henry Hunt and John Knight for their parts in the reform meetings of the previous year, the 'general strike' in Scotland in the spring, and the 'trial' of

---

[1] For a full account of the Burnley meeting of 15 November, see W. Bennett, *History of Burnley* (Burnley, 1948), III, 279–83.
[2] Read, *op. cit.* pp. 155–9.   [3] See above, pp. 104 and 130.

Queen Caroline, in whose cause he showed great enthusiasm. As late as October 1822, he reported the release of 'Mr Hunt' from Ilchester gaol, 'and to commemorate this day there is drinking, and shooting, and from Padiham there goes a balloon'.[1] But such sympathy did not, in the early 1820s, find expression either in the growth of organizations of committed reformers, as in 1816–17, or in large-scale public demonstrations, as in 1819.

At the depth of the handloom weavers' misery in 1826—which was certainly the most widespread and protracted slump to affect them—they again toyed with the possibility of ending their difficulties by securing the franchise, and other radical nostrums. On 9 February 1827, Joseph Hume presented a petition in the Commons on behalf of 'the starving weavers of Blackburn', who claimed that all the evils which added to their misery—the unjustifiable wars which ran up a huge national debt, the placemen and the army maintained by heavy taxation, and the class-motivated Corn Law—had 'originated from the people not being represented in that House'.[2] John Knight and other old radicals were active again, but the reform agitation was neither so well organized as in 1816–17, nor so widely supported as at Peterloo. And, once the worst of the depression had passed, the movement's edge was again blunted.

In the nation-wide disturbances which accompanied the new Whig government's resolution to bring in some measure of reform in 1830–2, the cotton handloom weavers seem to have played only a small part—a possible reflection of their diminishing importance in the labour force, especially near Manchester,[3] and of the lack of organization which their relative poverty inevitably involved. This is not to deny that individual weavers shared the prevailing 'anti-establishment' mood of the time, and entertained the widely-held hopes that great benefits would come from the reformed parliament. The interest of the Preston weavers, for example, is sufficiently attested by the fact that, on the occasion of William IV's coronation in September 1831, a mock funeral procession was arranged by the local radicals. In addition to the usual

[1] Bennett, *op. cit.* pp. 379–84. [2] *New Series Hansard*, vol. 16, col. 431.
[3] See above, p. 57, and below, p. 265.

reform slogans, 'there was exhibited a banner with the figures of the Queen and the Princess Victoria on one side, with their annuities marked below; and on the other, as a contrast, a weaver's wife and her daughter, with the alleged amount of their incomes also inscribed'.[1]

Handloom weavers seem also to have been involved on the side of John Fort, the Reform candidate, in the only major disturbance to take place in a predominantly weaving constituency during the Reform Act crisis—the Clitheroe election riot of 31 July 1832. When the Tory candidate, Mr Irving, visited the town, his carriage was attacked and the military had to be called in to restore order. The following doggerel, from a broadsheet called 'Fort's Advocate, or The People's Register', can be taken as an incitement by the reformers to the local weavers to cause trouble on Irving's visit:

> Ye Pendleton lads, now lift up your heads,
> Come jump off your looms, but piece no more threads,
> Yonder is Irving coming, let us give him a pill,
> Let us grunt him and groan him back to Clark Hill.[2]

But the reform agitation was one which seems to have drawn in most classes in the industrial areas, and there is little to suggest that the handloom weavers as an organized group played any outstanding part in it, or that their particular problems and grievances were brought out to justify the case for reform.

IV

Although the cotton weavers were at several times identifiable with the radical cause in the days of the unreformed parliament, the conclusion is inescapable that their interest and their enthusiasm —often, admittedly, quickly and passionately aroused—was usually rapidly dissipated without securing any concrete results. The handloom weavers, of course, differed little from most other groups of workers in this respect, for the mass reform movement as a whole

[1] *Manchester Guardian*, 17 Sept. 1831.
[2] Enclosure in a large bundle of documents relating to the Clitheroe disturbance in HO. 52. 18.

moved in fits and starts during the first three decades of the nineteenth century. Nonetheless, their particular behaviour requires some explanation before the rather special case of the weavers' radicalism after the great Reform Act is considered.

In the first place, it is important to realize that, even if some weavers were drawn into radicalism, others were not. Many, like Richard Needham of Bolton, remained basically 'loyalist' in regarding the structure of parliament as largely irrelevant to their particular local problems. Even in the Chartist days, when the remaining handloom weavers had endured many years of almost unrelieved misery and had been disappointed in the reformed parliament, there was still a certain element which refused to be drawn in.[1] It was therefore at all times less easy to secure unanimous support for the reform cause than for either peaceful petitioning for legislative help or industrial action.

Not only was it the case that many weavers held back, but it is also difficult to accept Mr E. P. Thompson's thesis that from the post-war slump to the Chartist movement 'the strength of the extreme reformers...lay in the handworkers' villages of the Midlands and the north'.[2] Although it can certainly be shown that the cotton handloom weavers did on occasions support radicalism, this is very different from proving that they were attached any more constantly or firmly to the cause than were other groups of workers.

Indeed, Mr Thompson's conclusion that 'weavers and stockingers were the worst victims of *laissez-faire*, and *therefore* [author's italics] they merited also the closest attentions of Lord Sidmouth' must rank as a classic *non-sequitur*.[3] The connexion between extreme poverty and extreme radicalism can never be assumed—the factors which determine an individual's political outlook and behaviour are far more complex than that. In every case, the link must be proved. Often it seems that the most depressed are also the most apathetic, and this was the case with some of the handloom weavers. Those who showed no initiative in getting out of a manifestly declining trade—and many of those who stuck to

[1] See below, p. 227.　　　　　　[2] Thompson, *op. cit.* p. 648.
[3] Thompson, *op. cit.* p. 649.

handloom weaving in the big factory towns in the 1830s did precisely that[1]—were hardly likely to show initiative in changing their political status, either.

It is difficult to avoid concluding that, over the first half of the nineteenth century, political radicalism on the whole was no more than a kind of lowest common denominator which all workers might seize upon when some temporary setback seemed particularly severe and when the more usual forms of defence seemed inappropriate or had proved unsuccessful. It is always difficult to assess the numerical significance of any one section of the working class in movements which appear to involve all sections, but there seems no reason to suppose that radicalism was not the same vague, imprecise, ill-thought-out last resort to the cotton weavers as it was to most other working men.

Secondly, political radicalism was a relatively minor weapon in the weavers' armoury because there were others which, tactically, had greater advantages and were more likely to be accepted by the bulk of the workers themselves. Apart from the purely practical difficulties of organizing a nation-wide agitation in a country where communications were slow and regional differences pronounced, all mass political movements of the early nineteenth century which sought political reform by peaceful means had to face the inevitable dilemma of what to do if their demands were rejected. No matter how much it might try to impress by the strength of its numerical support, no extra-parliamentary agitation could seriously hope to succeed unless there was inside parliament a general opinion prepared to accept reform. There was such an opinion in 1830–2 and in 1865–7, but it was absent in 1816–19 and in the 1840s.

But the reluctance to resort to parliamentary reform as a remedy for distress sprang from something even deeper than this uncertainty about what to do if their demands were not met. Parliament, London, and the great aristocratic families who controlled them were, after all, very remote—indeed almost wholly divorced —from the everyday experience of handloom weavers in small towns and villages in the north of England. The central govern-

---

[1] See below, pp. 253–4.

ment did little which directly affected their normal lives, whether for good or for evil, except occasionally to send down judges and soldiers as the symbol of its authority to keep order, and to levy taxes which seemed very burdensome in times of unemployment and high prices. Far more real to the weavers in their own localities, however, were the attitudes and actions of magistrates and manufacturers. The resentment of William Varley was never directed at my lords Liverpool, Eldon, Sidmouth, and Castlereagh, but it was very frequently levelled against 'the inhuman and relentless masters' and against the soldiers whom the local magistrates had caused to be stationed 'at their grand and populous but infamous town of Burnley'.[1]

It was these local men who had to be threatened and coerced, who had to be made to take a responsible attitude to wages whether as payers or as fixers, and whose sympathy and charity had in the last resort to be relied on. The J.P. and the employer, not the M.P. and the cabinet minister, were the 'higher powers' in the weavers' everyday experience, and it was to influencing *them* that their main efforts were necessarily directed. Appealing to parliament meant a long delay until committees had met, information had been gathered to enlighten ignorant legislators, and the rights and wrongs of any proposed action had been debated. Appealing to the goodwill, or overcoming the obstinacy, of the local political and economic 'establishment' was far more likely to produce short-term results.

For these reasons, particularly before the lessons of the 1826 slump had been driven home, the cotton handloom weavers were likely to try other remedies before they turned to political radicalism. They could always hope that parliament would 'do something', not by fixing wages itself, but by compelling local magistrates and masters to act. The whole rationale of the Arbitration Acts and of the various schemes for 'boards of trade' was to make prominent men in the weaving districts more aware of their responsibilities, or at least to enable those who already approached the weavers' problems in a 'responsible' way to prevail against those who did not. Then again, industrial action, difficult as it was,

[1] Bennett, *op. cit.* p. 379.

was never wholly ruled out. The cotton weavers managed two major strikes, and minor and often successful ones still occurred after 1826.[1] And finally, when there was a protracted industrial recession, it was on the charity of the wealthier members of the local community that those in distress primarily depended.[2] All three of these alternative methods of seeking to end poverty essentially involved influencing important local people.

Occasionally, when a major disaster made long-term plans more imperative than immediate *ad hoc* decisions, the weavers found these local channels inadequate, and turned their attention to such panaceas as parliamentary reform. But to take up such a remedy was in itself a sign of weakness and despair, not of strength. It meant deserting the specific, the practical, and the immediate for the vague, the imprecise, and the improbable. And on the whole, the cotton weavers were sufficiently realistic to see that they were more likely to advance their cause by strictly limited and practical means than by plunging into the unmapped wilderness of whole-sale political reform.

v

As is well known, the Reform Act of 1832 did little to quell the popular demand for further reform. The expectations which both working men and their sympathizers among the new radical M.P.s had entertained of the reformed House of Commons were un-fulfilled. Within a few weeks of the new parliament assembling, Mr Gillon, M.P., was complaining that 'a reformed parliament had now met six weeks, and not one measure having any or the least tendency to promote the prosperity of the people at large had yet been introduced, a fact which was but too likely to shake the confidence of the people in a reformed parliament'.[3] As if to confirm this view, as early as May 1833 'the working classes of the hundred of Blackburn', where the main concentration of hand-loom weavers was now to be found, held an open-air meeting near Padiham 'for the purpose of memorializing his Majesty, praying him to dismiss his present ministers, and for petitioning

---

[1] See above, chapter 8, *passim*.   [2] See below, pp. 239 *et seq.*
[3] *3rd Series Hansard*, vol. 16, col. 938.

the House of Commons for universal suffrage, annual parliaments, vote by ballot, and the abolition of the property qualification for M.P.s'.[1] The similarity between these demands and the 'six points' of the People's Charter is striking, and it is obvious that the call for political institutions over which they would have greater control and in which they would be directly represented would become increasingly loud as the new parliament demonstrated its inability, or, indeed, its downright unwillingness, to do anything to improve the weavers' position.

There was further evidence of this growing dissatisfaction at the time of the 1834 select committee. One Scottish witness observed that the Reform Act had 'not given them all they require' and that 'the generality of the weavers were favourable to a lower scale of franchise'.[2] Another commented sagely that he knew 'no conceivable reason why men should love the institutions of their country unless they insure to them a reasonable amount of social enjoyment'.[3] English weavers and manufacturers held similar views, John Makin reporting that 'the general cry is "Oh, parliament will do nothing for you"'.[4] Nor was it long before public men were warning of the consequences of failing to help the weavers. 'It was only by relieving their distresses', claimed Lord Dudley Stuart, in 1835, 'that their respect could be secured to the laws and institutions of their country, for if they found that by those laws and institutions they were not protected, was it to be wondered at that they should be guilty of some transgressions?'[5]

The brief prosperity of 1834–6, in which even the cotton hand-loom weavers shared,[6] did no more than postpone active demands for the franchise. With the slump of 1837, coupled with the attempt to implement the new Poor Law in the north of England, political radicalism emerged again in Chartism. Apart from the exaggerated fears, common to all sections of the working class, which greeted the introduction of that uninviting piece of Whig

---

[1] *Manchester Guardian*, 1 June 1833. The report suggests, however, that the meeting was not particularly well attended, although it took place on a Monday, normally a day when most weavers, if they had been interested, would not have found it difficult to attend.

[2] PP. *1834* (556) x, QQ. 2774–5.   [3] *Ibid.* Q. 2164.

[4] *Ibid.* Q. 5023.   [5] *3rd Series Hansard*, vol. 29, col. 1158.

[6] See above, p. 106.

social legislation into the manufacturing districts,[1] the handloom weavers had a private grievance against the inhumanity of the reformed parliament, since, despite the strenuous efforts of Fielden and Maxwell, the select committees of which so much had been hoped had produced no beneficial results.[2] By the late 1830s, it was quite obvious that neither boards of trade, taxes on steamlooms, state-aided emigration, a generous public policy towards poverty, nor any of the other standard remedies would be applied to the weavers' condition so long as parliament represented directly only a small proportion of the population, and so long as the majority of its members accepted the fashionable ideas of political economy.[3]

Given such a background, a renewed bout of political agitation among the handloom weavers was hardly unexpected, and it is not surprising that historians have always identified them among the staunchest supporters of the Chartist movement in the late 1830s and 1840s. Professor Briggs, for example, speaks of them as 'a key group in Chartist politics', who preferred those of the Chartist leaders who 'knew how to use and were willing to use militant, headstrong language'.[4] No attempt can be made here to write a narrative of the movement in the weaving districts; but it is possible to offer some general suggestions on the significance of the handloom weavers' contribution to the movement as a whole.

First, the place of the cotton weavers in society at large must be seen in its proper perspective, for although they may indeed have been zealous for the cause, numerically they were a minor element in the great labour force employed in the cotton industry by the late 1830s.[5] By the time the first national petition was drawn up at Birmingham in May 1838, their numbers were rapidly falling off; and they had virtually disappeared before Chartism died in the early 1850s. Even in the movement's early days, they were a significant element in the population in only a few districts—

---

[1] See below, pp. 248–9. 　　　　[2] See above, pp. 160–4.

[3] The radical *Bolton Free Press* realized this. Reporting the departure of Mr Muggeridge (5 May 1838), it expressed the fear that 'their [the weavers'] just claims will not receive much attention from a Legislature like the present'.

[4] *Chartist Studies*, ed. A. Briggs (London, 1960), pp. 7 and 9.

[5] See below, p. 266.

chiefly the towns of Paisley, Carlisle, Preston, Chorley, Bolton, Burnley, Colne, and the villages round about them.

The contribution of the handloom weavers is further weakened if we reject Professor Redford's thesis that, by the late 1830s, the bulk of the cotton handloom weavers were Irish.[1] For it is then no longer possible to boost the cotton weavers' role by stressing the connexions, recently emphasized by several historians,[2] between Irish nationalism and English Chartism, or by assuming that the mythical horde of Irish weavers had both national and economic motives for providing a bulwark of the Chartist movement. The real cotton handloom weavers in the late 1830s were confined to the few areas specified, and even here, many of their number were women and children who were unlikely to have strong political interests. Whatever their keenness, any numerical strength which they brought to Chartism was unlikely to be very significant.

VI

That many of the remaining cotton handloom weavers were closely associated with Chartism cannot be doubted.[3] O'Connor himself frequently commended their loyalty, and once described them as 'the originators, the ornaments, the prop and support of the Chartist cause'.[4] Nor is it surprising that the movement's propaganda repeatedly emphasized the miserable condition into which they had fallen. For their fate offered a grim warning to all working families of what might happen to them if they remained unrepresented in parliament. On an early visit to Carlisle in 1838, Feargus O'Connor claimed that, of 800 male weavers in the town over 21, only 19 possessed the vote, 'and consequently those 19 were but poor make-weights in the struggle with the money-

---

[1] The thesis is stated in A. Redford, *Labour migration in England, 1800–50* (Manchester, 2nd ed. 1964), p. 152. For an examination of it, see above, pp. 63–5.

[2] See, for example, R. O'Higgins, 'Irish influences on the Chartist movement' (*Past and Present*, no. 20 (1961), pp. 83–96), and D. Read and E. Glasgow, *Feargus O'Connor, Irishman and Chartist* (London, 1961).

[3] It should be stressed that the ensuing paragraphs deal only with *cotton* weavers. Studies of handloom weavers on other fabrics and in other districts may well show a different relationship with Chartism.

[4] *Northern Star*, 25 June 1842.

mongers for the complete dominion over their order. If,' he went on, 'the 800 handloom weavers had votes...the great improvement in machinery which displaces them from their position would be directed to the general comfort of man, and not to the advantage of those who trafficked upon labour because they had the franchise.'[1]

The fate of the handloom weavers also fitted excellently into the backward-looking social ideology—of a world of smallholding peasants and domestic craftsmen—which Chartism acquired under Feargus's domination. The evils inherent in the uncontrolled adoption of machinery which displaced men from their traditional employments and made them labour under monstrous conditions —unpleasant atmosphere, long hours of unremitting attention, separation from the rest of the family, and all the other horrors of the early factories—gave great scope for editorials in the *Northern Star*, the movement's chief newspaper.[2] O'Connor once wrote of 'the devouring enemy, machinery', as 'the assassin' which had already destroyed the weavers and now 'threatened also to slay every succeeding interest'.[3] With such an ideology, it is small wonder that the *Northern Star* castigated clergymen like the incumbent of Burnley when he appealed for funds to build a church to end the 'spiritual destitution' of the weavers in the nearby township of Briercliffe, and recommended him instead to 'direct his attention to the temporal wants and physical destitution of his charge',[4] or that recitations with such titles as 'The Downfall of the Handloom Weavers' and 'The Deserted Village' went down well at Chartist soirées and tea-parties.[5]

Some of the leading national figures in the Chartist movement took a special interest in the handloom weavers and acquired a particularly devoted following among them. O'Connor himself was very popular with the weavers; his reception in north-east Lancashire in June 1842, was, even allowing for the *Northern Star's* fulsome reporting, one of the most enthusiastic of his career. Among the more usual banners carried in procession on that

---

[1] *Ibid.* 21 July 1838.
[2] See above, p. 143.
[3] *Northern Star*, 25 June 1842.
[4] *Ibid.* 11 Sept. 1841.
[5] *Ibid.* 2 Sept. 1843.

occasion—'More Pigs and Fewer Parsons', and 'Sweep out the House of Corruption' (surmounted by a broom)—was the simple device 'The Handloom Weavers of Burnley'.[1] Julian Harney, again, was a particular favourite with the Carlisle weavers, whom he frequently visited;[2] and R. J. Richardson, of Manchester, devoted a good deal of his term of imprisonment to analysing the report of the royal commission on the weavers, his conclusions being published in a series of verbose letters in the *Northern Star* in the latter part of 1840.

Of the prominent local Chartists who emerge as something more than mere names, at least two, Richard Marsden and Joseph Broom Hanson, were themselves weavers. Marsden first appears in November 1838 as 'a handloom weaver of Bamber Bridge' when he took the chair at a meeting on Preston moor, and was elected as delegate for Preston at the first national convention.[3] After serving there, he is to be found in the spring of 1839 on an 'agitating tour' to spread the cause in Clitheroe, Padiham, Burnley, Chorley, and other towns and villages in the weaving area.[4] In the period of decline around 1840 he seems to have gone back to the loom first in Bolton and later in Preston again.[5] But in 1841, as the movement revived, he was re-engaged as a local lecturer by the National Charter associations of north-east Lancashire.[6] In 1843 he seems to have caused dissension among the faithful in that district by his opposition to the land scheme; but he represented 'Colne, Sabden, Clitheroe, etc.' at the Chartist convention at Birmingham in September of that year,[7] and was still active as a Chartist official in Preston as late as 1847.[8] J. B. Hanson, the leader of the Carlisle weavers, was equally prominent in industrial and political action during these years. He was foremost in presenting the weavers' case to the royal commission on Mr Muggeridge's visit to Carlisle in June 1838;[9] he was a member of the 1840

[1] *Northern Star*, 2 July 1842.
[2] A. R. Schoyen, *The Chartist challenge* (London, 1958), pp. 48, 74 and 104.
[3] *Manchester Guardian*, 7 Nov. 1838.   [4] *Northern Star*, 29 June 1839.
[5] *Ibid.* 2 Jan. and 21 Aug. 1841.   [6] *Ibid.* 11 Sept. 1841.
[7] *Ibid.* 26 Aug. and 9 Sept. 1843.
[8] *Ibid.* 16 Jan. 1847. Further details of Marsden's career in the national movement can be found in the standard histories of Chartism by Gammage and Hovell.
[9] *Carlisle Journal*, 23 June 1838.

Manchester conference which launched the National Charter association; and he was 'Chartist candidate' at the hustings in Carlisle in the general election of 1841.[1]

At a more humble level, too, handloom weavers were prominent in their own districts, for example, as movers of resolutions at political meetings. All but three of the speakers at the Preston meeting which elected Richard Marsden to the first national convention were weavers.[2] In Bolton it was asserted in 1840 that 'the radicals...are chiefly of that poor despised class called weavers'.[3] This was a startling development, for a weaver who had advocated universal suffrage and the ballot there in 1837 had been heard 'with mingled symptoms of applause and disapprobation';[4] but by September of the following year, at the meeting which first considered 'the propriety of supporting the People's Charter', two of the three speakers whose occupations are known were weavers.[5] Perhaps the fact that, in the interval between these two meetings, the royal commission's representative had been and gone without effecting any improvement in their lot was of some significance in bringing about this change in the Bolton weavers' outlook.

The best indication of the strength of Chartism in the weaving towns and villages, however, is the effectiveness of their local organizations. Here, everything suggests great vitality, particularly in the first phase, 1838–9. In north-east Lancashire, the first great pro-Charter meeting seems to have been at Colne on Monday, 22 October 1838, when J. R. Stephens and R. J. Richardson addressed an estimated crowd of 25,000, which had been swollen by processions from the surrounding townships.[6] Thereafter, activity was brisk, and in the closing months of the year, branches of the 'Northern Union' were formed in many of the nearby villages, most of which numbered their populations in a few hundreds only: Laneshaw Bridge, where the Primitive Methodists[7] were particularly active in the movement,

---

[1] *Northern Star*, 3 July 1841. [2] *Manchester Guardian*, 7 Nov. 1838.
[3] *Northern Star*, 24 Oct. 1840. [4] *Manchester Guardian*, 21 June 1837.
[5] *Bolton Free Press*, 22 Sept. 1838. [6] *Northern Star*, 27 Oct. 1838.
[7] For a general discussion of the relationship between the different branches of Methodism and political movements in this period, see E. P. Thompson, *op. cit.* pp. 350–400. The

was reported to have a branch in the *Northern Star* of 5 November; Marsden, Haggate, Barnoldswick and other places quickly followed.[1]

The financial contributions which these small and poverty-stricken places were able to make to various Chartist appeals— such as the 'national rent' and the J. R. Stephens defence fund— also indicate the enthusiasm felt in this centre of cotton handloom weaving for a cause which promised an immediate panacea for years of suffering. 'The noble but famishing handloom weavers of Haslingden' collected £7. 15s. 1½d. for the use of the first convention;[2] Sabden, where a population of 1,200 bought 44 *Northern Stars* weekly, sent £7. 10s. to both the convention and the Stephens fund;[3] and 12s. out of a total of £16 subscribed in Burnley on Stephens's behalf was given by 'a few poor handloom weavers of Mereclough, a small village near Burnley, who are determined to do their utmost to free themselves from the galling fetters that bind them'.[4] Similar financial sacrifices were made by the Carlisle weavers,[5] whose devotion to radical politics seems even to have pre-dated the establishment of the great 'Northern Union' and its branches. One of the remedies suggested to assistant commissioner Muggeridge by their leader, J. B. Hanson, was that 'the suffrage should be made universal, because this would give all classes an opportunity of supporting every legitimate interest in the Commons house of Parliament, instead of the exclusive principle that is now pursued with respect to legislation'.[6]

After the period of decline in 1840, there was again considerable activity in the weaving districts in the establishment of National Charter associations. At the beginning of 1842, William Beesley,

Methodist Unitarians, a small sect peculiar to north-east Lancashire, whose strongholds were Oldham, Rochdale, Todmorden, Rossendale, and Padiham, seem to have been particularly active in social and political movements. Their most noted adherents were John Fielden, M.P., and James Taylor, radical candidate at Rochdale in 1832 and subsequently a member of the 1838–9 Chartist convention; but their support came overwhelmingly from artisans and workmen, and in Padiham in particular from handloom weavers. See H. McLachlan, *The Methodist Unitarian movement* (Manchester, 1919), *passim*.

[1] *Northern Star*, 12 Nov., 10 and 17 Dec. 1838.
[2] *Ibid.* 2 March 1839. [3] *Ibid.* 29 June 1839.
[4] *Ibid.* 6 April 1839. [5] *Ibid.* 26 Jan. 1839.
[6] *Carlisle Journal*, 23 June 1838.

an Accrington bookseller, member of the 1842 national convention, and secretary of the north-east Lancashire group of Charter associations, reported new branches in many villages along the Lancashire–Yorkshire border—Oswaldtwistle, Baxenden, Grindleton, Sawley, Great Harwood, Settle, and Long Preston being among them. He contrasted their enthusiasm with their material poverty, which made it impossible to engage a district lecturer to keep interest alive. Of Sawley, a tiny village near Clitheroe, where Beesley spoke in a room under the Methodist Chapel on Christmas Day 1841, he wrote 'There is some brave fellows in that place, but God help them, they are in a miserable condition, being all of them handloom weavers, and not able to earn more than from 2 shillings to 3 shillings per week'.[1] By May 1842, the weavers in the Burnley area were holding regular outdoor meetings,[2] and in the end the language used by the speakers was said to be so violent that O'Connor was obliged to administer a rebuke and to urge greater moderation.[3]

Not quite all the cotton handloom weavers were Chartist, however, particularly in the big factory towns, where those still surviving in 1840 were likely to be either elderly and probably more 'conservative', or else shiftless and uninterested.[4] Blackburn, for example, was 'somewhat apathetic', even according to the Chartists themselves, in the 1838–9 phase.[5] At Preston, too, there were evidently divisions among the remaining weavers. One of their old leaders, John Lennon, a witness at the 1834 select committee, wrote a vitriolic letter to the Home Secretary in 1839 denouncing those who followed O'Connor as 'an infidel crusade, more bent on the upsetting of the present cabinet and more devoted to plunder than they are to wholesome laws and equal rights'.[6] It was therefore in the poorer small towns and villages, where a lack of employment opportunities meant that many of the weavers were still relatively young and energetic, that Chartism really took a firm hold.

[1] *Northern Star*, 1 Jan. 1842. [2] *Manchester Guardian*, 4 May 1842.
[3] *Northern Star*, 25 June 1842. [4] See above, p. 166.
[5] *Northern Star*, 30 March 1839.
[6] J. Lennon to Lord J. Russell, 21 Jan. 1839 (*HO. 44. 32*).

VII

The close relationship between many of the remaining cotton handloom weavers and the Chartist movement is clearly established. Two problems remain. First, were the weavers, as Professor Briggs suggests, more inclined than other groups of workers to be swayed by the violent 'physical force' men,[1] and secondly, did they remain more constant in their attachment to Chartism than did the cotton factory workers, as Dr Read implies?[2] In 1839, there was clearly much violent talk going round in Lancashire, and local authorities became alarmed. On 27 March, the Chartists of the little weaving village of Haggate, between Burnley and Colne, resolved that, if 'moral force' failed, the national convention would be 'justified in having recourse to means of a more decisive and physical nature, and shall, when called for, receive with promptitude the assistance of our right arms and entire physical energies';[3] within a few days, the Burnley magistrates had evidence that pikes were being manufactured in the village.[4]

By the summer of 1839, the magistrates of Colne were bombarding the Home Office with pleas for a barracks, on the grounds that careful inquiry had revealed the existence of between three and five hundred armed Chartists in a town of less than 10,000 people.[5] Risings among the Lancashire silk weavers were also expected: at Middleton, the local Chartist association, said to have 800 well-armed members in 1839,[6] was able to keep going even in the gloom of 1840;[7] and at Leigh, the other Lancashire silk-weaving centre, the 'state of insubordination amongst the weavers' was such in December 1838 that 'the lives of...clergymen, mill-owners, and Poor Law guardians' were held to be in danger.[8] But in none of these places did a political rising occur, either then, or in 1841–2.

[1] Briggs, *op. cit.* p. 9.
[2] D. Read, 'Chartism in Manchester', in Briggs, *op. cit.* p. 48.
[3] *Northern Star*, 13 April 1839.
[4] Enclosure in Rev. W. Thursby, J.P. (Burnley) to Home Office, 8 April 1839 (*HO. 40. 37*).
[5] H. Bolton, clerk to Colne magistrates, to Home Office, 7 Aug. 1839 (*ibid*).
[6] *Manchester Guardian*, 24 Aug. 1839.   [7] *Ibid.* 15 Aug. and 19 Sept. 1840.
[8] Rev. J. W. Edwards (Leigh) to Lord J. Russell, 12 Dec. 1839 (*HO. 52. 37*).

The handloom weavers were not unique among cotton workers in being violent in words, though not in deeds. As a group, the handloom weavers were in fact missing from the procession of Manchester trades which marched to the first great Kersal Moor meeting on 23 September 1838 and heard wild words from a succession of leading radical speakers.[1] Nor was Cooke Taylor, from whose one-day tour of north-east Lancashire the thesis that the handloom weavers were more violently inclined than the factory workers chiefly derives, wholly consistent.[2] Elsewhere on his travels, he contrasted 'the extraordinary violence and reckless-ness of the blockprinters', another declining group of male textile workers, with 'the patient submission of the handloom weavers'.[3] Moreover, it was not merely the handloom weavers of Burnley who went to be inspired by Feargus on his triumphal visit to north-east Lancashire in 1842, for 'the [factory] masters... set their hands at liberty', too, to hear him.[4]

The overall impression is that the handloom weavers, although no doubt inclined to enjoy both hearing and using violent lan-guage, were just as reluctant as any other group with similar tastes when it actually came to doing something violent. Their spirit may have been more willing, but their flesh was as weak as anyone else's; and there was no equivalent of the events at New-port or Llanidloes in the cotton-weaving districts. There was, indeed, one serious riot at Colne in 1840 in which a special constable was killed. But it had no political aim. It was directed against the newly-established county constabulary, whose repre-sentatives in Colne were apparently guilty of overbearing conduct.[5]

If the handloom weavers were no more violent in action than many other Chartist supporters, there is not much to suggest that they were any more loyal, either. The great falling-off of activity after the Newport rising appears to have been just as marked in the weaving districts as elsewhere, while after 1842 there was a

[1] *Manchester Guardian*, 25 Sept. 1838.
[2] W. Cooke Taylor, *Notes of a tour in the manufacturing districts* (London, 1842), pp. 64–5.
[3] *Ibid.* pp. 93–4.   [4] *Northern Star*, 2 July 1842.
[5] *Manchester Guardian*, 12 Aug. 1840. The Colne riot occurred at a time when Chartism everywhere was at a very low ebb. It is significant that it was first reported in the *Northern Star* under 'Keighley News', an indication that there was no correspondent in Colne at the time. Even this report was almost a verbatim copy of the *Guardian* account.

rapid collapse of interest and support—largely, of course, the result of the return of prosperity and of the great increase in factory employment in the years 1843–5.[1] A meeting of Chartist delegates in north Lancashire in September 1843 revealed a very sorry state of affairs: 'The Padiham delegate could not say that his district had made much progress of late...The Sabden delegate said his district had been in a declining state...The Bacup delegate said his locality was in a low condition; they had at present only about fifteen members', and at Accrington 'they had no place to hold their lectures in, their numbers were few, and they were in debt.'[2]

Other weaving districts showed a similar decline in interest in 1843: in March, the Bolton association's funds were said to have been 'materially injured',[3] while in Carlisle a meeting to elect a new committee to serve 'as a sort of rallying point for the Chartist body' was attended by 'not more than 40 to 50 persons'.[4] Had not economic developments caused their numbers to dwindle rapidly after 1842, then perhaps the hand-weaving areas might have remained more loyal to the declining radical movement. But there is in fact little to suggest that handloom weavers were prominent among such Chartists as were still active after 1842, and there are few signs of activity in the old weaving districts in Chartism's last flare-up in 1847–8.

VIII

Any connexion between the cotton handloom weavers and Chartism's main contemporary as an extra-parliamentary agitation—the anti-Corn Law League—was inevitably much more tenuous, for most of the League's energy was devoted to converting or cajoling parliamentary electors, among whose numbers weavers did not bulk large. However, the weavers' awful fate provided anti-Corn Law propagandists with suitable material to strengthen their general case: it was very easy to argue that, if food were cheaper at home, the weavers' wages would stretch further, and

[1] See above, p. 90. [2] *Northern Star*, 23 Sept. 1843.
[3] *Ibid.* 25 March 1843. [4] *Ibid.* 6 May 1843.

that if foreign markets for cloth were more certain, there would be less periodic unemployment.[1] Archibald Prentice, the League's first historian and a local politician always anxious to strengthen the links between the manufacturers and their workers, evidently had some success in his periodic efforts to arouse the remaining Manchester weavers, many of whom, of course, were weaving silk rather than cotton, against the Corn Laws:[2] for example, Edward Curran, a weaver prominent in working-class movements in Manchester in the 1830s, became a strong repealer, and presented a petition on behalf of the handloom weavers against the Corn Laws to the celebrated conference of clergymen which the League organized in August 1841;[3] Manchester handloom weavers provided a quarter of the 17,000 signatures to an anti-Corn Law petition organized by the Manchester trades in 1839;[4] and at least one of the League's paid lecturers, J. J. Finigan, was an ex-weaver.[5]

Yet most handloom weavers probably rejected the idea that repeal of the Corn Laws would in itself be sufficient to improve their condition.[6] The weavers of Carlisle were certainly lukewarm towards the League, and J. B. Hanson went so far as to argue that it was all a manufacturers' ramp to lower the price of food and so give an excuse for paying even lower wages.[7] C. P. Villiers, the leading parliamentary opponent of the Corn Laws before Cobden entered the Commons, admitted that the weavers were not sympathetic, although he tried to show a connexion between two of their major proposals—a tax on machinery and direct representation in parliament—and the Corn Law question, by arguing that the weavers had a strong case for each proposal so long as parliament was inconsistent and failed to give the same protection to weavers from machine competition as it gave to landlords from foreign competition.[8] But this was mere verbal

[1] This was the general trend of the speeches at a League tea-party in aid of the Manchester weavers, as reported in *Manchester Guardian*, 4 Sept. 1841.
[2] *Manchester Guardian*, 20 May 1838. [3] *Ibid.* 21 Aug. 1841.
[4] *Ibid.* 20 Feb. 1839. [5] *Ibid.* 4 Sept. 1841.
[6] For some of their arguments, see above, p. 112.
[7] *Northern Star*, 25 Sept. 1841. See also L. Brown, 'The Chartists and the anti-Corn Law League', in Briggs, *op. cit.* p. 350.
[8] *3rd Series Hansard*, vol. 54, col. 540.

fencing to minimize the basic differences which were bound to exist between the League and the weavers.

For there was really little to attract the handloom weavers to the anti-Corn Law agitation, which preferred manipulating the existing parliamentary system to seeking further doses of reform, and which found its strongest supporters among the employing classes. More comprehensive, if vaguer, objectives, expounded by apparently disinterested demagogues, were more to the weavers' tastes, and it is not surprising that—for all that they were not numerically important among its supporters, nor particularly violent or loyal in their attachment to it—it was Chartism which provided the most suitable channel for their last flare-up of despair and disillusion. In terms of results, of course, it was no more productive than any of the other channels they had previously tried. The franchise was not extended to working men in the 1840s, and by the time it was widened, more than twenty years later, the handloom weavers had ceased to be a social problem, because they had virtually vanished.

CHAPTER 10

THE PROBLEM OF POVERTY

ATTEMPTS to interest the legislature in their plight; industrial action against their employers; and spasmodic outbreaks of political radicalism: in none of these ways were the cotton handloom weavers successful in maintaining their position within the economic organization of early nineteenth-century Britain. But although there was no permanent relief to their long decline, there were temporary ones which at least prevented them from actually dying of want as they were forced out of the economic race. For England had at that time an elaborate structure of both public and private charity which served to keep the weavers alive even in their most miserable periods of depression. The present study does not seek to trace the history of Poor Law administration or to examine the aim and scope of private philanthropy in Lancashire in the early nineteenth century; both these vast fields still await the close attention of historians. Nevertheless, the attempts to mitigate the worst extremes of poverty to which many families were likely to sink at this time deserve some examination.

The problem of organizing charity on a sufficiently large scale to deal with the critical situations in which the handloom weavers frequently found themselves was enormous. The cotton weavers were numerous, and concentrated within a relatively limited area; in many of the country villages and small towns of Lancashire, the majority of the inhabitants found their employment at the loom. Thus, in a trade depression, unemployment became an acute regional problem. There had been such depressions during and just after the Napoleonic war; but they were increasingly persistent and serious after the first large-scale adoption of the powerloom in the 1820s. In 1826, 1829, 1832, 1837, 1839, and 1841–2, the cotton handloom weavers suffered bouts of heavy and protracted unemployment, and contemporary accounts leave no doubt as to the utter misery and demoralization which affected

233

entire communities—both towns and villages—in these years. It was reflected in countless ways. On the first Sunday of May 1829, for example, no banns of marriage were called at Burnley parish church, although the average each Sunday was normally between fifteen and twenty couples. 'No other reason can be given for this unusual circumstance', ran the newspaper account, 'except that the extreme poverty and wretchedness of the working people now prevent them marrying.'[1]

As the powerloom spread again in the early 1830s, the hand-loom weavers' position in the crisis years became even worse as a result of their marginal economic role. They had become 'always the first class of operatives in this county to feel the effects of a season of adversity, and perhaps the last to benefit by a return of prosperity'.[2] In 1837, John Fielden claimed that 'for the last two or three months at Colne the weavers had been placed in greater distress than they were in 1826'.[3] According to J. F. Foster, a Manchester magistrate, the transition from full employment to no employment at all in the weaving trade was, by the late 1830s, far more rapid than in the past.[4]

A further burden was added to the problem of preventing actual starvation with the drastic decline in piece-rates after the last phase of prosperity in the early 1820s. There had always been the periodic problem of large-scale unemployment according to the vicissitudes of the trade. But the permanent decline in piece-rates after the coming of the powerloom meant that, no matter how industrious, a weaver with a large family of young children could not earn enough to keep them decently, even when he was fully employed. Thus the machinery of charity had to face a dual problem: the periodic one whenever there was a depression in the cotton industry, and in later years the permanent one of helping those members of the weaving community who had heavy family responsibilities.

[1] *Blackburn Mail*, 6 May 1829.   [2] *Manchester Guardian*, 17 June 1837.
[3] *Ibid.* 29 July 1837.
[4] J. F. Foster to Lord J. Russell, 18 April 1837 (*HO. 52. 34*).

II

The apparatus of the old Poor Law could deal far more readily with the second problem than with the first. For handloom weaving had always fitted in well with the traditional patterns of public relief. In workhouses all over the country, weaving was one of the forms of labour to which the inmates were commonly subjected, whilst in the cotton-weaving districts, the ordinary provision for 'the poor in very deed'—the aged, the ill, the widowed, the orphaned, and the half-witted—was frequently geared to the nature of the staple local employment. The parish authorities would set up such paupers with looms, or repair their old implements, so as to enable them to earn their own living. This was, indeed, a 'normal' activity even in years of general prosperity, for there was always a residual army of true paupers to be taken care of by the overseers. Thus in 1814, the authorities at Barrowford, a small township near Colne, made the following outlays in providing or maintaining looms:

		£	s.	d.
6 Jan.	Paid Joseph Sutcliffe towards a pair of looms	1	10	0
21 July	Paid Henry Watson of Skipton towards Sarah Duckworth's looms	1	0	0
6 Aug.	Paid Thomas Blackey for setting up James Smith's wife's looms at John Pollard's		1	6
8 Nov.	John Sutcliffe of Matthews. A pair of looms and all gears [?]	1	12	0
14 Nov.	Roger Haworth of Stockport for a loom	2	0	0
19 Dec.	Paid Thomas Blackey for repairing John of Matthews' looms		4	11[1]

The parish authorities continued to regard the provision of the tools of the leading local trade as an essential part of their work in solving the normal problems of the paupers in their charge right

---

[1] The Barrowford overseers' accounts, 1813–20, are in the *Farrer MSS*, D. 88, Manchester Central Library. Other parish records show that the custom of providing or maintaining looms was widespread. See, for example, the *Billington parish records* (Lancashire Record Office, PR. 2386).

down to the late 1830s, when the new Poor Law came into operation in the north of England.[1]

In the agricultural parts of England, it had been very common since the end of the eighteenth century for the overseers to make up agricultural labourers' low wages to an agreed subsistence level, which depended on the current price of bread or the size of the family. Given this example, it was not surprising that, as the piece-rates fell markedly, a similar kind of 'Speenhamland system' was adopted in the handloom weaving townships. It was first described by the Rev. J. M. Turner of Wilmslow in his evidence to the 1827 committee on emigration. Before the slump of 1826, Turner claimed that there had been 'no adult healthy person receiving relief'.[2] After the slump, however, a weaver with a large family who failed to earn a given amount per week (2s. 6d. per head of family in the case of Wilmslow) had his wages made up to that total from the poor rates.[3] In addition, the members of the local select vestry, who were also incidentally the proprietors of the labourers' cottages, protected their own interests by ruling that weavers' cottage rents should also be paid in full by the parish—a policy which the emigration committee clearly regarded with distaste.[4] In spite of this disapproval, the payment of cottage rents seems to have continued to be widespread so long as the old Poor Law remained. In reporting on the administration in Lancashire to the select committee which considered the operation of the Poor Law in 1838, assistant commissioner Alfred Power affirmed that 'it was a very general course...throughout the West Riding and throughout Lancashire, to give relief in rents'.[5]

By the time assistant commisioner Henderson was reporting on the Lancashire Poor Law customs in 1834, making up handloom weavers' wages to an agreed subsistence level was standard practice. At Manchester, 'those employed on work of a common description usually make out a case for relief when they have three or more children under ten years of age; printed forms are used for the purpose of ascertaining from their employers the amount of

---

[1] Mr W. Spencer of Colne has provided me with examples of the practice continuing in the late 1830s, from the Colne parish records.
[2] PP. 1826/7 (237) v, Q. 552.   [3] Ibid. Q. 424.
[4] Ibid. QQ. 445–56.   [5] PP. 1837/8 (167) XVIII, part 1, Q. 2842.

their earnings and their character for industry; and after enquiring into their means of subsistence, the deficiency is usually made up to 2 shillings a head for each member of the family'.[1]

The comparison between the local allowance system which operated under the old law in the handloom weaving areas and the better-known Speenhamland system in the agricultural districts of the south and east should not, however, be pushed too far. For the former was less demoralizing, less widespread, and much less expensive. It applied to only a limited part of the labour force in one particular occupation in a fairly small and otherwise economically advanced area, and it was paid only when the applicant could satisfy the overseers that he was working as hard as was humanly possible. In spite of the allowance system, the cost of poor relief was lower, per head of population, in Lancashire than in any other part of the country.[2] Admittedly, the rates were probably higher in the predominantly weaving townships than elsewhere in the county, and it is a pity that very few of these townships seem to have completed the returns to the 1833 royal commission which Dr Blaug found so useful in his examination of the Speenhamland system.[3] Nevertheless, it would appear from the limited evidence that even these rates are likely to have been modest in comparison with rural areas elsewhere; at Padiham, for example, expenditure per head on poor relief was only 3s. 8d., in 1821, and 5s. in 1831.[4] Indeed, there was probably no part of the country where the day-to-day administration of the old Poor Law caused less offence to the commissioners than Lancashire.

III

The old Poor Law, then, was fairly adequate to deal with the normal problems of pauperdom in weaving areas, and after 1826 it also adjusted itself to allow for the special problems of the young

[1] PP. 1834 (44) XXVIII, p. 920. Alfred Power gave further details of the system to the select committee of 1838 (PP. 1837/8 (167) XVIII, part I, Q. 2866).

[2] PP. 1834 (44) XXVIII, p. 911; PP. 1837/8 (167) XVIII, part I, QQ. 2951–2.

[3] See M. Blaug, 'The myth of the old Poor Law and the making of the new', Journal of Economic History, XXIII (1963), the 'The Poor Law report re-examined', Journal of Economic History, XXIV (1964).

[4] PP. 1834 (44) XXX, pp. 284 and 639.

married weaver which sprang from the habitually low rates of pay. But the heavy unemployment of a slump year, when half the parish might be without work, was beyond its resources. It was in north-east Lancashire—the extensive calico-weaving area of small towns, villages and hamlets, remote from Manchester and the south Lancashire towns where the earliest cotton factories had tended to congregate—that this problem became most acute after 1826.

In the face of lengthy spells of large-scale unemployment in the 1820s and 1830s, parish funds were quickly exhausted. The *Manchester Guardian* wrote of north-east Lancashire in 1837: 'as the district in which the distress prevails is one where very few wealthy persons reside, the population consisting almost entirely of weavers and of farmers and artisans but one remove above the weavers, it will be almost impossible to raise in the neighbourhood funds for the relief of the existing pressure.'[1] The burden of the local poor rates soon became insupportable. On comparing the annual rental of farms with the poor rate at the end of 1826 the incumbent of Colne found that 'the average [poor rate] for the last eight months has been sixteen shillings and the present rate is about thirteen shillings in the pound per annum on the actual rental of the land'. Many of the ratepayers were small-farmer weavers, and were suffering themselves in part from the industrial depression; yet, the incumbent added, 'when a poor farmer has received the weekly earnings of his family, to the amount of from six to nine shillings, it is a very common occurrence for the overseer of the poor to follow him home and demand the whole or nearly the whole of it for the poor rate'.[2] The Grand Jury of Lancashire pointed out the intolerable burden of the poor rates in a memorial to the Home Office on 12 August 1826; in two extensive weaving townships on the hills above Burnley—Cliviger and Briercliffe—1,400 and 1,353 persons out of a total population of 1,500 and 1,611 respectively were receiving parish relief.[3] Under circumstances of this kind, it is little wonder that local landowners such as William

---

[1] *Manchester Guardian*, 17 June 1837.
[2] Rev. J. Henderson, 2 Dec. 1826; enclosed in T. Littledale to R. Peel, 5 Dec. 1826 (HO. 40. 21).   [3] *Ibid.*

Hulton, J.P., of Westhoughton, told the select committee on emigration with pride of his attempts to stop any more people from gaining settlements in this weaving village, and thereby becoming a future burden on the rates.[1]

The extraordinary problems of a general industrial slump, therefore, necessitated the supplementation of the old Poor Law by large-scale private charity. Inevitably, such charity had to begin at home in the extra exertions and sacrifices of the wealthier inhabitants of the stricken areas. Great noblemen gave up their packs of hunting hounds, whilst lesser mortals such as the rector of Thornton, on the border of Lancashire and Yorkshire between Colne and Skipton, told the Home Office in 1826 that 'our whole family, including two noblemen who are my pupils, have agreed to abstain from wine and beer and to apply the saving to the relief of those around us...'.[2]

The creation of local *ad hoc* committees, raising their own funds by subscription and spending them in the ways thought most likely to reduce distress, was the first admission that a serious slump was in progress. The periodic existence of such bodies can be traced in the local press throughout this period, and in all parts of the weaving area. The motives behind their activities were, naturally, a mixture of genuine charity and frightened ransom-paying. As the Rev. Dr Calvert, warden of the Collegiate Church, told the Manchester relief committee of 1826, 'his impression was that charity to the poor was not only a Christian duty, but he held it to be the best policy: for when the poor saw their wealthier neighbours sympathizing with them in their sufferings, the edge of envious feeling became blunted, and they perceived that they had an interest in the funds reserved in the pockets of the rich, who were as stewards for the poor'.[3]

But whatever the motives, there can be no question as to the very great exertions and successes of these local voluntary associations in tackling the problems of heavy cyclical unemployment which the public system of relief could not solve single-handed.

[1] *PP. 1826/7 (237)* v, Q. 2103.
[2] Rev. M. Barnard to Home Office, 29 April 1826 (*HO. 40. 19*).
[3] *Wheeler's Manchester Chronicle*, 11 March 1826.

Many individuals were noted for their exceptional generosity to their less fortunate neighbours in these circumstances. Outstanding amongst them was Ann Ecroyd, of Marsden, near Colne, whose devotion to charitable works was warmly praised by Cooke Taylor when he visited Lancashire in 1842.[1] From the end of the Napoleonic war to the early 1850s, Miss Ecroyd, who belonged to a prominent Quaker family, was the moving force behind every voluntary charitable effort in the Colne district, and the record of her activities has survived in the notebooks in which she meticulously chronicled the exact state of the poor and the relief she organized for them.[2] The money she spent for these purposes came not only from her family resources, but from donations from Quakers all over the country.

The proceeds of voluntary subscriptions were rarely, if ever, given out to the unemployed in cash, but rather in the form of food and clothing. In the early years of the nineteenth century, the soup kitchen became a highly popular 'good cause' in Manchester, but in so critical a year as 1826 a much more elaborate system of relief in food had to be organized. From the beginning of the slump to the end of August 1826, the Manchester relief committee spent over £19,000 in providing food; nearly £11,000 worth of meal, £6,000 of bacon, and £1,000 of peas had been given away.[3] In a typical week, ending 2 June, 13,263 families had received food at eight stations in different parts of the town: 97,459 lb of oatmeal, 14,261 lb of bacon, and $197\frac{1}{2}$ measures of peas, at a total value of £1,065, being distributed.[4] Similarly, in Blackburn, 'fourteen thousand individuals, more than half the population of the township, have been relieved weekly with food' over a period of nine weeks in the early months of 1826.[5] Voluntary charity on this scale was indeed an immense undertaking.

The distribution of clothing, of which the weavers were often said to be in greater want than they were of food, was usually the responsibility of a ladies' sub-committee of the local relief organi-

---

[1] W. Cooke Taylor, *Notes of a tour in the manufacturing districts of Lancashire* (London, 1842), pp. 73–4.
[2] The collection of notebooks is in the *Farrer MSS*, D. 96, Manchester Central Library.
[3] *Wheeler's Manchester Chronicle*, 2 Sept. 1826.
[4] *Ibid.* 2 June 1826.   [5] *Ibid.* 15 April 1826.

zation. Ann Ecroyd particularly specialized in this kind of charity, giving away lengths of cloth, made-up clothing, and bedding, and also repairing shoes and clogs. The activities of the Lower Darwen committee in 1830 gave some indication of what a distribution of clothing involved: it gave away '382 blankets, 346 pairs of clogs, 279 yards of blue baize in 79 women's petticoats, 140 yards of flannel for waistcoats, and 62 boys' suits of clothes'.[1] The charitable had, however, a major reservation about giving relief in clothing rather than in food; the poor might pawn or sell their new clothing, and use the proceeds indiscriminately.

Whenever the charitable process went beyond the mere distribution of food, in fact, problems of this kind multiplied. For the rich were unwilling in the last resort to go on being charitable indefinitely; they would be generous and even self-sacrificing only so long as their efforts seemed relevant, effective, and appreciated. Thus, much of the money subscribed for 'charitable' purposes was spent in providing the unemployed, not with doles to maintain them in idleness, but with alternative work. As a Scottish landowner told the 1843 select committee which inquired into distress in Paisley, 'we must have labour for any money that we paid'.[2] Often the work provided was weaving: as early as 1811, 'the gentlemen of Kinross-shire...in a most generous manner, resolved to purchase on their own risk cotton and linen yarns to give out to the weavers to be manufactured into cloth...£4,000 have already been subscribed',[3] and a similar weaving fund was established in Paisley as late as 1842.[4] On one occasion, Ann Ecroyd tried a variant of this policy in the Colne district. At the end of the slump of 1829, she purchased and repaired forty-two old handlooms from Liverpool at a total cost of £77, and gave them to needy local weavers, who paid for them at a rate of sixpence a week.[5]

At a time of depression in the textile industries, however, it was

[1] *Manchester Guardian*, 3 April 1830.   [2] *PP. 1843 (115)* VII, Q. 406.
[3] *Manchester Mercury*, 5 Feb. 1811.
[4] *PP. 1843 (115)* VII, QQ. 304–5 and 932–4.
[5] *Farrer MSS*, D. 96. Miss Ecroyd did not, of course, make any profit on the transaction. She herself paid for the carriage of the looms from Liverpool, and at the end of 1833 remitted any debts still outstanding on the loom account.

often unsuitable to provide weaving work for the unemployed, and other outlets had to be found. Outdoor labouring was the most popular form of alternative work. At Stockport in 1816, the unemployed were set to work 'in levelling a large piece of ground near the town, for which they receive low wages'.[1] In 1826, there were many such projects. Samuel Oldknow, for example, suggested that the unemployed of Mellor might be occupied in finishing the Macclesfield canal, and tried to persuade the government to facilitate the resumption of work by sending down Telford the engineer to superintend it.[2] The form of outdoor work most frequently provided for the unemployed, however, was on the roads. In 1826, McAdam, the famous road-builder, spent a considerable time in Lancashire supervising the construction of new roads for the local turnpike trusts.

Raising money to relieve the effects of heavy local unemployment, whether by providing the poor with food or clothing or by finding them alternative work, was not entirely a matter of local charity. The resources of national private charity, too, were mobilized in bad years, and money was sent into the distressed areas by voluntary committees elsewhere. Districts not themselves directly affected by the weavers' unemployment opened subscriptions on their behalf—Liverpool, for instance, was prominent in this respect in 1826.

The greatest of these organizations was the London manufacturers' relief committee, set up in May 1826 after a meeting at the City of London Tavern at which the Lord Mayor of London, Archbishop of Canterbury, Home Secretary, and other leading public figures were present. Among the first subscribers to its fund were King George IV, who gave £2,000; Sir Robert Peel, Snr., £500; Mr Secretary Peel, £300; the Lord Chancellor and the Prime Minister, £200 each; and Messrs Canning and Huskisson, £100 each.[3] The London committee's work was described to the emigration committee of 1827 by W. H. Hyett, who acted as its

---

[1] P. M. Giles, *The social and economic development of Stockport, 1815–36* (M.A. thesis, Manchester 1950, unpublished), p. 173.

[2] S. Oldknow to R. Peel, 22 July 1826 (*HO. 44. 16*).

[3] *Wheeler's Manchester Chronicle*, 6 May 1826. For other notable contributors, see *ibid.* 13 May 1826.

secretary. Local relief committees came to depend heavily on large donations from the London body as their own funds became exhausted. Between 2 May and 15 July 1826, the London committee had received a total of £126,575 in subscriptions, and had made grants totalling just over half that sum.[1] At first, it was content 'to make liberal remittances to the suffering districts', which might be spent locally on food and clothing.[2] In the summer of 1826, however, it began to insist on outdoor work as a condition of relief. McAdam worked closely with Hyett on the Lancashire road schemes of that year; the engineer told the local Manchester committee in August that 'the London relief committee will give £1 for every £3 paid for labour only by the trustees of roads, the proprietors of canals, or private gentlemen who would employ the distressed manufacturers'.[3] But grants for clothing and bedding were resumed as the supply of outdoor work dwindled in the winter. At the beginning of 1827, the London committee was estimated to have given away £120,000, over half of it going to Lancashire, and a further quarter to Yorkshire.[4] Without outside help on this scale, the committees in the weaving districts would have been very much restricted in their capacity to tackle what was, after all, primarily a matter of local responsibility.

IV

This pattern of relief—the subsidization of low wages from the poor rates where necessary, and the supplementation of the public system from the wide resources of local and national charity at times of stress—can be traced throughout the last years of handloom weaving. How effective was it in preventing actual death by starvation in the periods of distress? Certainly, in the worst years, poverty (meaning a lack of adequate food, clothing, and heat) may well have lessened the weavers' resistance to disease and caused some premature death. During 1826, the Blackburn relief committee was very concerned lest the great influx of 'countrymen'

[1] W. H. Hyett to H. Hobhouse, 17 July 1826 (*HO. 40. 20*).
[2] *PP. 1826/7 (237)* v, Q. 2350.
[3] *Wheeler's Manchester Chronicle*, 26 Aug. 1826.
[4] *Ibid.* 13 Jan. 1827.

into the town to share in the distribution of food and clothing might lead to 'an epidemic complaint...from their being crowded together (sometimes three families in one cottage)...'.[1] In February 1827, William Varley recorded woefully in his diary that 'sickness and disease prevails very much, and well it may, the clamming and starving and hard working which the poor are now undergoing...The pox and measles takes off the children by two and three a house'.[2] But it seems unlikely that Mr E. P. Thompson's suggestion—that the great fall in the numbers of cotton weavers in the 1830s was achieved not by their being drafted into new jobs but by death, whether natural or premature —has any real validity.[3]

The argument that the institutions of public and private charity were so inadequate as to have permitted many of the handloom weavers to have died of want looks very dubious when it is remembered that both contemporaries and later historians actually maintained an opposite view: that the treatment of poverty was so effective that it in fact encouraged weavers to stay in the trade instead of seeking alternative work.[4] Assistant Poor Law commissioner Henderson, for example, complained of the generosity of the overseers at Burnley, and recounted an incident which occurred on his visit there in 1833. 'A stout young man applied for relief...; it appeared he was a weaver, with a wife and four children, who had been sent at considerable expense by the parish to work at a colliery at a distance; the wages he received there at first were 18s. a week, but were afterwards lowered to 13s., and although he could not earn above 5s. at Burnley, he brought his family back and presented himself at the vestry; after some reproof, he was ordered 5s., a pair of looms, and a house belonging to the parish.' The commissioner drew an obvious moral: 'the prospect for this part of the country is melancholy, if handloom weavers with youth, strength, and opportunities of gainful employment reject the means of independence and are suffered to remain

[1] Enclosure from J. W. Whitaker, Blackburn, 7 July 1826, in W. H. Hyett to R. Peel (HO. 40. 20).
[2] W. Bennett, op. cit. pp. 379–89.
[3] E. P. Thompson, The making of the English working class (London, 1963), p. 302.
[4] See, for example, T. S. Ashton, The industrial revolution (London, 1947), p. 117.

burthensome to the public.'[1] It is by no means certain how typical this case was; but there was at least one good reason for this weaver's returning to his old home in 'the fear of the cholera, which had broken out among the colliers'. Perhaps the generosity of the old Poor Law did keep a number of weavers too long in their trade, and stifled their initiative to look elsewhere; but there are other more tangible factors which made it very difficult for some of them to abandon their old occupation.[2]

In any case, the basic contradiction is clear: the self-same system of poor relief which, according to some, was so inefficient as to have caused death by starvation cannot also have been so generous as to have encouraged the outmoded trade to survive too long. There are, however, at least three valid criticisms which can be brought against the methods applied to relieving the handloom weavers' distress. In the first place, the custom of making up low earnings may have encouraged over-production, in that the manufacturers, knowing that their workers were sure of a 'living wage', possibly gave out more work and paid lower rates than the state of the market really demanded.[3] The allowance system possibly helped to reinforce this tendency, since a weaver only had his earnings subsidized if he could prove that he was very industrious: 'the fact unquestionably is', wrote Henderson, 'that the weavers are stimulated beyond their powers under the allowance system'.[4] The situation became still worse when Poor Law officials or relief committees insisted on providing weaving work as a condition of relief.[5]

More importantly, the whole concept that relief must be earned by some kind of labour, whether weaving or not, created unnecessary complications. At the end of 1826, the incumbent of Colne asserted that 'since the time the London relief committee began to require outdoor labour in return for the relief granted from their funds, we have been able to avail ourselves but little of their liberality, in consequence of the difficulty of finding a sufficiency of outdoor employment, and the unfavourable season of

[1] PP. 1834 (44) XXVIII, p. 923.   [2] See below, pp. 254–7.
[3] PP. 1826/7 (237) V, QQ. 1972 and 2088.
[4] PP. 1834 (44) XXVIII, p. 909.
[5] L. Simond, Journal of a tour...(Edinburgh, 1815), I, 223; PP. 1826/7 (237) V, Q. 2275 and PP. 1843 (115) VII, QQ. 304–5 and 933–4.

the year'.[1] Suitable work could not always be provided for the unemployed, and the north Lancashire weavers, when they maintained in 1826 that 'it is the cruelty and oppressive disposition of the magistrates, clergy, and better sort of inhabitants that require work from them', were surely being more sensible than McAdam, the road-builder, who lamented that 'the money that has been bestowed gratuitously either in money or provisions has done much evil'.[2] Even when outdoor labouring or roadwork could be provided, it was rather pointless to make the weavers do it, since it was a type of labour to which they were generally unsuited, and often performed ineffectively.[3]

Thirdly, the attitude of the central government in the 1820s and 1830s to the problems of exceptional regional distress was profoundly unhelpful. There were many who argued that the government ought to intervene directly to relieve the consequences of heavy local unemployment. Thus Lord Milton urged in the Commons on 2 May 1826 that 'the people of Lancashire might be considered the poor of England, and the whole nation as the parish to which they belonged. They were in justice chargeable not on the parishes of Blackburn or Bolton but on the country at large'.[4] The weavers themselves were at that moment advocating 'a parliamentary grant of as much money as will purchase the surplus of goods in the market, to have them deposited in warehouses, there to be kept until a renumerating price can be obtained'[5]—in other words, the government, and not private charity, should attempt to remedy the present defective state of the cotton industry's markets.

The government, however, maintained a general policy of non-intervention, on lines laid down by Peel in a letter to the Blackburn magistrates in 1826: 'from...a general consideration', he

---

[1] Enclosure from the Rev. J. Henderson in T. Littledale to R. Peel, 5 Dec. 1826 (HO. 40. 21).

[2] Enclosure from J. McAdam in J. C. Herries to R. Peel, 10 Sept. 1826 (ibid.).

[3] See *Wheeler's Manchester Chronicle*, 30 Sept. 1826: of 1,350 weavers who had recently applied for roadwork in Manchester, 400 quickly gave it up. See also *PP. 1843 (115)* VII, Q. 412, on the alleged unsuitability of Paisley weavers for outdoor labouring.

[4] *New Series Hansard*, vol. 15, col. 808.

[5] Printed enclosure from 'the outdoor weavers' of Stockport, in General Byng to R. Peel, 11 May 1826 (HO. 40. 19).

wrote, 'they [the government] are strongly impressed with the conviction that the direct interference of the government for the relief of the unemployed poor (even if the pecuniary means existed) would be much less effectual than the exertions that are made locally in concert with the committee at the City of London Tavern.'[1] J. C. Herries even argued in 1826 that 'any...measure for increasing the funds of the [London] committee at this time would have the effect of encouraging the masters in their systematic endeavours to keep down the price of labour and thereby to prolong the evil with which we are contending'.[2] Thus there were no direct money grants from the government to either public or voluntary charitable organizations in the handloom weaving districts. Yet the situation, certainly in 1826, was surely critical enough to have justified emergency measures and the temporary abandonment of the creed of 'non-intervention'. Nor would such an action by the government have been entirely without precedent: in a public letter in 1826, Sir John Sinclair, who had been M.P. for Caithness at the time, recalled that the government had made financial grants to the northern districts of Scotland and the Orkney Islands at a time of bad harvest in 1783.[3]

The government was not wholly inactive, however. The Home Secretary was personally responsible in 1826 for distributing the king's own donation;[4] he insisted that local committees should not give money to anyone implicated in the loom-breaking of that year;[5] and a quantity of surplus military clothing—including 3,000 coats, 10,000 pairs of trousers, 2,500 pairs of shoes, and 5,000 blankets—was made available by the government to the London relief committee, which transmitted it to the distressed localities.[6] But apart from a fair amount of reasonably sane advice to hard-pressed local magistrates and clergymen, the central government did nothing further to relieve the cotton handloom weavers in their most critical moments.

---

[1] 28 July 1826 (*HO. 41. 7*).
[2] J. C. Herries to R. Peel, 25 Oct. 1826 (*HO. 40. 21*).
[3] *Wheeler's Manchester Chronicle*, 23 Aug. 1826.
[4] See various letters from Peel in May 1826 in *HO. 41. 7*.
[5] *Ibid.*
[6] *Wheeler's Manchester Chronicle*, 23 Aug. 1826.

V

In 1834, however, the central government did initiate a major change in the whole system of public charity by the Poor Law Amendment Act. 'The Legislature which felt itself unable to offer [the weavers] any measure of relief struck directly and actively at their conditions... the effect was truly catastrophic'; thus Mr E. P. Thompson.[1] But was it catastrophic? Were the cotton handloom weavers noticably less well treated under the new Poor Law than under the old? Certainly, it was widely felt that the weavers would suffer dreadfully if, as the Act implied, all outdoor relief was to be abandoned. And in the four years which elapsed between the passing of the Act and the attempt at its enforcement in the industrial north in 1838, a strong movement, in which the weavers played a prominent part, and which ultimately merged into Chartism, grew up, seeking to prevent the application of the odious Act and its inhuman provisions.

Throughout Lancashire, there were many who would have agreed with a certain Rochdale radical when he confessed that 'he was at a loss to tell how the damnable Poor Law bill could be passed in such a gospel-preaching, church-building, psalm-singing age',[2] and from the end of 1837 there was a strenuous agitation, in which John Fielden took a leading part, to secure the new Act's repeal.[3] There was a series of protest meetings early the following year in most of the weaving towns and villages of north-east Lancashire; and many petitions for the Act's repeal were sent to parliament as a result.[4] At Padiham, for example, the local Unitarian leader, 'after detailing the horrible state of the weavers of

---

[1] Thompson, *op. cit.* p. 302.   [2] *Manchester Guardian*, 1 May 1839.

[3] For a general account of the movement, see C. Driver, *Tory Radical: the life of Richard Oastler* (Oxford, 1946). Repeal was a feasible objective for the Poor Law's opponents, since the Act had been passed for five years only and would be due for renewal, or be allowed to lapse, in 1839 (Spencer Walpole, *History of England* (London, 1890), IV, 363–6).

[4] Petitions against the Act were sent, *inter alia*, from the following north Lancashire and West Riding weaving towns and villages during the session 1837–8: Bolton-by-Bowland, Blackburn, Barnoldswick, Barrowford, Bashall Eaves, Colden-in-Hepton-stall, Chipping, Chatburn, Clitheroe, Downham, Foulridge, Gisburn, Grindleton, Heptonstall, Marsden, Newchurch, Padiham, Preston, Ribchester, Rimmington, Sawley, Slaidburn, Trawden, Twiston, Todmorden, Whitewell, Whalley, Waddington, and Walton-le-Dale (*PP. 1837/8 (681)* XVIII, part 1, pp. 48–9).

this district, hoped that heaven would spare them from the operation of the cruel and unchristian law: for he feared that, if inflicted upon them, it would drive the people to the commission of acts endangering the public tranquillity'.[1] This group of meetings in the weaving district does not appear, however, to have been spontaneous, but was arranged by a deputation from the south Lancashire anti-Poor Law association—an indication of a certain apathy among the weavers at this stage. Once aroused, however, the 'countrymen' were zealous opponents of the law; from Colne in 1838 came reports of a plot to assassinate Mr Wharton, the relieving officer, and a rate-collector was actually beaten up.[2]

Before the new Poor Law was applied, therefore, there were certainly grave apprehensions among the handloom weavers as to its probable effects. But in practice, was Lord Brougham right when he asserted in March 1839 that 'the effect of this measure had necessarily been to render the condition of the handloom weavers worse than it was under the old law'?[3] Addressing an anti-Corn Law League tea-party in aid of the weavers in 1841, Alderman Brooks of Manchester said he was 'glad to find that the guardians were very liberal; and that the working of the new Poor Law was not different from the old'.[4] Recent research on the Poor Law in north-east Lancashire bears out the Alderman's opinion.[5] Until the outdoor relief regulation order of 25 August 1852, the central Poor Law commissioners seem to have been satisfied to allow the principle of outdoor relief to continue unchecked, so long as the new machinery of administration had been set up, and the union and the guardians had replaced the township and the overseers. Thus at Bolton and at Burnley in the early 1840s the guardians and relieving officers continued to supply poor weavers with the tools of their trade,[6] and in most of the east Lancashire unions the low wages of handloom weavers with heavy family

---

[1] *Northern Star*, 30 Jan. 1838.   [2] *Manchester Guardian*, 29 Dec. 1838.

[3] *3rd Series Hansard*, vol. 46, col. 872.   [4] *Manchester Guardian*, 4 Sept. 1841.

[5] R. Boyson, *The new Poor Law in north-east Lancashire, 1834–71* (M.A. thesis, Manchester 1960, unpublished). Mr Boyson's conclusions are embodied in an article in *Trans. Lancashire and Cheshire Antiquarian Soc.*, LXX (1960), 35–56.

[6] Boyson, *op. cit.* pp. 242–3. For a general discussion of the various 'allowances', see M. E. Rose, 'The allowance system under the new Poor Law', *Economic History Review*, XIX (1966), 607–20.

responsibilities continued to be subsidized. The latter practice continued at Bolton even after the order of 1852, which attempted a stricter regulation of outdoor relief.[1] Indeed, assistant commissioner Alfred Power had admitted in 1838 that the outdoor relief system could not be abolished overnight in the weaving districts of Lancashire, and had merely advised the select committee of that year that any future relief should be given in provisions rather than in money.[2] Thus the willingness of the new Poor Law officials to ignore the letter of the law and to relieve handloom weavers with tools, food, and subsidized wages seems, in short, to have continued for as long as the weavers remained a serious social problem.

Under neither the old nor the new Poor Laws, therefore, were the cotton handloom weavers treated unsympathetically. In the worst years of industrial depression, particularly 1826 and the late 1830s, conditions were undoubtedly grim, physical suffering and spiritual demoralization were certain enormous, and the local machinery of both public and voluntary charity was subjected to tremendous strain. But at least the system proved adequate to keep the weavers from starving and sharing the fate of the Indian handloom weavers when first subjected to competition from the superior British industry,[3] or of the wretched Irish peasantry in the great famine of the 1840s. To be kept alive only in order to suffer again at no distant date is perhaps a dubious privilege. But before we blame the early nineteenth-century state for not being more positive in its efforts to help the handloom weavers, we should remember that the legitimate comparison is not with the welfare state of today, but with what was happening elsewhere at that time. And on that test, society's efforts on the weavers' behalf, although terribly limited, were not unsuccessful.

[1] Boyson, *op. cit.* pp. 176, 178 and 182.
[2] *PP. 1837/8 (167)* XVIII, part 1, Q. 2873.
[3] R. M. Martin, a prominent economist of the 1830s maintained (*PP. 1834 (556)* X, Q. 4001) that, 'with the entry of English cotton into the Indian market after 1815, upwards of two millions of handloom weavers have there not only been thrown out of employment, but have mainly perished...'. Professor M. D. Morris, of the University of Washington, Seattle, is currently undertaking a re-appraisal of the fate of the Indian handloom weavers in the nineteenth century.

CHAPTER II

DISPLACEMENT AND DISAPPEARANCE

ONE last problem remains. The cotton handloom weavers failed to keep their trade alive: from being probably the most numerous single group of workers in manufacturing industry in the 1820s they dwindled within thirty years into a picturesque anachronism, encountered only in small numbers and in odd localities. How quickly had this change been brought about, and where had the weavers gone? Largely because of the thinness of the evidence, there has been no adequate examination of these two problems. Yet even if it is possible to offer only general suggestions on this topic, it must be clear from the outset that some of the more facile explanations will not suffice. Mr E. P. Thompson, for example, has suggested that the majority of the handloom weavers left the trade in the 1830s simply because they died off, either of old age, or prematurely as a consequence of their reduced economic circumstances.[1] There is, however, a great deal of evidence to show that, in fact, many of the weavers were sufficiently wise and realistic to heed the lessons of 'political economy', and sought more secure and remunerative employment elsewhere.

How successful were they in finding new jobs? There has always been a school of thought among historians which suggested that the weavers' misery was protracted unnecessarily because of their blindness to the economic facts of life, which made them 'reluctant' to take up the most readily available alternative work in the ever-expanding cotton factories.[2] This theory is both plausible, and, up to a point, demonstrable from contemporary evidence. The *Manchester Guardian*, for example, frequently asserted in the 1830s that it was 'mere shiftlessness'[3] which accounted for

[1] See above, p. 244.
[2] See, for example, T. S. Ashton, *The industrial revolution* (London, 1947), p. 117.
[3] *Manchester Guardian*, 26 Jan. 1833.

the weavers' failure to change their occupation; 'it is their own want of energy in seeking to improve their circumstances, quite as much as the competition of women and children or of machinery, or any other cause, to which they have really to attribute their depressed and suffering condition'.[1]

But apathy was only one of a number of factors which might explain the handloom weavers' reluctance to go into mills. 'No man would like to work in a powerloom [shed]', Richard Needham told the 1834 select committee; '. . . there is such a clattering and noise, it would almost make some men mad; and next, he would have to be subject to a discipline that a handloom weaver can never submit to.'[2] Others objected to the factories because of their bad effects on the health, morals, and education of the young: John Scott, a Manchester silk weaver whose son had been killed in a mill accident, declared himself 'determined. . . that if they will invent machines to supersede manual labour, they must find iron boys to mind them'.[3] John Fielden himself had a simple explanation of the alleged reluctance to take factory work when it was available: 'it is scarcely necessary to do more than read Dr Kay's own description of the factory given in his pamphlet of 1832 to account for the disinclination'.[4] Fielden was not entirely consistent in his explanation of the handloom weavers' attitude to factories: at one time he claimed that 'except for a very few comparatively' they 'will neither go into them, nor suffer their children to go',[5] but elsewhere he stressed that alternative work, even if desired, was simply not available in many cases.[6]

It is clear that some handloom weavers failed to take factory work when the opportunity was offered. In 1843, the relieving officer of the Chorlton Poor Law Union complained that 'the handloom weavers who live in the outdistricts seem to expect the

[1] *Manchester Guardian*, 1 Aug. 1835.   [2] *PP. 1834 (556)* x, Q. 5473.
[3] *PP. 1835 (341)* XIII, Q. 2644.
[4] J. Fielden, *The curse of the factory system* (London, 1836), p. 66. The 'pamphlet of 1832' was, of course, J. P. Kay, *The moral and physical condition of the working classes employed in the cotton manufacture in Manchester*. Kay became a frequent object of attack in the late 1830s because of his work as an assistant commissioner under the new Poor Law. His attempts to persuade agricultural labourers to migrate to Manchester and take factory work accorded ill with the black picture of Manchester life which he had painted a few years earlier.
[5] *Ibid.* p. 68.   [6] See below, p. 255.

trade to go to them; I have urged upon people repeatedly, and offered to find them a house if they would follow me to Manchester, and that I would undertake to find them subsistence, and their children and wives work in factories, but they prefer staying eight or nine miles off in the country'.[1] Unwillingness to move one's home as well as to change one's job is perhaps understandable, but in some cases, town weavers who might have continued to live in their old houses still refused to take factory work. Henry Ashworth of Turton, a noted philanthropic factory master, claimed in 1840 that Bolton weavers 'would not walk across the street to get 10 shillings per week by working in a mill'.[2] Likewise, handloom weavers at Droylsden refused to take advantage of the opening of a new hat factory in 1835, and as a result the new mill changed over to cotton spinning.[3]

In the boom years of the mid-1830s, the demand for factory workers in and around Manchester was almost certainly greater than the supply.[4] Indeed, during the mania for company promotion in 1836, a company with a capital of £1 million was floated to establish the cotton industry outside Lancashire and Cheshire. Entitled 'the South British manufacturing company', its promoters, apparently believing that cotton would 'continue to increase to almost an unlimited extent', argued that it could only expand in the south of England, as there was now insufficient new labour in the traditional cotton areas.[5] Under these conditions, all but the most elderly of the handloom weavers in these factory towns would have found no difficulty in obtaining alternative work had they been prepared to go into the factories. The fact that the Poor Law commissioners organized a migration scheme to bring in agricultural labourers from the south is sufficient proof of the absence of local labour willing to man the new

[1] *PP. 1843 (402)* VII, Q. 1109.
[2] *PP. 1840 (314)* X, Q. 4857. This was a rather special case, however, since Ashworth evidently expected the weavers to be willing to work as blacklegs when the local factory workers were on strike; threats of beatings-up or of social ostracism, rather than a 'reluctance' on grounds of hostility to the system, may well be the true explanation of their behaviour on this occasion.
[3] R. Speak and F. R. Witty, *History of Droylsden* (Stockport, 1953), p. 91.
[4] See, for example, *Manchester Guardian*, 21 March 1835.
[5] *Ibid.* 9 July 1836.

mills in 1835–6.[1] To remain at the handloom in such a situation was a mark either of extreme apathy or of inveterate hostility to the whole factory system.

And yet, by the mid-1830s, although there still were handloom weavers in the towns near Manchester, their numbers were very few.[2] Only a minority of the former weavers were now working at their old trade; the great bulk of the army of domestic weavers had, in fact, found themselves more promising occupations. Thus the terms 'apathy' and 'reluctance' can be used only as regards a very small element among the handloom weavers in and around Manchester.

II

In some districts, however, handloom weavers survived as a numerically important element in the population until the 1840s. Was this the result of shiftlessness, or of hostility to the factories? According to a host of witnesses from the time of the 1827 emigration committee, it was not. Bishop Blomfield of Chester was quite emphatic that in many places the question of alternative employment simply did not arise. 'In the larger towns', he told the emigration committee, 'the handloom weavers are more ready to take advantage of the least increase in the facilities of labour afforded by the powerlooms, and...they are absorbed in the powerloom population. There is no such opportunity afforded to the handloom weavers in the villages.'[3] W. H. Hyett, of the London manufacturers' relief committee, also lamented that the weavers had 'very little chance of ever finding employment again, especially those who are resident in the distant townships'.[4]

The lack of alternative work on the fringes of the vast cotton-weaving area became a factor of crucial importance after the slump of 1826. Men of enterprise and capital sufficient to build factories and so create new employment were lacking in the small country towns and villages. The original spinning factories had

[1] For migration from the agricultural areas to the factory towns under the new Poor Law, see A. Redford, *Labour migration in England, 1800–50* (Manchester, 2nd ed. 1964), pp. 97–117.
[2] See above, p. 57.
[3] PP. 1826/7 (237) v, Q. 2271.
[4] *Ibid.* Q. 2351.

tended very much to congregate in the south Lancashire towns, and it was one of the peculiarities of the introduction of the power-loom in cotton that the new sheds also grew up first in the traditional, factory district, rather than in the old hand-weaving areas such as Paisley, Carlisle, Bolton, or north-east Lancashire.[1] John Fielden himself admitted that 'work in the factories was not so easily obtained as the members of the [1834 select] committee seemed to suppose', and recalled that 'before I came up to Parliament I was applied to weekly by scores of handloom weavers who were so pressed down in their condition as to be obliged to seek [factory] work, and it gave me and my partners no small pain to have the applications and be compelled to refuse work to the many who applied for it'.[2] Even in 1842, William Cooke Taylor was surprised to discover that in north-east Lancashire 'there are not labour and wages so abundant in any one occupation in the country to absorb and supply a new horde of immigrants', with the result that handloom weavers who stayed in the district were obliged to stick to their old trade.[3] As the cotton industry recovered from its great stagnation of 1837–42, and many more factories were set up, the chances of finding new jobs in the former weaving districts increased. But for nearly twenty years after 1826, commentators on the weavers' position frequently stressed the particular problems facing the country weaver, whose children might still have to be put to the loom long after it ceased to offer a prospect of remunerative employment.[4]

It can, of course, be argued that the country weavers were unenterprising in not migrating to the factory towns a mere ten or fifteen miles away, and that the word 'reluctance' can be stretched to imply an unwillingness to leave the paternal home. However, the census figures from 1821 to 1851 show that a good many of the country weavers were not unwilling to move away into other districts. Between 1821 and 1841, some three-fifths of the townships in the extensive hundred of Blackburn experienced an actual

[1] See above, pp. 90–2. [2] Fielden, *op. cit.* p. 68.
[3] W. Cooke Taylor, *Notes of a tour in the manufacturing districts of Lancashire* (London, 1842), p. 72.
[4] *PP. 1826/7 (237)* V, QQ. 34–6, 505, 1970–1, and 2094; *PP. 1833 (690)* VI, QQ. 9452–6, 11163, and 11268.

decline (which in some cases was later reversed) in population.[1] The fall in numbers took place in precisely those remote weaving villages where alternative employment opportunities were lacking; one of them, for example, was Higham, where William Varley, the weaver-diarist of the 1820s, lived. In these twenty years after 1821, the population of Lancashire as a whole (and even of the whole hundred of Blackburn) was increasing, in the case of the county by about 25 per cent per decade. Yet from the villages around Pendle Hill or on the moors above Bolton and Bury there was a marked exodus of people seeking work elsewhere, and resulting in a substantial shift in the distribution of population within Lancashire. Obviously, not all the country weavers moved out. It would, however, be rash to maintain that those who stayed were foolish in preferring the pleasant traditional life of their small Pennine communities to the rootless existence in the over-crowded and unhealthy factory towns. There comes a point when even political economists must accept 'reluctance' as a natural and forgivable aspect of human nature.

The location of the earliest factories was not the only problem in finding new work for the handloom weavers. The general effect of new machinery in both cotton spinning and weaving in the 1830s was 'to increase the demand for the labour of young persons, and to diminish the demand for the labour of persons past the prime of life'.[2] As Gaskell pointed out, 'it is well known that steamlooms do not require an adult labourer, but that they are supplied by young women and girls'.[3] In spinning mills, too, the chief demand was for the unskilled labour of women and children as the large self-acting mules came to be introduced.[4] As a result, adult men did find it relatively difficult at this period to get factory work, and this factor must naturally have hampered

---

[1] The census figures for Lancashire are most readily accessible in the *Victoria County History of Lancashire* (1920), vol. II. For a detailed discussion of changes in population distribution in Lancashire and Cheshire in the first half of the nineteenth century, see the articles by J. T. Danson and T. A. Welton in *Trans. Lancashire and Cheshire Historical Society*, IX–XI (1857–8), particularly X, 15–21.

[2] *PP. 1834 (44)* XXVIII, p. 920.

[3] P. Gaskell, *Artisans and machinery* (London, 1836), p. 36.

[4] See, for example, the evidence of R. Gardner, Bolton manufacturer, to s.c. handloom weavers (*PP. 1835 (341)* XIII, QQ. 2332–6).

the absorbtion of the older weavers into the mills to some degree. One should not, however, accept too many of the tales of adult men unable to find work being maintained in large numbers by the labour of their wives and children—stories which Engels and other commentators very readily put about.[1] For in the towns, there were always plenty of jobs for men only in the skilled trades, in general labouring, in warehousing, and so on; and in any case women and children had for many years provided the bulk of the labour force among domestic weavers, too. Nonetheless, the nature of much factory work did add somewhat to the difficulties of transferring directly from domestic weaving to the mill.

There were other difficulties, too. The attitude of other trade unions, such as that of the Glasgow spinners, was often said to be at best unhelpful, if not downright hostile, to the handloom weavers' efforts to find new jobs. Naturally, the other trades feared that their employers might use the handloom weavers as cheap blackleg labour.[2] Richard Needham told the 1833 select committee on manufactures that 'all the other trades combine together to prevent weavers' children coming into their trade, and if a master was to take a weaver's child an apprentice, they would turn out against him'.[3] Another factor was also alleged by Needham to add to the problems of weavers who wanted to put their children into new jobs, particularly in the spinning factories: 'the children of spinners are always preferred before the children of weavers, because they work with their parents.'[4]

III

Taking these factors together, we can see that the survival of cotton handloom weaving is much more than a case of either apathy or positive unwillingness on the part of the weavers to abandon their old habits of working and living. Yet in the course

[1] F. Engels, *The condition of the working class in England* (English edn. by W. H. Chaloner and W. O. Henderson, Oxford, 1958), pp. 162–65.
[2] *PP. 1833 (690)* VI, QQ. 5625–6; *PP. 1837/8 (488)* VIII, Q. 1953.
[3] *PP. 1833 (690)* VI, Q. 11790.
[4] *Ibid.* Q. 11793.

of time the weavers did disappear, and many were able to overcome the various obstacles which had made it difficult to find alternative work. Where did they find new employment? When it was available, factory work was the most obvious outlet, and some handloom weavers were taking advantage of it even in the early 1820s. In Stockport, it was said that 'a great many handloom weavers are gone to the steamlooms' as early as 1824.[1] With the great burst of factory building in the mid-1830s, any weaver in the immediate vicinity of Manchester who was prepared to take factory work did not lack opportunities. By 1840, Henry Ashworth could tell John Fielden that his Turton mills had absorbed 'all [the handloom weavers] we could bargain with',[2] while James Thomson, cloth printer, of Clitheroe, claimed in 1833 to have 'many dyers, washers and labourers in our works that were formerly handloom weavers'.[3] In Glasgow, in the late 1830s, weavers' children went into spinning mills: to refute the statements that the spinners' union prevented weavers from finding new jobs, it was alleged in 1838 that 'there are no less than 1305 children of handloom weavers employed as piecers to 950 spinners in Glasgow and its vicinity at this moment'.[4]

The kind of factory work most suited to the handloom weavers, however, was at the powerloom. Immediately after the loom-breaking of 1826, an anonymous commentator on the events in Blackburn proclaimed 'that man will be a benefactor to his country who shall assist in rescuing the handloom weavers from the thraldom of Egyptian task masters and in providing for them a description of labour suited to their habits, and affording a renumeration equal to their industry', and added: 'whether the powerloom might not assist in accomplishing this beneficial change in the condition of the weavers is a subject well worth their consideration.'[5] W. R. Greg told the 1833 committee on manufactures that he preferred to employ handloom weavers on his powerlooms, and asserted that 'as handloom weavers have been accustomed to

[1] *PP. 1824 (51)* v, p. 421. [2] *PP. 1840 (314)* x, Q. 4861.
[3] *PP. 1833 (690)* vi, Q. 3976. [4] *PP. 1837/8 (488)* viii, Q. 2846.
[5] Eight-page pamphlet, anon., entitled *Remarks on weaving, with reflections on the recent events in Lancashire*, found in *HO. 40. 19*. It was probably originally enclosed in a letter to the Home Office from local magistrates.

care and minute attention, they are most in demand for that species of occupation'.[1]

Many handloom weavers, particularly women and children, must have found employment in this way. A small decline in population at Chadderton between 1831 and 1841, for example, was specifically attributed to 'the removal of nearly twenty families of handloom cotton weavers who have become power-loom weavers at Oldham'.[2] In fact, at Oldham the select vestry which operated under the old Poor Law took 'great pains to shift... [handloom] weavers to more profitable occupations. Situations had been procured for many of them in the powerloom factories, their families having been maintained by the township whilst they were learning to work at the powerlooms, which requires about a fortnight. Thus', Mr Henderson concluded his report on this enterprising custom, 'their number has been diminished as the powerlooms, of which there are now [1834] several thousands, increased in number.'[3]

Apart from actual weaving work in the new factories, it would appear that some old handloom weavers found employment in those ancillary trades inside the mills—such as looming and twisting—which had not yet been mechanized, and to which their dexterity might fairly easily be adapted. For in 1859, the loomers and twisters of Blackburn applied for an advance of wages, which their employers unanimously rejected on the grounds that 'if the old men, mostly old handloom weavers, would work constantly, they might earn sixteen shillings per week; but it seems they are pretty much their own masters, and do not work much on Monday'. The masters further argued that 'the work could be better and cheaper done by females and young persons; and the old men are kept on rather to keep them off the parish funds, than for any other reason'.[4]

Another, albeit less permanent, source of new employment came from changing over to weaving, by hand, a fabric other than cotton. Some of the calico weavers in Preston and Blackburn in

[1] PP. 1833 (690) VI, QQ. 11364-5.   [2] Manchester Guardian, 23 June 1841.
[3] PP. 1834 (44) XXVIII, pp. 917-8.
[4] Burnley Advertizer, 24 Sept. 1859. It is interesting to note that the casual habits of hand-loom weaving could still be accommodated to these ancillary factory jobs.

the 1830s found a new, if brief, lease of life in the dandyloom shops, where harder and more regular work at least provided a reasonable wage.[1] But a cotton handloom weaver might also profit for a time from any sudden increase in demand for some other fabric to which the powerloom had not yet been applied. In Manchester, there was a substantial turnover from cotton to silk hand weaving in the 1820s. J. F. Foster, a local magistrate, told the Home Office that in 1823 'there were about 2,500 looms employed in goods composed altogether of silk, and about 3,000 looms in goods with warp composed of silk and shot [with] cotton, worsted, or linen'; five years later, 'the number of the former was not less than 8,000 and of the latter 3,000 to 4,000'.[2] William Haynes, a Manchester silk merchant, provided the 1833 committee on manufactures with further information about this important trend: the silk industry in Manchester, he said, had developed almost entirely within the previous ten years; latterly, there had been 'a constant change of employment from cotton to silk', where the wages were better; and it was the better type of cotton weaver—formerly employed on nankeens, ginghams, or muslin—who had been first to make the transfer.[3]

The change to silk was not confined to Manchester. As the slump of the mid-1820s drew near, the Bolton weavers also made an effort to attract the silk industry to their town, even advertising in the press that 'the town of Bolton-le-moors contains from 5,000 to 7,000 as expert weavers in the plain and fancy line as can be found in the three kingdoms; any respectable house in the silk trade wishing to extend their connexions, might, by establishing a concern in Bolton, be supplied with any number of excellent workmen, within the number specified above'.[4] The silk industry did not, however, come sufficiently quickly to Bolton to prevent heavy unemployment in 1826; in February of that year, Colonel Fletcher, its leading magistrate, told the Home Office that the hopes of 'an improvement in the weaving trade by the introduction of silk' had 'completely vanished'.[5] After 1827, however, silk

---

[1] See above, pp. 83–5, and pp. 134–5.

[2] J. F. Foster to R. Peel, 1 June 1829, *HO. 40. 24.*   [3] *PP. 1833 (690)* VI, QQ. 5131–6.

[4] *Wheeler's Manchester Chronicle*, 12 March 1825.

[5] R. Fletcher to H. Hobhouse, 23 Feb. 1826, *HO. 40. 19.*

weaving did spread rapidly in the district around Bolton and Leigh. According to the *Manchester Guardian*, 'an absurd combination [of Manchester silk weavers] against Messrs Walk was the means of setting on silk goods hundreds of looms in the neighbourhood of Leigh which had been previously employed on cotton fabrics'.[1] Two years later, the same paper reported 'a regular and constant conversion of cotton into silk weavers... to a great extent amongst the muslin weavers in the neighbourhood of Leigh', adding that 'of late, several silk houses have begun to put out work amongst the cotton weavers in Bolton and the neighbourhood'.[2] The older-established Lancashire silk weavers in Manchester and Middleton came in fact to resent the spread of their trade to new areas, claiming that the weavers at Leigh, who numbered 8,000 in 1838, 'had always woven at a halfpenny per yard lower than at Fails-worth and Middleton'.[3]

Silk was not the only other fabric to which displaced cotton weavers might turn in the hope of better wages. Sir Sidney Chap-man's assertion that 'the cotton weavers in Scotland, and perhaps those in England, did not attempt to transfer their labour to the woollen industry, partly for lack of enterprise, partly because they could not give the few days requisite for learning the new work, or afford to remount their looms', is in several respects very mis-leading.[4] Obviously, the whole body of cotton weavers could not simultaneously have changed to woollens: they could only be absorbed in the sister industry if an expansion of the cloth market created a demand for extra labour, as in fact it did. In both England and Scotland in the later 1830s, many cotton weavers started weaving 'mousseline-de-laine', a new fashionable dress fabric made from a mixture of cotton and worsted. In north-east Lanca-shire it first caught on in 1838, when the *Blackburn Gazette*, under the heading 'trade at Colne', spoke of 'a new manufacture... being introduced into that town, the warp of cotton and the weft of worsted;... some of the weavers have made 12/- a week by weaving it'.[5] Mousseline-de-laine also spread rapidly in Scotland:

---

[1] *Manchester Guardian*, 15 Dec. 1827.   [2] *Ibid*. 24 Oct. 1829.
[3] *Ibid*. 23 May 1838.
[4] S. Chapman, *The English cotton industry* (Manchester, 1904), p. 47.
[5] *Blackburn Gazette*, 24 Jan. 1838.

in the same year, 1838, it was said that 'nearly one half of the handloom weavers in Scotland are in full operation in manufacturing the cloth'.[1] In both areas, the new fabric came to employ a very large number of the former cotton weavers during the following decade, and as late as 1850, factory inspector Leonard Horner could still speak of it as 'a description of manufacture which has greatly extended, and in which there is at present great activity'; those who wove it, he had been informed, could earn from 14s. to 20s. a week.[2]

The two most obvious channels through which the cotton weavers obtained new and better-paid employment were, therefore, factories and other textiles. But there were others. Agricultural labour, if sometimes only seasonal, might provide opportunities in some of the villages in both England and Scotland during these early years of 'high farming', although, of course, the number of openings here *in toto* is unlikely to have been very large.[3] For example, James Orr, a Paisley weaver, cited in 1833 the case of Ouston, a village a few miles west of Paisley, 'where three or four years ago they had 150 looms, and now there are not more than 40'. Fortunately for the weavers, Ouston was 'a country village surrounded with gentlemen's estates' where the weavers' apprentices had 'got employ in agricultural labour'.[4]

Healthy young men might become general outdoor labourers, and a number even became coalminers. Weavers from Burnley and Padiham were brought in by the mineowners during a colliers' strike in the Oldham district in 1831,[5] whilst Joseph Gott, underlooker at a 'mountain mine' near Rochdale, informed the 1842 royal commission on the employment of children in mines that 'the parents, who are often weavers, come and beg to thrust their children in, before they are fit to go'.[6] Some of the more able did even better, and found work as warehousemen, clerks, and schoolteachers;[7] whilst the most fortunate few, who are known

---

[1] *Manchester Guardian*, 17 Oct. 1838.   [2] *PP. 1850 (1239)* XXIII, p. 278.
[3] Various witnesses in 1834 spoke of the drift into farm work around Perth, Paisley, and Preston (*PP. 1834 (556)* X, QQ. 1689, 3054, and 6251).
[4] *PP. 1833 (690)* VI, Q. 11991.   [5] *Manchester Guardian*, 2 July and 20 Aug. 1831.
[6] *PP. 1842 (380)* XV, p. 27, para. 79.
[7] J. Fielding, *Rural historical gleanings in South Lancashire* (Manchester, 1852), pp. ii, iii, and 31.

to us as individuals by virtue of their published works—such as John Fielding, reporter of the *Manchester and Salford Advertiser*, William Thom, the Scottish 'weaver poet',[1] David Winstanley, the Manchester schoolmaster,[2] and, of course, Samuel Bamford, the radical of Peterloo—became writers and journalists. In short, if individual case histories are followed up, former handloom weavers might be found, according to their aptitude and ability, in any of the whole range of occupations appropriate to a rapidly developing industrial society.

IV

How quickly did the bulk of the cotton weavers disappear, and for how long did their last survivors hold out? The often-quoted statement of commissioner Hickson after his brief tour of the weaving districts in 1838, that the number of cotton weavers was still 'almost as great as at any former period' is surely misleading,[3] since it directly contradicts the opinions of Alfred Power, the much more knowledgeable assistant Poor Law commissioner, to a select committee in the same year. Power argued that 'the class of handloom weavers of cotton has been for some time a diminishing class, very considerably, for some years in Lancashire', and that 'the most distressed class of handloom weavers, namely the weavers of calico, are not in any very great proportion anywhere with reference to the whole population'.[4] The fact is that the total number of cotton handloom weavers fell continuously after 1826, but that the progress of decline was irregular, varying greatly from place to place and from year to year. After that disastrous slump, it was widely recognized that there was no future in handloom weaving. William Feilden, J.P., of Blackburn, for example, told the 1827 emigration committee that 'handloom weaving in that district [was] almost at an end as a means of subsistence', and

---

[1] For more details of Thom than are given in the introduction to his *Rhymes and recollections of a handloom weaver* (2nd edn, London, 1845), see Thomas Cooper, *Life, written by himself* (London, 1872), pp. 313–15. Cooper, like Thom, won popularity as a poet in the 1840s.

[2] For Winstanley, see D. Winstanley, *A schoolmaster's notebook* (ed. E. and T. Kelly, Chetham Society, Manchester, 1957).

[3] *PP. 1840 (639)* XXIV, p. 650.

[4] *PP. 1837/8 (167)* XVIII, part 1, Q. 2863, and *PP. 1837/8 (183)* XVIII, part 1, Q. 3382.

that there was 'no distinct prospect of any relief being afforded'.[1] Bishop Blomfield was more cautious, and, in the event, more accurate. He recognized that 'the decay of that branch of trade will by no means be so sudden as has been apprehended', and that 'some considerable time must elapse before the handloom weaving will be quite extinct'.[2]

The parliamentary inquiries of 1833–5 furnish a good deal of evidence of decline within the labour force as a whole since 1826. Assistant Poor Law commissioner Henderson reported that it was 'gratifying to observe...that few young persons are now brought up to weaving...and [that] nothing is more common than to see a solitary weaver working amidst vacant looms which have been deserted for other occupations'.[3] Likewise, Robert Gardner, a knowledgable spinner and handloom manufacturer with connexions at both Bolton and Preston, claimed that no new handlooms had been manufactured in the ten years previous to 1835; that a quarter of the looms in Bolton, and between 10 and 15 per cent in Chorley, Preston, and Blackburn, were standing idle in that year; and that in ten years, the total number of cotton weavers in Lancashire had fallen by a third.[4]

It is impossible to build up an exact picture of the declining numbers. The trade statistics give little help, since they deal with exports only, and give no indication of the amount of handloom cloth still being made for the home market. After the large-scale adoption of the powerloom in the early 1830s, there was a marked change in the types of cotton cloth still woven by hand: the coarse calico branch of the trade—the so-called 'printers' cloths'—where the early powerloom was most successful, fell away very quickly; and in 1838, George Dewhurst, a veteran radical reed-maker, asserted that 'there is no printers' cloth made by the hand' in his native town of Blackburn, formerly centre of the calico trade, and that the remaining weavers were working at fancy jaconnets and cambrics.[5] This broad change is reflected in the available export figures, which show a decline in the export of printed calico after

[1] *PP. 1826/7 (231)* v, QQ. 1962–3.   [2] *Ibid.* QQ. 2262 and 2282.
[3] *PP. 1834 (44)* XXVIII, p. 910.   [4] *PP. 1835 (341)* XIII, QQ. 1759–60.
[5] *Blackburn Standard*, 1 Aug. 1838.

1825 and a shortlived increase in the 1830s in exports of ginghams, velveteens, and other fancy cloths.[1] But it is impossible to use such figures to indicate the rate of decline of the labour force.

The census figures, again, suggest the general drift away from handloom weaving in the 1830s, but still do not enable an exact statement to be made. Many of the smaller country townships in the hundred of Blackburn, where handloom weaving had formerly prevailed, suffered an absolute decline in population between 1821 and 1841,[2] and a number of others grew hardly at all. Colne was the most notable among the latter: it had a population of 7,272 in 1821 (twice as many as it had had in 1801), yet it had still not passed the 9,000 mark in 1851. On the other hand, the factory towns of south Lancashire were growing rapidly.

The whole subject is complicated, however, because the fall in the number of weavers was far more rapid in some places than in others. In 1834, assistant commissioner Henderson reported that 'the number of weavers is diminishing (though in various degrees) in all the large towns', and it is this 'variety of degrees', together with the 'large towns', which needs to be stressed.[3] It has already been shown that handloom weavers were no longer a numerous element in the population of Manchester and its neighbouring towns by the mid-1830s, and that, of those remaining, many were weaving silk rather than cotton.[4] Absorption into other occupations must have been rapid in the later 1820s and early 1830s. In 1834, James Brennan, a Manchester silk weaver, declared that in his street there were only forty-six weavers as compared with 112 a few years earlier; and William Longson alleged a fall in the number of weavers in Stockport from over 5,000 in 1818 to only 400 in 1834.[5] The fact that as early as 1829 the Stockport factory masters tried to import handloom weavers from north-east Lancashire to break a mill workers' strike suggests that there was no comparable cheap labour available locally.[6]

[1] R. Burn, *Statistics of the cotton trade* (London, 1847), table 6.
[2] See above, p. 256.   [3] *PP. 1834 (44)* XXVIII, p. 910.
[4] See above, p. 57 and p. 260.   [5] *PP. 1834 (556)* x, QQ. 6525 and 6741.
[6] *Manchester Guardian*, 18 April 1829. The factory workers are said to have bribed the immigrant weavers with money to go away again.

In the more remote factory towns, the fall in the number of hand weavers was probably less noticeable immediately after 1826, but became marked in the early 1830s. At Bolton, where the handloom trade was brisk in 1835, there was actually a shortage of fancy weavers, who had to be bribed back to the loom by a bounty over and above the normal piece-rate if they completed a given quantity of work in a specified time.[1] This boom was shortlived, for in 1838 the secretary of the Bolton weavers' union told Mr Muggeridge that 'there had been a constant diminution in the numbers of weavers employed since 1836. In many cases, whole shops were entirely shut up...Weavers generally sent their children to work at the factory as soon as they are old enough.'[2] The Preston weavers were said by their leader, Richard Marsden, to have dwindled to only 1,500 by 1838;[3] and in the same year it was reported that at Blackburn 'the number was decreasing daily',[4] those remaining in the trade being predominantly old people, relatively less able and willing to take new work. By 1841, the handloom weavers of Blackburn numbered little more than 1,000.[5]

The decline was slowest in the country places, whose falling populations attest the hopelessness which was facing entire communities. In 1838, Alfred Power reported: 'My impression is that the worst part of Lancashire with reference to the distressed handloom weavers is about Colne, Burnley, and Padiham', although he considered that 'in this district the number of handloom weavers in cotton has been very materially reduced'.[6] In spite of a drop in absolute numbers, however, it is likely that in some of the villages the remaining handloom weavers still formed the predominant element in the population. As late as 1833, James Grimshaw, spinner and manufacturer at Barrowford, near Colne, affirmed that the number of weavers there was increasing, rather than falling;[7] and there were said to be still as many looms at work in Carlisle in 1838 as there had been in 1824, although the number had fallen off in the surrounding villages.[8] Most of the Scottish

---

[1] *Manchester Guardian*, 24 Oct. 1835.
[2] *Bolton Free Press*, 28 April 1838.
[3] *Preston Observer*, 2 June 1838.
[4] *Blackburn Standard*, 23 June 1838.
[5] *Manchester Guardian*, 4 Dec. 1841.
[6] *PP. 1837/8* (174) XVIII, Q. 3298.
[7] *PP. 1833* (690) VI, QQ. 10172–4.
[8] *Carlisle Journal*, 23 June 1838.

witnesses at the select committees of 1833–4 also had the impression that there had as yet been no noticeable reduction in the number of weavers in Scotland.[1] Not until the very heavy increase in the capacity of both spinning and weaving factories which began after 1842 and continued strongly through the 1850s were these last pockets of domestic weavers mopped up.

Certainly, by the late 1840s, the cotton handloom weaver had become a comparatively rare species. In a few isolated places, small groups of elderly ones might be found, but they had become a mere handful after the cotton famine of the 1860s. Fielden brothers of Todmorden (John Fielden himself died in 1850) still retained fifty-three old handloom weavers on their books in 1861, but they stopped giving out work in that year, and pensioned off the survivors.[2] By 1870, a diligent search would have been necessary to locate even isolated individuals still weaving cotton by hand: in the remoter parts of Rossendale, a few might have been encountered as late as 1880;[3] about 1890, the German writer Schulze-Gaevernitz found fifty very aged counterpane weavers in Bolton;[4] and in the years 1885–90, Richard Marsden, a historian of the powerloom, reckoned that there might have been three or four working in villages of the Ribble valley around Longridge and Ribchester, but was doubtful whether at the date he was writing, 1895, there would be a single survivor. Marsden's own conclusion on the weavers' disappearance remains perhaps the most eloquent that has been penned. 'Thus passed away', he wrote, 'a type of industry, picturesque far beyond its successor, that from 1750 to 1850 found employment for several millions of people. Though it has only just disappeared, it has hardly left as many footprints behind it as have the Roman legions that sixteen or seventeen hundred years ago tramped over the country in which it was carried on.'[5]

[1] *PP. 1834 (556)* x, QQ. 1344 and 2149–50.
[2] D. A. Farnie, *The English cotton industry, 1850–1896* (Manchester M.A. thesis, unpublished, 1953), p. 47, where there are other references.
[3] G. Tupling, *Economic history of Rossendale* (Manchester, 1927), p. 211; D. Halstead, *Haslingden's history* (Haslingden, 1929), p. 51.
[4] G. von Schulze-Gaevernitz, *The cotton trade in England and on the Continent* (London, 1895), pp. 104–6.
[5] R. Marsden, *Cotton weaving. Its development, principles, and practice* (London, 1895), p. 232.

The traditional picture of the extinction of the handloom weavers suggests a long and painful process of gradual displacement after terrible years of laborious competition with the powerloom. In fact, the evidence indicates that this is false, for two major reasons: first, the handloom weavers suffered long before the powerloom came into operation, and in these early years their position was the more hopeless because they had little prospect of escaping from the capricious trade in which they found themselves; secondly, as compared with the experience of other industrializing countries later in the nineteenth century, England's cotton handloom weavers disappeared with remarkable speed and ease. Whereas in 1875 two-thirds of Germany's cotton weavers were using handlooms, and whereas as late as 1914 France still had 25,000–30,000 cotton handlooms,[1] few of England's old cotton weavers survived into the second half of the nineteenth century. Although England scarcely knew the powerloom in 1820, by the late 1830s the remnants of the once-numerous force of the cotton weavers constituted a serious social problem only in northeast Lancashire. Thus the speed with which the handloom weavers disappeared, rather than the protraction of their agony, is the really notable feature of their history—although since Lancashire was at the time the world's most advanced industrial region we should hardly be surprised to find that labour there redeployed itself so easily.

v

The economic changes of the late eighteenth and early nineteenth centuries, which transformed a predominantly agrarian into a predominantly industrial society, form the central event in recent English history. From the manifold aspects of what has recently been called 'the greatest discontinuity in history'[2] have stemmed most of the political problems of the past century and a half. A development of this magnitude has necessarily been both complex and controversial. At the present time, economic historians are

---

[1] J. H. Clapham, *Economic development of France and Germany* (Cambridge, 1936), pp. 247–8, and 297.

[2] R. M. Hartwell, 'Causes of the industrial revolution', *Economic History Review*, xviii (1965), 165.

concerned more with complexity than with controversy,[1] and are more anxious to analyse causes than to criticize consequences; thus they study entrepreneurship, capital formation, foreign trade, population change, and the other ingredients necessary to the process of economic growth. And they do so from a more strictly economic viewpoint than has hitherto been the case, in order to discover exactly how and why the mechanics of the whole process got under way.

Contemporaries, however—and some economic historians of an earlier generation—were more aware of the controversial aspects of the industrial revolution. To most public men in the early nineteenth century, 'machinery'—what we would call 'technology'—was the outward symbol of economic change. Machinery meant increased output, which involved new, complex, and delicate relationships within both the national and the international economies. Machinery meant recruiting, training, and redistributing labour. Machinery also meant factories; factories meant industrial towns; and industrial towns meant a whole range of pressing problems which the old order had largely been able to ignore. The solution of these problems naturally caused grave discussions. In detail, there were controversies about each individual problem—education, public health, the tariff, and so on—as each in turn demanded attention; and, in general, there was the wider controversy as to whether economic change had been really beneficial to the country as a whole.[2] Unlike the present generation of economic historians, the men of the time were more troubled by the consequences of recent economic growth, which they had to handle, then by its causes, which are purely a matter of speculation.

If we again see the classic industrial revolution of 1780–1850 in the way that contemporaries tended to see it—as the consequences of the coming of 'machinery'—the significance of the handloom weavers' history is all too clearly reasserted. For the cotton weavers appear at first sight to have been the most numerous and the most obvious victims of technological progress in the first half of the nineteenth century. Their fate obliged even Ricardo to reconsider

---

[1] Except for the recent revival of interest in the standard of living of the working classes— a controversy which has so far generated heat rather than light.

[2] See above, pp. 139–47.

his views and admit that 'the opinion entertained by the labouring class that the employment of machinery is frequently detrimental to their interests, is not founded on prejudice and error, but is conformable to the correct principles of political economy'.[1]

To what extent can the conclusions of the present study claim to alter the traditional picture of the displacement of the handloom weavers? No one would attempt to deny that they were adversely affected by the process of economic change. Their sufferings were certainly great, although we may suggest that such figures as exist for the course of their actual earnings need to be used with the greatest circumspection. But it is surely time to discard a number of myths which have grown up over many generations of distorted polemical discussion of this and kindred topics.

Perhaps the first casualty should be the idea—if it still persists—that cotton handloom weavers were trained craftsmen whose skill was now to be entrusted to machines which women and children could tend. The Hammonds were never more misleading than when they consigned their account of the weavers' political and industrial agitations to a volume entitled *The skilled labourer*.[2] Cotton handloom weaving, from its earliest days, was an unskilled, casual occupation which provided a domestic by-trade for thousands of women and children, whose earnings were normally quite low. The initial recruitment of its labour force—which was just as much a consequence of one set of technological advances as its displacement was of another—provides a salutary reminder that the classic 'industrial revolution' did not necessarily mean the coming of the factory system, but in many industries simply involved the multiplication of low-grade, low-paid, casual, domestic hand workers. The whole attitude to work of this vastly swollen body of traditional outworkers was so completely different from that which was coming to apply among the new factory hands, that comparisons between the two classes as regards earnings and living standards are very deceptive.

A second myth which deserves to be dropped is the theory that

---

[1] D. Ricardo, *Principles of political economy and taxation* (Everyman edn (1911), p. 267).

[2] They are doubly misleading, since elsewhere they were ready to admit that 'handloom weaving was not a mysterious or difficult art' (*The town labourer* (London, 1917), p. 296).

the deterioration in the material well-being of the handloom weavers was simply the result of the coming of the powerloom. For it could be argued that they suffered at least as much in the years before 1820, when, as we have seen, the powerloom was of little importance, as they did after that date. Indeed, it is possible to go further and argue that in reality the powerloom was a blessing and not a curse to the handloom weavers, and that their problems were greatest in the earlier period, not because 'the machine' was displacing them, but because it was *not* displacing them. Certainly there was terrible suffering in some districts in the 1820s, 1830s, and early 1840s; but since this was really very localized and most of the handloom weavers in the cotton industry were absorbed into alternative employment with remarkable speed and ease, the position in the later years was far less hopeless than during the wars with revolutionary and Napoleonic France and in the immediate critical post-war period. Defenceless against employers who could easily pass the burden of suffering during recurrent trade depressions on to their workers, and driven by repeated bouts of poverty to a demoralizing competition amongst themselves which rendered effective united action almost impossible, the early handloom weavers were trapped in a squalid and wholly unromantic trade—'trapped' in the sense that, whether pushed by the pressure of a growing population or attracted by shortlived boom-time wages, they could easily get into it, but once in could extricate themselves only with great difficulty. The extension of factory employment which the powerloom, the self-acting mule, and other machines made possible from the early 1820s provided the first escape route from this hopeless dead-end job. More than any other group, the cotton handloom weavers demonstrate that the real 'black spots' of Britain's classic industrial revolution are to be found, not in the early textile factories or even in the mines (bad as both these were) but in the swollen armies of unskilled domestic outworkers in those trades still unaffected by new machines and new methods. At a time of rapid population growth, a considerable increase in industrial output was attainable simply by the wholesale extension of existing techniques, and in these expanded labour-intensive industries where no great skill was

required, the position of the labourer was bound to be precarious. Thus, if the workers of England really did suffer in the first half of the nineteenth century, as often as not they did so, not because 'machinery' was making rapid progress, but because its progress was not rapid enough.

Thirdly, there seems to be a need for a substantial revision of the accepted account of the weavers' reaction to a deteriorating economic position. A labour force which contained so large a casual and apathetic element could hardly have represented the 'cohorts of revolution', as Professor Briggs has reminded us.[1] The weavers' contribution to various working-class political movements in the period needs to be kept in perspective, and their chief reliance on more orthodox local channels of expressing grievances and seeking redress—by petitioning parliament or by taking industrial action—needs to be recognized.

Finally, there is no need to be melodramatic about the undoubted distress and poverty which many of these unfortunates suffered, and certainly no occasion to talk of their being starved to death or inhumanly neglected by the community in which they lived. As things worsened, many of them were able to take advantage of new employment opportunities offered by an expanding economy, and only a part of the whole labour force, confined to specific areas, was obliged to suffer long. Poverty and misery were still seen as the normal lot of most of society, as they had always been, and public men probably did the best that could be expected with the administrative machinery to hand and with the prevailing framework of ideas. By our own standards, their best was not good enough; for, fatalistically, they accepted some degree of misery as the inevitable result of economic laws which they believed could not be controlled. But if the sufferings of the handloom weavers contributed anything at all to swelling a feeling that man must learn to understand and control economic laws, just as he was learning to control the physical world around him, they were surely not in vain. For it is on the basis of past experiences, usually of an unpleasant kind, rather than of future hopes, however bright, that societies come to deem certain situations to be intolerable.

[1] A. Briggs, *The age of improvement* (London, 1959), p. 302.

APPENDIXES
BIBLIOGRAPHY
INDEX

SOME PIECE-RATE SERIES

The following are the full series of piece-rates for 60-reed Bolton muslin, as summarized in table 2, chapter 5, p. 99.

Date	J. Honey-ford s. d.	R. Needham and W. Pilling s. d.	W. Gifford and R. Ellison s. d.	R. Guest s. d.	Average to nearest 6d. s. d.	Index (1805 = 100)
1795	—	33 3	35 0	—	34 0	136
1796	40 0	33 3	35 0	—	36 0	144
1797	34 0	29 0	30 0	—	31 0	124
1798	28 0	30 0	30 0	—	29 0	116
1799	27 0	25 0	28 0	—	27 0	108
1800	25 0	25 0	28 0	31 6	27 6	110
1801	24 0	25 0	28 0	30 0	27 0	108
1802	32 0	29 0	32 0	32 6	31 6	126
1803	19 0	24 0	22 0	34 6–28 0	24 0	96
1804	23 0	20 0	22 0	26 0	23 0	92
1805	26 0	25 0	18 0	28 0–32 0	25 0	100
1806	24 0	22 0	16 0	30 0–26 0	22 6	90
1807	22 0	18 0	14 0	22 0–18 0	18 6	74
1808	12 0	14 0	13 0	18 0	14 0	56
1809	—	16 0	18 0	18 0–20 0	18 0	72
1810	—	19 6	20 0	25 0–19 0	20 6	82
1811	—	14 0	12 0	16 0	14 0	56
1812	—	14 0	12 6	18 0	15 0	60
1813	—	15 0	20 0	21 0–32 0	21 0	84
1814	—	24 0	20 0	28 0–20 0	23 0	92
1815	—	14 0	12 0	17 0	14 0	56
1816	—	12 0	8 0	17 0–14 0	12 0	48
1817	—	9 0	8 6	14 0	10 6	42
1818	—	9 0	11 0	14 0	11 0	44
1819	—	9 6	8 0	12 0	10 0	40
1820	—	9 0	8 6	12 0	10 0	40

For sources, see text, as above.

The series of calico piece-rates, on which table 3, chapter 5, p. 105, is based, are as follows:

Date	J. Grimshaw s. d.	J. Fielden s. d.	G. Smith (1) s. d.	G. Smith (2) s. d.	W. Ecroyd s. d.	Average s. d.	Index (1815 = 100)
1814	6 6	8 0	5 10	—	—	6 9	162
1815	4 3½	—	4 1	—	—	4 2¼	100
1816	3 4½	2 6	2 10	—	—	2 10¾	70
1817	3 0¼	2 6–3 6	2 8	—	—	2 10¾	70
1818	3 7¼	4 0	3 3	—	—	3 7½	87
1819	3 1¼	3 9–2 6	2 5	—	—	2 10½	69
1820	2 11	2 6–3 0	2 7	3 3¾	—	2 10¾	70
1821	3 1¾	3 0–3 3	3 2	3 3½	—	3 2	76
1822	2 6½	2 9	2 7	2 10¼	—	2 8¼	64
1823	2 4	2 6	2 2½	2 8¼	—	2 5¼	58
1824	2 1½	2 6	1 10	2 5	—	2 2½	53
1825	2 1½	2 6–2 0	2 2½	2 6	—	2 4	56
1826	1 3¾	1 6–1 9	1 3	1 5¾	—	1 4½	33
1827	1 7½	1 3–2 0	1 5	1 10	—	1 8	40
1828	1 7½	2 0	1 8	1 10½	—	1 9½	43
1829	1 2	1 1½	1 1	1 3¾	—	1 2	28
1830	1 6	1 3	1 5	1 7¼	—	1 5½	35
1831	1 7¼	1 3	1 7	1 10⅛	1 10½	1 7¾	39
1832	1 3¾	1 3	1 3½	1 6¼	1 7⅝	1 4¾	33
1833	1 4	1 3	1 5	1 8	1 7½	1 5½	35
1834	—	—	—	—	1 9⅜	1 9⅜	43
1835	—	—	—	—	1 9¾	1 9¾	44
1836	—	—	—	—	1 8⅜	1 8⅜	41
1837	—	—	—	—	1 2¾	1 2¾	29
1838	—	—	—	—	1 3⅜	1 3⅜	31
1839	—	—	—	—	1 3¾	1 3¾	32
1840	—	—	—	—	1 3	1 3	30
1841	—	—	—	—	1 1⅞	1 1⅞	28

For sources, see text, as above.

THE PIECE-RATE AND THE
PRICE OF FOOD

Fluctuations in the piece-rates paid for cotton weaving were far wider than changes in the price of food, and the long-term drop in piece-rates in the post-1815 period was far sharper than the fall in the cost of living. Sufficient materials to construct a reliable cost of living index for this period are not available. But enough is known about the retail price of particular commodities, such as oatmeal, which was a staple element in the weavers' diet, to enable a useful comparison to be made between piece-rates and food prices. Although this cannot provide an exact summary of the widely different progresses of wages and of the cost of living in this crucial phase of the industrial revolution, a comparison based on these materials can serve the same general function as Professor Rostow's famous 'social tension' chart, by indicating when the weavers' distress was most acute.[1] The indices for the piece-rate and the retail price of oatmeal are closest in 1821–2, which are years of notable calm; and they are furthest apart in 1817, 1826, and 1829, years of known distress and disturbance.

The index for oatmeal has been constructed from four sources, three in the parliamentary papers of the early 1830s, the fourth, covering only the first few years, in the *Manchester Mercury* of 18 January 1819. Each source provides several series of retail commodity prices over periods of several years, and the oatmeal series have been selected as being most relevant to the cotton handloom weavers. 1815 is taken as the base year for the oatmeal index, and for the calico piece-rate, which is examined in chapter 5. In the case of food prices, 1815 seems suitable because it marked the lowest year between the period of scarcity just before the war ended and the difficult years immediately before the 1820s; and in the case of piece-rates, 1815 stands midway between the inflated prices of the 1813–14 boom and the slump of 1816–17. In table 2, these two indices are given, together with the Silberling price index (also converted to a base in 1815) for purposes of general comparison.[2]

---

[1] W. W. Rostow, *The British economy of the nineteenth century* (Oxford, 1948), pp. 123–5.
[2] The Silberling index is from J. H. Clapham, *The early railway age* (Cambridge, 1930), p. 602.

TABLE I. *Retail price of oatmeal in Lancashire, 1815–33, per 12 lbs*[1]

Date	(1) Manchester Mercury s. d.	(2) J. Makin s. d.	(3) J. Grimshaw s. d.	(4) J. Milne s. d.	Average s. d.
1815	2 2	1 $7\frac{1}{4}$	1 $10\frac{1}{4}$	1 $11\frac{1}{2}$	1 $10\frac{3}{4}$
1816	2 1	1 $8\frac{3}{4}$	1 $9\frac{1}{2}$	2 $0\frac{1}{2}$	1 11
1817	3 2	1 6	3 6	2 1	2 $6\frac{3}{4}$
1818	2 8	2 6	2 6	2 5	2 $6\frac{1}{4}$
1819	2 3	1 $10\frac{3}{4}$	1 11	2 $0\frac{3}{4}$	2 $0\frac{1}{4}$
1820	—	1 $8\frac{1}{2}$	2 $0\frac{1}{2}$	2 0	1 11
1821	—	1 $4\frac{1}{2}$	1 $6\frac{1}{4}$	1 $7\frac{1}{2}$	1 6
1822	—	1 $3\frac{1}{2}$	1 $5\frac{1}{2}$	1 $7\frac{1}{2}$	1 $5\frac{1}{2}$
1823	—	1 6	2 $0\frac{1}{2}$	1 $8\frac{3}{4}$	1 9
1824	—	1 $8\frac{1}{2}$	2 $1\frac{1}{4}$	1 $11\frac{3}{4}$	1 11
1825	—	1 $9\frac{1}{2}$	1 $9\frac{1}{2}$	1 $11\frac{3}{4}$	1 $10\frac{1}{4}$
1826	—	2 $4\frac{1}{2}$	1 $8\frac{3}{4}$	1 $11\frac{3}{4}$	2 $0\frac{1}{4}$
1827	—	1 $8\frac{1}{2}$	1 $11\frac{3}{4}$	2 1	1 11
1828	—	1 $7\frac{1}{4}$	1 6	1 $8\frac{3}{4}$	1 $7\frac{1}{4}$
1829	—	1 $7\frac{1}{2}$	1 9	1 $10\frac{1}{2}$	1 9
1830	—	1 $6\frac{1}{2}$	1 11	1 $11\frac{3}{4}$	1 $9\frac{3}{4}$
1831	—	1 $8\frac{1}{2}$	1 $10\frac{1}{2}$	1 $11\frac{3}{4}$	1 $10\frac{1}{4}$
1832	—	1 $2\frac{1}{2}$	1 $4\frac{3}{4}$	1 $7\frac{1}{2}$	1 5
1833	—	1 $2\frac{3}{4}$	1 3	1 $4\frac{1}{2}$	1 $3\frac{1}{2}$

[1] Sources of table 1, above:
 (1) *Manchester Mercury*, 18 Jan 1819.
 (2) Evidence of J. Makin (Bolton), PP. *1834* (*556*) x, p. 396.
 (3) Evidence of J. Grimshaw (Barrowford, near Colne), PP. *1833* (*690*) vi, p. 608.
 (4) Evidence of J. Milne (Oldham), *ibid.* p. 665.

TABLE 2. *Movement of piece-rates and other prices, 1815–40*

Date	Calico piece-rate Index	Oatmeal index	Silberling index	Date	Calico piece-rate index	Oatmeal index	Silberling index
1815	100	100	100	1828	43	85	72
1816	70	101	90	1829	28	92	71
1817	70	135	101	1830	35	96	72
1818	87	133	106	1831	39	98	74
1819	69	107	96	1832	33	75	73
1820	70	101	88	1833	35	68	71
1821	76	80	77	1834	43	—	68
1822	64	77	67	1835	44	—	66
1823	58	92	74	1836	41	—	74
1824	53	101	75	1837	29	—	74
1825	56	98	85	1838	31	—	79
1826	33	107	74	1839	32	—	82
1827	40	101	73	1840	30	—	81

G. H. WOOD'S ESTIMATES OF AVERAGE WEEKLY EARNINGS

Date	s. d.	Date	s. d.	Date	s. d.
1797	18 9	1811	12 3	1825	8 3
1798	19 9	1812	14 0	1826	7 9
1799	18 6	1813	15 0	1827	7 6
1800	18 9	1814	18 6	1828	7 3
1801	18 6	1815	13 6	1829	7 3
1802	21 0	1816	10 3	1830	6 3
1803	20 0	1817	8 9	1831	6 0
1804	20 0	1818	8 3	1832	6 0
1805	23 0	1819	8 3	1833	6 0
1806	20 0	1820	8 3	1834	7 0
1807	17 3	1821	8 3	1835	6 3
1808	13 3	1822	8 3	1836	6 3
1809	14 0	1823	8 3	1837	6 3
1810	14 3	1824	8 3	1838	6 3

From G. H. Wood, *History of wages in the cotton trade during the past hundred years* (London, 1910), p. 112.

BIBLIOGRAPHY

A. Manuscript sources.
B. Parliamentary Papers.
C. Newspapers.
D. Contemporary printed works.
E. Secondary books, articles, and theses.

A. MANUSCRIPT SOURCES

I. *Business Papers*

The Samuel Oldknow MSS, 1782–1811 (John Rylands Library, Manchester).
Wage-book of D. Millar, Colne, 1845 (loaned by W. Spencer, Colne).
Anonymous Wage-book from Foulridge, Colne, 1852 (loaned by W. Spencer, Colne).

II. *Local Government Records*

Home Office Papers in the Public Record Office, London
HO. 40. Correspondence, Disturbances, 1812–55.
HO. 41. Disturbances, Entry Books.
HO. 42. Correspondence, George III, 1782–1820.
HO. 44. Correspondence, George IV and later, 1820–51.
HO. 52. Correspondence, Counties, 1820–50.

Parish Records
Overseers Accounts of the Township of Barrowford (Farrer MSS, D. 88, Manchester Central Library).
Great Harwood Parish Papers, 1826 (Lancashire County Record Office, Preston).
Billington Parish papers (*ibid.*).

III. *Miscellaneous*

Notebooks of Ann Ecroyd, of Marsden, Colne, 1815–52. (Farrer MSS, D. 96, Manchester Central Library.)
Manuscripts and Papers of the Manchester Statistical Society, 1833–40. (Manchester Central Library.)
The Household Accounts of William Varley, calico weaver, of Higham, Burnley, 1819–22. (Transcript by W. Bennett, in Burnley Central Reference Library.)
The Autobiography of David Whitehead. (MS in Rawtenstall Public Library. Limited typescript edition, Rawtenstall, 1956.)

B. PARLIAMENTARY PAPERS

Hansard's Parliamentary Debates, 1st Series, New Series, and 3rd Series.

PP. *1803* (*114*) III, part 4. Minutes of Evidence Taken before the Committee to whom the Several Petitions Presented to the House in this Session, relating to the Act of 39 and 40 George 3 'for Settling Disputes between Masters and Workmen Engaged in the Cotton Manufacture', were Referred.

PP. *1804* (*41*) IV, part 1. Report from the Committee Appointed to Consider the Most Speedy and Effectual Mode of Adjusting such Differences as may arise between Masters and Workmen Engaged in the Cotton Manufacture.

PP. *1808* (*177*) II and PP. *1809* (*111*) III. Reports from the Committee on the Petitions of Several Cotton Manufacturers and Journeymen Cotton Weavers.

PP. *1808* (*179*) III. Report from the Committee on Dr Cartwright's Weaving-machine.

PP. *1810/11* (*232*) II. Report of the Committee on the Petitions of Several Weavers, etc.

PP. *1812* (*21*) and (*231*) III. Reports of the Committees of the Whole House on the Petitions against the Orders in Council.

PP. *1816* (*397*) III. Report of the Select Committee on the State of the Children Employed in the Manufactories of the United Kingdom.

PP. *1817* (*141*) XIV. Statement of the Quantity of Cotton Yarn Exported from Great Britain.

PP. *1817* (*482*) XIV. Copies of all the Memorials Presented to H.R.H. The Prince Regent during the Present and Last Year, on the Exportation of Cotton Yarns.

PP. *1824* (*51*) V. Report of the Select Committee on Artisans, Machinery, and Combinations.

PP. *1826/7* (*404*) IV and PP. *1826/7* (*88*), (*237*), and (*550*) V. Reports of the Select Committee on Emigration from the United Kingdom.

PP. *1830* (*590*) X. Report of the Select Committee Appointed to Consider the Means of Lessening the Evils Arising from the Fluctuation of Employment in Manufacturing Districts.

PP. *1833* (*450*) XX. Report of the Royal Commission on the Employment of Children in Factories.

PP. *1833* (*690*) VI. Report of the Select Committee on the Present State of Manufactures, Commerce, and Shipping in the United Kingdom.

PP. *1834* (*44*) XXVIII. Report of the Poor Law Commission, including the Reports of Assistant Commissioners.

PP. *1834* (*44*) XXX to XXVI. Appendixes to the Report of the Poor Law Commissioners.

    Appendix B 1. Answers to Rural Queries.

    Appendix B 2. Answers to Urban Queries.

PP. 1834 (556) x. Report of the Select Committee on Handloom Weavers' Petitions.

PP. 1835 (341) xiii. Report of the Select Committee on Handloom Weavers' Petitions.

PP. 1836 (24) xlv. A Return of the Number of Powerlooms used in Factories in the Manufacture of Woollen, Cotton, Silk, and Linen Respectively, in each County of the United Kingdom Respectively, so far as They can be Collected from the Returns of the Factory Commissioners.

PP. 1837/8 (488) and *(646)* viii. Reports of the Select Committee on the Working of the Act of 6 George 4 cap. 129, and Generally into the Constitution, Proceedings, and Extent of any Trades Union, or Combination of Workmen or Employers of Workmen.

PP. 1837/8 (681) xviii (parts 1–3). Reports of the Select Committee to Inquire into the Administration of the Relief of the Poor under the Orders and Regulations Issued by the Commissioners Appointed under the Provisions of the Poor Law Amendment Act.

PP. 1839 xlii; *PP. 1840* xxiii, and xxiv; and *PP. 1841* x. Reports of the Royal Commission on the Handloom Weavers.

PP 1840 (220) xxiv. Report from R. M. Muggeridge on the Condition of the Handloom Weavers of Lancashire, Westmorland, Cumberland, and parts of the West Riding of Yorkshire.

PP. 1840 (639) xxiv. W. E. Hickson's Report on the Condition of the Handloom Weavers.

PP. 1841 (296) x. Final Report of the Royal Commission.

PP. 1840 (203), *(227)*, *(314)*, *(334)*, *(419)* and *(504)* x. Six Reports from the Select Committee on the Act for the Regulation of Mills and Factories.

PP. 1842 (380) xv. Report of the Commission for Inquiring into the Employment and Condition of Children in Mines and Manufactories.

PP. 1843 (115) vii. Report of the Select Committee on Distress in Paisley.

PP. 1843 (402) vii. Report of the Select Committee on the Labouring Poor (Allotments of Land).

PP. 1850 (745) xlii. Returns of the Number of Cotton, Woollen, Worsted, Flax, and Silk Factories subject to the Factories Act in each County.

Quarterly and Half-yearly Reports of the Factory Inspectors, 1835–50.

C. NEWSPAPERS

I. *Long runs*

Manchester Mercury, 1778–1827.   *Northern Star*, 1838–48.
Manchester Guardian, 1826–42.

II. *Short runs and individual years.*

Blackburn Mail (later *Blackburn Gazette*).   *Bolton Chronicle*.
Blackburn Standard.   *Bolton Free Press*.

BIBLIOGRAPHY

Carlisle Journal.   Manchester Observer.
Wheeler's Manchester Chronicle.   Preston Chronicle.
Manchester Exchange Herald.   Preston Observer.

D. CONTEMPORARY PRINTED WORKS (largely pre-1850)

Adshead, J. Distress in Manchester. Evidence (tabular and otherwise) of the state of the labouring classes in 1840–2 (London, 1842).

Agricultural and Industrial Magazine (London, 1834–5).

Aikin, J. A description of the country from 30 to 40 miles around Manchester (London, 1795).

Babbage, C. On the economy of machinery and manufactures (London, 1832).

Baines, E. Address to the unemployed workmen of Yorkshire and Lancashire on the present distress and on machinery (London, 1826).

Baines, E. History of the cotton manufacture (London, 1835).

Bamford, S. Passages in the life of a radical (Heywood, 1843).

Early days (London, 1849).

The dialect of South Lancashire (Manchester, 1850).

Homely rhymes, poems and reminiscences (London, 1864).

Black, J. Summary of Statistics of Bolton, Lancashire (from Trans. Provincial Medical and Surgical Association, London, 1837).

Burn, R. Statistics of the cotton trade (London, 1847).

Butterworth, J. The fustian manufacturer's and weaver's complete draught book (Manchester, 1797).

The antiquities of the town, and a complete history of the trade of Manchester (Manchester, 1822).

A complete history of the cotton trade (Manchester, 1823).

The condition of the working classes in an extensive manufacturing district in 1834–6 (Report of Manchester Statistical Society, London, 1838).

Cooper, T. The life of Thomas Cooper, written by himself (London, 1872).

Coulthart, J. R. Report on the Sanatory Condition of the Town of Ashton-under-Lyne (Ashton, 1844).

D'Eichthal, G. 'Condition de la classe ouvriere en Angleterre (1828)'. Printed in Revue Historique, vol. 79, Paris, 1902.

Dickson, R. W. A general view of the agriculture of Lancashire, with observations on the means of its improvement (London, 1815).

Duncan, J. Practical and descriptive essays on the art of weaving (Glasgow, 1808).

Engels, F. The condition of the working class in England in 1845 (English edn by W. H. Chaloner and W. O. Henderson, Oxford, 1958).

Fielden, J. The curse of the factory system (London, 1836).

Fielding, J. Rural historial gleanings in South Lancashire (Manchester, 1852).

Gammage, R. G. History of the Chartist movement (2nd edn, Newcastle, 1894).

Gaskell, P. *The manufacturing population of England* (London, 1833).
Artisans and machinery (London, 1836).

Greg, W. R. *Not overproduction, but underconsumption the source of our sufferings* (London, 1842).

Guest, R. *A compendious history of the cotton manufacture, with a disproval of the claim of Sir Richard Arkwright to the invention of its ingenious machinery* (Manchester, 1823).

Holt, J. *A general view of the agriculture of the county of Lancaster* (London, 1795).

Kay, J. P. *The moral and physical condition of the working classes employed in the cotton manufacture in Manchester* (London, 1832).

Kennedy, J. *Observations on the rise and progress of the cotton trade in Great Britain* (1815). (Reprinted in *Miscellaneous papers on subjects connected with the manufacture of Lancashire*, privately printed, Manchester, 1849.)

Maxwell, J. *Manual labour versus machinery* (London, 1834).

McCulloch, J. R. 'The rise, progress, present state and prospects of the British cotton manufacture', *Edinburgh Review*, XLVI (1827).

'Mercator' (pseud.). *A letter to the inhabitants of Manchester on the exportation of cotton twist* (Manchester, 1800).

Napier, Sir W. *The life and opinions of General Sir Charles James Napier* (4 vols. London, 1857).

Ogden, J. *A description of Manchester* (Manchester, 1783).

'Operator' (pseud). *The petitioning weavers defended, in remarks on the Manchester police meeting of 13 January 1817* (Manchester, 1817).

Prentice, A. *Historical sketches and personal recollections of Manchester* (London, 1851).

Radcliffe, W. *The origin of the new system of manufacture commonly called power-loom weaving, and the purposes for which this system was invented and brought into use, fully explained in a narrative, containing William Radcliffe's struggles through life to remove the cause which has brought this country to its present crisis* (Stockport, 1828).

Scrope, G. P. *Political economy versus the handloom weavers* (Bradford, 1835).

Simond, L. *Journal of a tour and residence in Great Britain during the years 1810 and 1811, by a French traveller* (2 vols. Edinburgh, 1815).

Stanley, E. *Statistical Report on the Parish of Alderley* (In 'Papers of the Manchester Statistical Society', London, 1838.)

Taylor, W. C. *Notes of a tour in the manufacturing districts of Lancashire* (London, 1842).
Handbook of silk, cotton, and woollen manufactures (London, 1843).
Factories and the factory system (London, 1844).

Thom, W. *Rhymes and recollections of a handloom weaver* (London, 1844, with enlarged editions 1845 and 1847).

Twiss, T. *Two lectures on machinery* (Oxford, 1844).

Ure, A. *The philosophy of manufactures* (London, 1835).
  The cotton manufacture of Great Britain investigated and illustrated (London, 1836).
White, G. *A practical treatise on weaving by hand and powerlooms* (Glasgow, 1846).
Whittle, P. A. *Blackburn as it is* (Preston, 1852).
Winstanley, D. *A schoolmaster's notebook* (ed. E. and T. Kelly, Chetham Society, Manchester, 1957).
'Wish-em-well, W.' (pseud.). *A journey to Blackburn* (Leeds, 1826).
Young, A. *Six months tour of northern England* (2nd edn London, 1771).

E. SELECT LIST OF SECONDARY WORKS (post-1850)

I. Books

Abram, W. A. *History of Blackburn* (Blackburn, 1877).
Andrew, S. *Fifty years cotton trade* (Oldham, 1887).
Ashton, T. S. *An economic history of England: the eighteenth century* (London, 1955).
  Social and economic investigations in Manchester, 1833–1933 (London, 1934).
  The industrial revolution (London, 1947).
Aspinall, A. *The early English trade unions* (London, 1949).
  Politics and the press (London, 1949).
Barlow, A. *History and principles of weaving by hand and by power* (London, 1878).
Bennett, W. *History of Burnley* (4 vols. Burnley, 1947–9).
  History of Marsden and Nelson (Nelson, 1957).
Briggs, A. *The age of improvement* (London, 1959).
Brown, L. *The Board of Trade and the free-trade movement, 1830–42* (Oxford, 1958).
Chapman, S. J. *The Lancashire cotton industry* (Manchester, 1904).
Clapham, J. H. *The early railway age, 1820–50* (2nd edn, Cambridge, 1930).
Clarke, S. *Clitheroe in the old coaching days* (Clitheroe, 1897).
Clokie, H. M. and Robinson, J. W. *Royal commissions of inquiry* (Stanford, 1937).
Collier, F. *The family economy of the workers in the cotton industry, 1784–1833* (ed. R. S. Fitton, Manchester, 1964).
Court, W. H. B. *A concise economic history of Britain since 1750* (Cambridge, 1954).
Crouzet, F. *L'économie britannique et le blocus continental* (2 vols. Paris, 1958).
Daniels, G. W. *The early English cotton industry* (Manchester, 1920).
Darvall, F. O. *Popular disturbances and public order in Regency England* (London, 1934).
Deane, P. and Cole, W. A. *British economic growth, 1689–1959* (Cambridge, 1962).
Driver, C. *Tory radical: the life of Richard Oastler* (Oxford, 1946).
Ellison, T. *The cotton trade of Great Britain* (London, 1886).
Fitton, R. S. and Wadsworth, A. P. *The Strutts and the Arkwrights* (Manchester, 1958).
Fong, H. D. *Triumph of factory system in England* (Tientsin, 1930).

Foster, G. F. *Ashton-under-Lyne, its story through the ages* (Ashton, 1947).

French, G. J. *Life and times of Samuel Crompton* (London, 1859).

Gilboy, E. W. *Wages in eighteenth-century England* (Harvard, 1934).

Habakkuk, H. J. *American and British technology in the nineteenth century* (Cambridge, 1962).

Halevy, E. *England in 1815* (English paperback edn, London, 1961).

Halstead, D. *Haslingden's history* (Haslingden, 1929).

Hamilton, H. *The industrial revolution in Scotland* (Oxford, 1932).

Hammond, J. L. and B. *The town labourer, 1760–1832* (London, 1917).
    The skilled labourer, 1760–1832 (London, 1919).
    Lord Shaftesbury (4th ed. London, 1936).

Harland, J. *Ballads and songs of Lancashire* (London, 1865).

Holden J. *History of Todmorden* (Manchester, 1912).

Hovell, M. *The Chartist movement* (Manchester, 1925).

Mantoux, P. *The industrial revolution in the eighteenth century* (English revised edn, London, 1961).

Marsden, R. *Cotton weaving. Its development, principles, and practice* (London, 1895).

Matthews, R. C. O. *A study in trade-cycle history* (Cambridge, 1954).

McLachlan, H. *The Methodist Unitarian movement* (Manchester, 1919).

Miller, G. C. *Blackburn: evolution of a cotton town* (Blackburn, 1951).

Mitchell, B. R. and Deane, P. *Abstract of British historical statistics* (Cambridge, 1962).

Newbigging, T. *History of the forest of Rossendale* (London, 1868).

Piggot, S. *Hollins: a study of industry, 1784–1949* (Nottingham, 1949).

Pinchbeck, I. *Women workers and the industrial revolution, 1750–1850* (London, 1930).

Read, D. *Peterloo: the massacre and its background* (London, 1958).
    Chartism in Manchester (in 'Chartist Studies', ed. A. Briggs (London, 1960)).
    Press and people, 1790–1850 (London, 1961).

Read, D. and Glasgow, E. *Feargus O'Connor, Irishman and Chartist* (London, 1961).

Redford, A. *Labour migration in England, 1800–50* (Manchester, 2nd ed. 1964).
    Manchester merchants and foreign trade, 1794–1858 (Manchester, 1934).
    An economic history of England, 1760–1860 (2nd edn, London, 1960).

Rostow, W. W. *The British economy of the nineteenth century* (Oxford, 1948).

Schoyen, A. R. *The Chartist challenge* (London, 1958).

Schulze-Gaevernitz, G. von. *The cotton trade in England and on the continent* (London, 1895).

Singer, C., Holmyard, E. J., Hall, A. R. and Williams, T. I. (eds.). *A history of technology*, vol. IV: *The industrial revolution* (Oxford, 1958).

Smelser, N. J. *Social change in the industrial revolution* (London, 1959).

Smith, D. Walker. *The protectionist case in the 1840s* (Oxford, 1933).

Speake, R. and Witty, F. R. *History of Droylsden* (Stockport, 1953).

Stigler, G. J. *Five lectures on political economy* (London, 1949).

Thompson, E. P. *The making of the English working class* (London, 1963).

Tupling, G. H. *An economic history of Rossendale* (Manchester, 1927).

Turner, H. A. *Trade union growth, structure, and policy* (London, 1962).

Unwin, G. *Samuel Oldknow and the Arkwrights* (Manchester, 1924).

Wadsworth, A. P. and Mann, J. de L. *The cotton trade and industrial Lancashire, 1600–1780* (Manchester, 1931).

Walpole, S. *History of England from the conclusion of the great war in 1815* (revised edn, 6 vols. London, 1890).

Ward, J. T. *The factory movement, 1830–55* (London, 1962).

Ware, C. F. *Early New England cotton manufacture* (New York, 1931).

Webb, S. and B. *History of trade unionism* (revised edn, London, 1920).

Wells, F. A. *The British hosiery trade* (London, 1935).

Wood, G. H. *History of wages in the cotton trade during the past hundred years* (London, 1910).

Woodcroft, B. *Brief biographies of inventors of machinery for the manufacture of textile fabrics* (London, 1863).

Woodward, E. L. *Age of reform* (2nd edn, Oxford, 1962).

II. *Journals, articles*

Ashton, T. S. 'Some statistics of the industrial revolution', *The Manchester School*, XVI (1948).

Blaug, M. 'The empirical content of Ricardian economics, *Journal of Political Economy*, LXIV (1956).

'The productivity of capital in the Lancashire cotton industry during the nineteenth century', *Economic History Review*, XIII (1961).

'The myth of the old Poor Law and the making of the new', *Journal of Economic History*, XXIII (1963).

'The Poor Law report reconsidered', *Journal of Economic History*, XXIV (1964).

Clapham, J. H. 'The Spitalfields Acts, 1773–1824', *Economic Journal*, XXVI (1916).

Daniels, G. W. 'The cotton trade during the revolutionary and Napoleonic wars', *Trans. of the Manchester Statistical Society* (1915–16).

Danson, J. T. and Welton, T. A. 'The population of Lancashire and Cheshire and its local distribution during fifty years, 1801–51', *Trans. Lancashire and Cheshire Historical Soc.*, vols. IX and X (1857–8).

Davies, H. W. C. 'Lancashire reformers, 1816–17', *Bulletin John Rylands Library*, X (1926).

Hartwell, R. M. 'Interpretations of the industrial revolution in England', *Journal of Economic History*, XIX (1959).

Hobsbawm, E. J. 'The machine breakers', *Past and Present*, I (1952).

Hutt, W. H. 'The factory system in the early nineteenth century', *Economica*, VI (1926).

Jewkes, J. 'The localization of the cotton industry', *Economic History*, II (1930).

Marwick, W. H. 'The cotton industry and industrial revolution in Scotland', *Scottish Historical Review*, XXI (1923–4).

Merttens, F. 'Hours and cost of labour in the cotton industry at home and abroad', *Trans. Manchester Statistical Society* (1893–4).

Mitchell, G. M. 'The English and Scottish cotton industries. A study in inter-relations', *Scottish Historical Review*, XXII (1924–5).

Nelson, E. G. 'The putting-out system in the English framework-knitting industry', *Journal of Economic and Business History*, II (1930).

Pollard, S. 'Factory discipline in the industrial revolution', *Economic History Review*, XVI (1964).

Rodgers, H. B. 'The Lancashire cotton industry in 1840', *Trans. Institute of British Geographers*, XXVIII (1960).

Rose, M. E. 'The allowance system under the new Poor Law', *Economic History Review*, XIX (1966).

Smith, R. 'Manchester as a centre for the manufacture and marketing of cotton goods, 1820–30', *University of Birmingham Historical Journal*, IV (1953–4).

Taylor, A. J. 'Concentration and specialization in the Lancashire cotton industry, 1825–50', *Economic History Review*, I (1949).

III. *Unpublished theses*

Boyson, R. *A history of Poor Law administration in north-east Lancashire, 1834–71* (M.A. Manchester University, 1960).

Farnie, D. A. *The English cotton industry, 1850–96* (M.A. Manchester University, 1953).

Giles, P. M. *The economic and social development of Stockport, 1815–36* (M.A. Manchester University, 1950).

Hartwell, R. M. *The Yorkshire woollen and worsted industries, 1800–50* (D.Phil. Oxford University, 1955).

Taylor, A. J. *Concentration and localization of the British cotton industry, 1825–50* (M.A. Manchester University, 1947).

INDEX

Accrington, 51, 92, 123, 200, 230
Addington, Henry, *see* Sidmouth, Lord
agriculture
  combination of, with handloom weaving, 13, 16, 45, 46, 58, 59, 60, 122, 180
  effects of growth of cotton industry on, 45 n. 5
  loss of weavers to, 262
  recruitment of weavers from, 45, 46, 52, 252 n. 4, 253, 254
Aikin, John, topographer, 22, 47, 49, 54
Alderley, 56 n. 6
Alison, Archibald, magistrate, 178
allowance system, *see* Speenhamland system
Althorp, Lord, M.P., 160
anti-Corn Law League, 90, 99 n. 2, 230–2, 249
apprenticeship, 16, 33, 34, 37, 48, 52, 53, 155 n. 4, 183
arbitration, industrial, 150, 151, 152, 153
  see also Cotton Arbitration Act
Arkwright, Sir Richard, inventor, 40, 68
  see also water-frame
Ashley, Lord, *see* Shaftesbury, Lord
Ashton, Thomas, of Hyde, factory owner, 91
Ashton, T. S., 4 n. 1, 5, 6, 7, 11, 18, 102, 103
Ashton-under-Lyne
  development of powerloom at, 7, 57, 92
  handloom sheds at, 33 n. 4
  strikes at, 179, 184, 187, 188 n. 2, 195
  wages at, 97
Ashworth, Henry, of Turton, factory owner, 253, 258
Ashworth, John, of Rossendale, manufacturer, 163 n. 1
Aspinall, A., 23, 176 n. 1
Attwood, Thomas, M.P., 159, 160

Babbage, Charles, mathematician, 21, 72, 141, 144
Bacup, 201, 230
Baines, Edward, journalist, 3, 8, 22, 87, 141, 204
Balladenbrook, 37
Bamber Bridge, 224

Bamford, Samuel, weaver and radical, 22, 36, 38 n. 2, 43 n. 4, 58 n. 2, 124, 166, 263
Bamford, 45
Barley, 56
Barnard, Rev. M., rector of Thornton, 239
Barnoldswick, 226, 248 n. 4
Barrowford, 235, 248 n. 4, 266
Bashall Eaves, 248 n. 4
Baxenden, 227
Bayley, Mr, of Manchester, J.P., 150 n. 1
bed-quilts
  areas producing, 28, 87
  weavers of, 55, 184
Beesley, William, of Accrington, Chartist, 226, 227
Birley and Hornby, of Blackburn, factory masters, 29
Birmingham, 33 n. 4, 221, 224
Black, James, physician, 55
Blackburn, hundred of,
  migration of population in, 255–6, 265
  number of handlooms in, 56
  radicalism in, 219
  strikes in, 196
  unemployment in, 123
Blackburn, town of,
  development of powerloom at, 7, 92
  embezzlement at, 124
  growth of population at, 49
  handloom factories at, 33 n. 4
  Irishmen at, 64
  number of handlooms at, 264, 266
  patriotism at, 206
  petitions from, 149, 214, 248
  poor relief at, 240, 243–4, 246
  radicalism at, 227
  riots at, 190, 200–1, 203, 258
  strikes at, 186, 187, 188 n. 2
  types of cloth produced at, 28, 29, 50, 51, 264
  visit of royal commission to, 166
  wages at, 97, 126, 129, 259
  weavers' workshops at, 36
blackleg labour, 179, 253 n. 2, 257, 262, 265
Blanketeers, march of the, 19, 211–12
Blomfield, Bishop, 30, 157, 254, 264
boards of trade, *see* wage regulation

291
19-2

Cambridge 69-003850 lal.69 75/-

7.500